BOLLYWOOD BLONDE

Gené Gualdi

MF BOOKS JOBURG

First published by MFBooks Joburg,
an imprint of Jacana Media (Pty) Ltd in 2014

10 Orange Street
Sunnyside
Auckland Park 2092
South Africa
+2711 628 3200
www.jacana.co.za

ISBN 978-1-920601-44-7

Cover design by publicide
Set in Sabon 11/14pt
Printed and bound by Creda Communications
Job no. 002300

See a complete list of Jacana titles at www.jacana.co.za

Thank you India for sharing so much of yourself with me.

And to my late granny Topsy, thank you for showing me how to throw myself to the wind and just be me.

Head in the clouds

I clutch my boarding pass stub in my hand 3 500 metres above the ground. Back in Cape Town, I made a deal with The Producer that I would buy the ticket to Mumbai and he would take care of the rest. My mind feels like it's mounted on those spinning teacups you find at the funfair. I'm giddy with excitement and fear. The Hindi squawking of women wrapped, rolled, folded and tucked into saris on top of the droning of aeronautical engines beside me is too much for my feather brain. I still have not admitted to myself exactly where I am going, I may get cold feet and not go at all. I keep reminding myself that it's the land of movies, exotic fruit, curry and red-turbaned servants fanning my sweating bronzed body. I see myself on set, directing my debut feature film, a vervet monkey sitting on my left shoulder just for luck.

The food trolley arrives. The 'makeshift curry in a foil sleeve' smell replaces the 'sterile meets floral' smell of insecticide spray that the airhostess has sprayed throughout the cabin. The meal disappoints. It is the dehydrated, powderised version.

"Just add water, watch it grow with explosive exotic burst of Eastern flavour. Your choice, veg or non-veg. Take your pick!"

I choose to have another 'voddie' instead. I'm too anxious to eat anyway.

I plug into my CD player and turn the volume to max because I was born deaf in my right ear. My beloved Leonard Cohen blares into my one and only working eardrum, rasping about loaded dice and everybody rolling with their fingers crossed.

That's all I can do now: roll with my fingers crossed into the unknown; there is no turning back.

I am quite aware that "there is no such thing as a free lunch".

Pretending to yourself that you do not know stuff is so much worse than admitting what you know. I know from before I have even boarded what The Producer's true intentions are. I have known from the moment we conversed in the company of that stray cat. I'm going to have to give him exactly what he wants because what he has to offer me is far greater than what I have to offer him. I distract my worry by making child-like pictures with the clouds accumulating outside the bulging aeroplane window. The vodka helps my turning imagination. I replay Leonard's song and how I got to this point in the first place.

How I find myself sitting on this flight begins a little earlier, on a film set in Cape Town where I am trying my hardest to break into the film industry. Having moved from art school in Italy to Durban, I major in photography purely because I want to be in an ever-changing place and film does just that.

As a child I believed Enid Blyton's story of *The Magic Faraway Tree*. The tree had different, constantly changing lands on the top of its branches. By climbing to the top of the tree you could be in a different land every day of the week. Now as an adult I know there is no magic tree and I have to make my world an ever-changing place that will revolve and evolve within me.

I soon find out that there are no hot-shot producers falling from the sky inviting me onto their casting couch. My 'magic faraway tree' is going to be a lot harder to find than I had initially thought. I am forced to settle for an ordinary day job as a photographer at Media24, Cape Town's biggest media and magazine house.

In my spare time I do a loader's course, clean lenses and wash floors after hours at a film gear rental house, MCC. Then I wait. I wait to be noticed. Finally I am noticed by one of the industry's top directors of photography, who operates best when high on cocaine. He invites me to train as a loader. I am thrown onto a set with a vicious crew. It's brutal. I am surrounded by Stephen King's version of creatures from his *Pet Cemetary*.

I learn everything the hard way. I am sent to find a skyhook. I search everywhere only to learn that a skyhook does not exist. The grips have a field day at my expense. I learn that a doughnut is not found at the craft food table, but rather in the camera department – it is a protective cloth the shape of a doughnut that rings around the lens. I lug, haul, pull, push and clean up everyone's mess. I have to score their drugs for them and get them home when they are too trashed, but I soon find I love it! I start calling in sick at Media24 so that I can go onto set with my 'bloodhound gang'. I sense my calling in sick way too many times is going to get me fired from clickedy-click land. Just before the elastic is stretched too far, 'SNAP', I find myself being catapulted onto the set of an Indian 'Pickle Perfect' bread spread commercial.

Why they have to come all the way to Camps Bay beats me. But the actor sits at an all-white kitchen counter spreading his Pickle Perfect spread with the emerald blue Cape Peninsula sprawled out behind him. With a clear, crisp sky and bleached white boulders dotted with penguins, a seagull flies past, the infinity pool disappears behind the deck as the white shutters separate perfectly angled shafts of sunlight. The start to a perfect day ... with the perfect Pickle Perfect spread on warm buttered toast ... Aaa the joys of advertising!

There I am, hauling, lifting, pulling, pushing like one of the bloodhounds, when he touches my shoulder to get my attention. Big hand.

"Hi there, I'm The Producer."

I have noticed him talking in Hindi on his mobile phone, picking his teeth with the stylus, while the rest of the Indian crew slave away.

He must be the 'Big Wig'.

"Hi, I'm Gené, like the genie in a bottle."

I always say this after my name because everyone always gets it wrong. People end up calling me Jenny, Ginny, Gina, but never Gené pronounced genie, which is why I spell it out with an unforgettable image attached.

He smiles. A deep set of dimples charm their way into my heart. It's beguiling, but his eyes remain stern, serious and in control. His voluptuous lips pout behind a neatly trimmed salt-and-pepper moustache.

I know that smile. It's the one that smears across every man's face when I say 'genie in a bottle'. The comeback is usually standard: "Does that mean you can give me three wishes? Where shall I rub you and how many times?"

His nose dominates his face as a main feature. He is very broad across his slightly hunched shoulders and much too heavy for his height. I notice his oversized hands again. His balding head catches the 'fall off' light from the set up of film lights in the kitchen. It is shaved clean, a small cut and a few older scars revealing the evidence of a very close daily shave. Less rotund and with more hair he would be an uncanny version of Alfred Molina.

He is not young.

"What do you do on set 'Gené in a bottle'?"

"I'm an assistant loader, and you?"

"I pay for all of this."

"I gathered that."

So this is what a real producer looks like. I wonder whether his casting couch will fall from the sky.

"I own a small production house in Bombay. I have been watching you. We could do with hard-working people like yourself."

He hands me a black card with 'Luna Films' printed on it in foiled silver. 'The Producer' is boldly embossed on the corner of the card with his mobile number next to it.

I move away from the crew at lunch to share my food with a stray cat. He is there again, watching, questioning and flirting.

"Do you like animals?"

His English accent has a rich curry flavour to it, but with an American twang.

"Yes, I do."

"I have a Rottweiler named Roti that I imported from America."

I smile sweetly. 'America' is the name of the drug dealer I score cocaine from, for my bloodhounds.

"Really."

"Yes, in India we have many dogs, but if you want pedigree you have to import."

"Wow, what's India like?"

"Why don't you come and see for yourself. Roti would love to meet you."

I run my hand nervously across the cat's spine, then pull the cat's fluffy tail through my hand and all the way up to its tip as I stand.

"Wow, that sounds amazing, maybe one day I will."

"One day? Why not now? I fly out tomorrow morning so let's have dinner later and discuss your options."

Now I am on an aeroplane barely two weeks later, after one encounter on a film set, a two-hour dinner date full of promises and a reassuring email from The Producer to my father telling him that I will be staying in the company guesthouse where I will be more than safe and comfortable. I will also be earning a sufficient salary to enable me to enjoy India to the full.

I hope India will be the branch that will take me to the top of my 'magic faraway tree'.

Bombay

I land in Mumbai, India in September 2003. I'm twenty-four years old. From the plane, through customs to the conveyor belt, I have already been blood-sucked by the common tropical mosquito six times. I'm itchy all over and irritable because I'm nervous and the fucking wheels on my trolley are retarded, going in opposite directions; they jam and stick. I keep coming to sudden halts, ramming my fear further down my dry throat. The trolley is dinky and has no breaks. It's made of flimsy round bars that remind me of weedy men with thin feminine fingers.

If the quality of airport trolleys in India is anything to go by then the reassuring and very frequent phrase "this is of very best quality, madam, just for you" leaves a lot to be desired. This rule of thumb generally applies to anything that gets sold or made in India.

It's 2am in the morning, three-and-a-half hours ahead of South Africa. I have no idea where I'm going to lay my head yet or what awaits me on the other side. Maybe he has kept his promise to my father about the guesthouse? Maybe it's fancy, maybe it's a hole. Maybe this is all a crock of shit and there are five big men waiting to put me in a van, fill my veins with heroin and sell me as a sex slave on the Asian market.

One more scanner to go and then I'll be rounding the corner into the chaos of the Mumbai Arrivals hall. I am the only white thing in the room. In and among the wave of brown faces and searching eyes, all craning their necks to spot their loved ones, I see him.

Oh god he's here, now what?

I want to turn around and run the other way, but I can't. He stands out, swaying as he tries to balance on his tippy toes for extra height to see over the crowd. His flamboyant shirt catches my attention. Radiant yellow linen with big green palm trees shooting off in different directions. Unmistakably a Banana Republic design, it's buttoned low, exposing his greying chest hairs. Mutton dressed as lamb.

Is it just me, or does he seem older than when I met him two weeks ago? I did not even think to ask him his age in Cape Town. Thank god there is no gold dollar-sign chain around his neck.

I wish I knew what he was thinking.

I hug him as he approaches. There is a brief moment of surprise in his eyes. His downward smile fixes on me as he beckons me to move forward.

I have dyed my hair auburn red. Is he disappointed? Does he also remember me differently?

A short portly man in navy slacks and a pale blue shirt takes my trolley and stares blankly ahead as he pushes with purpose through the crowds. We follow. There are clouds of '*miggies*' all over; I try to keep my mouth closed. The smell of India needs getting used to. It stays inside of you and no matter how much you blow out hard through your nose, it has a penetrating effect that lingers. I see skinny dogs and rag-wrapped bodies on pavements under the dirty yellow light of street lamps. It is all so busy for 3am in the morning.

I am too tired to notice much besides the cute little black-and-yellow tuk-tuks. I can hardly think.

The short portly man opens the back door of a gleaming gold BMW X5. Better in that than being drugged in a van with no windows, I think – if I go down, at least I do it in style. We share the lush leather back seat. The car is cool. Outside, the humidity has already got to me. I'm sweating from pores I did not know I had.

The short portly man drives. He cranks the air conditioning up. It gets icy. The Producer sits next to me, asking random questions about my trip. I answer monosyllabically. I can feel my mind whizzing past what's happening now. Tired as I am, I want to know what will happen next.

The Producer passes me his turquoise mobile phone. "Phone your family and tell them you're okay."

"Are you taking me to the company guesthouse now?" I manage to string a sentence together.

"Aaa, no, actually sweets, I decided you will be more comfortable staying at my place until you are more familiar with where you are. This country is very different to yours, and in any case, we fly to Kuala Lumpur day after."

We pull into a five-storey grey building. It's dark, but the moss casts shadows in patches like patterns across its walls. As the car door opens Indian men rush to grab luggage. I can smell and feel the damp coming off the building walls.

"Come."

The men are all looking at me, bowing slightly, palms facing up in the 'Namaste' greeting. I'm about to do the same back but The Producer grabs my arm.

"Come." He leads me up the wide marble stairs.

We go to the first floor. There is a massive Buddha statue at the entrance and a marble plaque with the family name engraved in black. The Producer rings the door bell. It sounds tinny and clanks more than it rings. As if he were standing directly behind the door, waiting, a man opens it almost immediately. I enter a low-lit room. The room is colossal. It stretches forward with recessed ceilings and mood lighting. There are two opulent wooden doors on either side of this immense space that branch off like a cross, it's all open-plan. The whole space is encased in marble and mirror. I am led to a wooden door on the left.

The handle is a naked woman stretching backward in brass. My thumb nestles between her breasts when I push the heavy door forward.

It is chilly in the room. The air conditioner hums with the odd rattle as the fan takes strain in the humidity. I notice an opulent king-size mattress embedded in an exotic wooden frame. Balinese style. The side lamps glow a gentle yellow on either side of the bed. Slippery blue silk sheets are pulled taut across the bed. One side of the bed has been invitingly turned down.

"The servants have put this glass jug of water for you to drink from. It is safe and clean."

"Thank you."

"Whatever you do, do not drink the water from the taps, or anywhere else for that matter. Only if I say you can drink it, then drink it. Always ask, okay?"

"Okay."

The silky pillows shimmer under the soft glow. There are wall-to-wall cupboards with mirrored doors along the longest wall of the room. I am too shy to look into them.

"This will be your room while you stay with me."

He opens another majestic wooden door leading off the bedroom. The bathroom is fresh looking. It's clad with green frosted glass. There are 'twirly' green bamboo stalks in beautiful tubular glass vases. The basin floats on top of the frosted counter. The counter is laden with every girl's dream items. Lancôme lipstick set of three. Dior shadow combo. Lancôme mascara. A bottle of Clinique Happy. There is a well-lit mirror against the marble wall and a smaller one for applying makeup. The shower is all glass and takes up half the space.

"These products are yours to use, please don't be shy. Now get some sleep. We will leave for the office by 9am. I will wake you at 8am. It's almost 4am – that gives you four good hours of sleep."

"Thank you, you are very kind."

"You don't have a phone to set an alarm right?"

"No, you told me to leave it behind 'cause you were not sure if we were on a different system or something."

"Ya, that's fine. We'll sort you out with one when we return from Kuala Lumpur."

The servant who opened the main door pads softly across the room with my suitcase and gently places it on the sideboard next to the sound system. He has a pair of scissors in his hand. He snips the cable ties off, unzips the lid and walks out without a word.

"There is a bell next to your bed; use it if you need something. One of the servants will attend to you. Now sleep sweets. And, oh, welcome to India."

"Thank you."

He walks out and I am so relieved. I can hardly believe my luck. He checks out. My veins are all in tact, and I have not been sold yet. I dance around a little and come to sit on my slippery bed. Fuck, look at me, I'm in Bollywood baby, for real! This is my life – I'm gonna live it!

I pull my new 'specially bought for India' jammies on from Woolies. They are made of baby-blue towelling material. It's a two-piece. Tank top and hot-pants bottoms.

The silk sheets are cool and smooth on my skin. I slip around trying to get used to them. I am so happy this has all checked out, I think I have found my favourite land so far. This time I want to stay. Maybe forever. I fall asleep in India to the drone of an air conditioner that struggles with a rusted fan choking in its throat.

Long drop down

My nose brings me out of my dog-tired dreams. It becomes aware of a rich, seductive scent, with spicy Eastern undertones. It demands my attention. I open my eyes. The Producer is standing over me, freshly shaven, a leopard-print gold-rimmed mug with four gold balls as feet in his hand. The aroma of coffee wafts past me. I am self-conscious and quickly wipe my sleepy eyes, trying to look alert and enthusiastic. Lying down seems submissive and vulnerable to me. I stand up, but, realising how skimpy my outfit is, quickly sit down again.

"Nice pyjamas," he says, winking. I squirm, but I'm not in the least surprised, sooner or later it was bound to happen. For now, I'm so relieved that most of who he is has checked out.

The coffee is strong, rich and very sweet. There's rich foam on the top sprinkled with raw granules of coffee cutting the sweet with its bitterness. For an Italian, this meets the mark.

We are back in the golden bullet, encapsulated in an air-conditioned, leather-clad monstrosity that seems too ostentatious for these streets. I am cut off from the heat, the smells and the loudness of the chaos happening around me. I feel like I am watching a silent movie. The sun is bright, but there is still a muggyness about the light; yellow-tinged smog hangs above us. They say that breathing in one day of Bombay's air is like smoking forty cigarettes in one go. I'm dying for a cigarette – I have not had one since I left South Africa.

Today The Producer sits in the front seat. He plays chess on his mobile phone, randomly picking his teeth with the stylus. The same portly man from last night drives. He must be the official driver.

We drive for over an hour, battling it out through the traffic. My flesh is soon icy from the air conditioning. I shift to the other side of the back seat into a ray of sun. I stare out the window, transfixed by what I see.

The roads are narrow, untarred, potholed and bumpy. We move so slowly that I am almost a part of what is happening outside. I resist, trying not to see too much, just yet. I leave again tomorrow. The more I see now, the less I have to look forward to when I come back. It's also almost too much to absorb. Everywhere is dense with people, dogs, cows and colour.

There is an unnerving loudness about the silence in the car. I want to break it, but I don't know what to say. There is no acknowledgement whatsoever between the boss and the driver, it's as if he does not exist.

I am shaken out of my awkwardness by the constant tapping on my window by very poor-looking street children. They push their clammy hands and faces up against the glass, demanding money as they throw their hands open towards my face staring back at them, banging more violently until we move on. I stare at the smudged glass. It suddenly seems too much. I look down into my lap and plug into my CD player for a while. The only person I know in all this pandemonium is sitting in front of me and I don't even know yet what I know about him.

I have arrived at the tail end of the monsoon.

We step out onto what seems to be a pile of concrete rubble, the pavement. The heat and smell of stagnation hits me, though nothing stands still. Everything is so busy, so crowded, so loud mouthed and in my face. All eyes are on me.

I follow The Producer down a side alley. A man in a vest stands behind a makeshift trolley, smashing pineapples in a wooden press. The sweet fruity smell mingles with the rancid waft of garbage. Avoiding murky puddles, we pass through a roller door and into a giant warehouse. Its dark mouldy walls loom high up into a metal rooftop. Exposed pipes and grotesque foil-like ventilation tubes hang snake-like high above. A few floodlights mounted on stands light up the vast open space at angles. There are some scattered red-and-white plastic garden chairs, a plastic table and an abundance of thin metal trunks stacked along walls. Some stand alone and are being used as seats.

There is a lot of coming and going. Everyone is dark. I feel like a glow worm. I am introduced to no one and no one introduces themselves to me. I guess for now I don't have to try to make friends or familiarise myself too much around here. I am a rolling stone. I leave again tomorrow morning.

We go to Bangalore for a production meeting with the client and agency, then on to Chennai to catch a connecting flight to Kuala Lumpur. I don't think too much is expected of me yet. I don't even know what my role in all this is going to be.

The Producer is on his mobile phone talking in Hindi. He points to an empty red plastic chair and beckons me to sit down. I obey. My eyes become accustomed to the light. There is a strange set up in the corner of the room: a red curtained-off area with a spotlight behind it. I see Indian girls dressed in sexy Western clothes move in and out from behind the curtain. Their silhouettes strike poses behind the red, growing big and distorted as they move. What is going on back there? Are they shooting a sex movie? Just when I thought I was in the clear.

When The Producer is off the phone, I walk over to his plastic desk. "Is there anything I can do?" Protruding eyes follow me; everyone almost slows down to stare.

"No, why don't you grab a chai or coffee and wait over there." He points back at a chair.

I sit back on my chair with a permanent smile plastered on my face. I want people to think I'm nice. Nobody approaches me, except the man who makes me my coffee (I later learn that these men in fawn uniforms are called *peons*). It's in a tiny little glass. It's sickly sweet.

A weedy man enters. He reminds me of an airport trolley. He is very dark and keeps his sunglasses on. He has a huge gold Rolex on his wrist and a ring on every finger, including big pearl rings protruding off his pinkie fingers. His pinkie fingernails are long. Long and filed like little spades for digging. I squirm, digging in which hole, for what? He clutches a crinkly yellow plastic bag with 'Diwali Sweets' written repeatedly all over it in red. He has a gold chain around his exposed hairless chest.

The Producer is on the phone again, he stops for a second and they exchange quiet words. The man places the bag on the floor next to The Producer's feet and leaves.

When The Producer is off the phone, he beckons me to come and sit across from him. He puts the plastic bag onto the plastic table. "Count these."

I open the bag, confused, until I see what I'm counting. Two brick-thick piles of American Express traveller's cheques. Each to the value of $500.00.

All this money and we are working on garden furniture?

I am back in my chair, my exaggerated smile in place.

A short stocky girl peeps out from behind the red curtain. She looks straight at me and giggles. She walks toward me holding a camcorder. Oh God, am I next? Is this really happening? At least the camera operator is a girl and seems nice, if I have to take my clothes off. She is wearing a denim mini skirt and a tight-fitting top that hugs her robustness. A huge '?' in red glitter bounces between her voluptuous breasts.

"Hi, my name is Nisha. You must be Gené right?"

"Yes, how did you know?"

"I like your clothes. You're a size 10 right?"

God, here we go … "Um yes, how did you know?"

She giggles. "I'm really good with sizes. There's a surprise waiting for you at The Producer's house, he asked me to pick it up for you."

"Nisha, you fat cow, are you using that gym membership I bought you? It does not look like it, *yaar*."

The Producer is off the phone again. Nisha giggles and makes her way toward The Producer. He leans forward and pinches her waistline hard. She squeals and buckles forward.

"Yes, I'm trying, you know it's hard with these long hours and all."

"One tight slap and you won't find it hard."

He looks across at me, "Gené, Nisha, Nisha, Gené."

He tugs on her skirt, "And you must stop wearing such short skirts, you have not got the body for it, *yaar*. When you look like that" – he points at a very tall skinny model leaving – "then we can talk."

She laughs, "I will never look like that unless you buy me a new body with very long legs."

She moves off, still giggling. This makes me feel better. His staff are obviously happy here. I recall the words in his email to my father: "Although we are extremely professional in our work, we run a close-knit production house which is more like a family and having spent time with Gené during our shoot in Cape Town, I am more than certain that she would fit in very comfortably within our organisation and make friends almost immediately."

I sit and I sit and I sit. Eventually, the small man in the fawn uniform and three others begin to lay newspaper down onto one of the plastic tables. On it, they place a bunch of metal spoons, cans of diet cola and an array of little round tin containers filled with what seem to be different curries.

All the men and women that were busily working around me gather around the table. They chat enthusiastically among themselves in Hindi.

"Come." The Producer hands me a plate. Everyone else is tucking in. They all eat with their hands. I'm almost shocked, but then remind myself that this is what they do. I am shy as I have never done this before. It seems so wrong. I take a spoon.

The Producer briefly introduces each dish to me. "This is dal, chicken and *palak paneer*, which is a kind of cheese in spinach." I try them all. The food is rich and spicy. I have never had such good curry before.

I ask for the bathroom and am pointed in the right direction by a very gentle-looking woman who understands English.

The first door I push is a urinal, filled with little pink camphor blocks. I move out quickly. The second door has a hole in the floor. The floor is tiled bright orange. It is wet. Urine maybe. There are brown zig-zag shoe prints in all this wet. I gag. I squat over the hole, holding my breath and trying not to get the bottoms of my jeans sodden in urine. I am left to drip dry with no toilet paper in sight. My thighs burn, trying to hold 'the position'. I lose my balance; in a frantic attempt not to fall into all the 'siffness' I grab onto a bucket full of water next to me. It topples over with my weight and my shoes get drenched. There's a little measuring jug that was floating on top of the water in the bucket. I lose it down the hole of the long drop. "Fuck it!"

I walk out of there in a huff. My feet suck into my shoes which are squidgy and heavy with the weight of water inside them.

It's dark. We finally leave to go home. The young crowd are still frantically working. They are prepping for our trip to Kuala Lumpur. I still don't understand what is going on around me, but there will be time for me to learn, when I return.

Sheridans and rice

The same servants from yesterday are scrambling to attention when we arrive. It is almost 10pm. It has taken us over two hours to get home in the traffic. The office is only 16 kilometres from the house. We live in Juhu and work in Worli.

I can't wait to get my waterlogged shoes off my feet. My feet are so sore and wrinkly from the wet. I go straight to my room. There is a beautiful Indian three-piece outfit spread out on my bed. It is a deep dark red, heavily worked with sequins and coloured stones and embroidered with gold thread. The workmanship is magnificent. I learn later that it's called a *salwar kameez.*

There's a knock on the door. The Producer pops his head through. "*Khānā* is ready," he says, indicating that the food is ready.

I hold up the top. "This is so beautiful, thank you."

"Good you like it, is the size right?"

"I think so."

"Well, don't thank me, thank Nisha, she made it for you, she was really excited when I told her about you."

"She's so sweet and very pretty."

"She needs her ass kicked."

"Why do you give her such a hard time?"

"Because she's my responsibility and I care about her health and how she looks, I don't want her ending up looking like a fat slob, she's still so young."

"Your responsibility?"

"My driver found her in a dumpster on the beach when she was two weeks old. I took her in and brought her up like my own. When I got too busy with work she went to live with my mother and my cousin. It's a more stable environment for her there; my mother has more time for her."

"How old is she?"

"Twenty'"

A pink label in the collar catches my eye, 'Nisha'.

"Adopting a stranded baby is a very generous act."

"One should always give back in life; it seemed like the right thing to do."

"You're a good man."

"I have my days just like everybody else."

I follow him to the dining room table. Two servants are carrying various dishes through. I recognise one from last night. He opened the door and brought my suitcase into my room. He is young and tall. Well built. The other is much older. He is really stocky and has a huge belly. They tiptoe barefoot around us. I look down. The short one has real troll feet. I try not to think about it, but his toes look cheesy. They place bowls and bowls of food around us. I look across into the mirrored wall. We sit back, just the two of us at this huge round dining room table. One black. One white. Near the front door there is a lit-up glass statue of a woman and man embracing. The man is made of black glass; the woman in his arms is made of white glass. How ironic!

I bring myself back to the table and realise that, out of respect, I am going to have to eat with my hands. I remind myself, right hand – food hand, left hand – arse-wiping hand. Got it! This can't be too hard. "Can I give you some butter chicken?"

"Yes please."

"And some rice?"

"No thank you. I would prefer a *roti.*" I say this thinking I can use it as a scooping tool for the butter chicken. Rice seems too messy to start with.

He spoons the butter chicken onto my plate and beckons to the tall servant to drop a piping hot *roti* onto my plate.

"We actually call these *chapatis* here in Bombay. *Roti* is a more universal word for all the different breads, and the name of my dog of course. Can I serve you up some of this too? It's called *baingan bhurta*, which is eggplant."

"Yes please."

"And some dal?"

As the short servant places a bowl of rice peaked into the shape of a mountain down onto the table, The Producer begins to shout loudly in Hindi. I have taken my first bite of butter chicken. I stop chewing and begin to panic. Don't use arse hand, right hand only, fuck is he shouting at me? Before I know it, he is pushing his sizeable rounded body away from the table, face contorted with anger. Scraping chair on marble, voice booming, he has the short stocky servant by the collar of his shirt. He frog marches him across the room to the front door and pushes him hard down the stairs. He spins round, slams the door and comes back to the table. My eyes begin to water, I have swallowed the butter chicken down the wrong way. Some of the contents of my *chapati* has also fallen out onto the table. I quickly hide it by moving my plate over it, discreetly.

"*Bhenchod*! Sorry about that, the fucker was scratching his balls while serving my rice."

The young, tall servant has disappeared into the kitchen. We continue eating.

"So what did you think of your first day in India?"

"I love it already."

"Well, you've seen nothing yet. Give it time. I notice that you are very comfortable with the food – most foreigners find it too spicy. If your stomach can handle the food, then you have overcome one of India's biggest obstacles."

The Producer rings the bell on the table, the tall servant returns, on edge. The Producer mumbles something to him in Hindi and he goes back into the kitchen. This time he returns with a mammoth black Rottweiler on a chain.

"Sweets, meet Roti, he is my imported Rottweiler I was telling you about."

The tall servant hands The Producer six slices of white bread. The Producer rises from the table and leads the chained dog a few metres away into an open space in the room. He begins taunting Roti, throwing his body forward and landing hard on both feet. Then he moves back and repeats this motion, this time he begins to slap Roti playfully on the side of his jowls. The hound begins to salivate. He becomes excited and starts leaping forward. There's a tussle between these two heavy males. The Producer holds one of the slices of bread against the dog's nose, then moves it quickly up into the air. He repeats this a few times before he allows Roti to grab it as he leaps. His body crashes down hard onto the marble floor, the force vibrating through his massive limbs. He quivers briefly and then goes up for the next piece. This performance ends when every slice of bread has been inhaled.

The Producer, the dog and I retire to the terrace. The terrace is large and is surrounded by palm trees. There is a view of Juhu beach and its murky Indian Ocean, but it is dark now.

The tall servant arrives with a tray. On it are two shot glasses, a bottle of Sheridan's, a pack of cards and a bell.

"Shall we play a game of blackjack? Winner, best out of three, gets to wish for something from the loser. This wish must be granted when we get to Kuala Lumpur."

Roti's face is level with mine. The more I try to avoid his intense stare, the closer he edges toward me.

I agree to the deal with a sweet smile. "Okay, sounds like fun." I've had many years around the Sunday lunch table with my family playing blackjack using coffee beans as money.

"Can you wish for anything, even expensive shoes?"

"Yes, anything, why? What shoes do you want?"

"Well, there's a Camper store in the famous Petronas Towers, so that's what I would want if I win: a new pair of Campers."

We play. The Producer wins two out of three.

"That settles it then. I've won."

The Producer begins to pour the shots. I watch the black coffee liqueur pour out first, then the white chocolate float on top.

"Cheers."

I hesitate. "Can't we play best out of six?"

"No ... we can't. A deal is a deal."

"So what's your wish? And don't ask me for three."

"Don't act dumb, Gené-baba. You know what my wish is. Don't ruin it by making me spell it out."

He swigs his shot back. I follow. I refuse a second, but he twists my arm to it.

"Bedtime, I will show you to your room."

"But I know where my room is."

"Come. I suggest you repack for Kuala Lumpur. We are only there for six days of shoot. Pack light, I will take you shopping; I hate the clothes you are wearing – they make you look fat. The top of your arms look like a bodybuilder's in that silly top with the frills."

He turns round and without warning pushes me up against the wall. His prickly moustache and whacking lips press against mine. His tongue begins to pry my little lips apart until he is inside my mouth.

I manage to squirm out from under him. "Not now!" is all I can think of to say.

He looks at me with a smirk.

"Remember, a deal is a deal and you lost. It's almost 2am. Pack and get some sleep. We leave in four hours for the airport."

We leave for Kuala Lumpur to shoot two commercials.

I have never flown business class before.

A deal is a deal

I know exactly what will happen in the hotel room in Kuala Lumpur. There are no surprises here.

In the adjoining room the showerhead spills down hard onto the stone floor. I can hear a shifting in its water flow as it runs down various parts of his beefy grotesque nakedness. The mirror is steaming up, but not enough for my liking. If I look up from my seated position I will see. I will see, and still it is no surprise because I know exactly what I will see: penis, hair, bum, testes, penis, hair, bum, testes ... lips, hands not still, but wandering ... dark not light, dark not light ... different ... Indian and a great deal older ... in fact, exactly double my age ... double my size in width.

But it's not like he's forcing me; it's much more like manipulated consent from both sides. By coming to India I have inadvertedly agreed to the chain of events that will play out in front of an audience that consists of hotel room furniture and a team of soccer players on the flat-screen TV in front of me.

I begin to untie my laces, slowly pulling the soft cream strands through the fingers of my right hand. Feeling the laces pull through my fingers reminds me of the stray cat's tail I pulled through my hand when we first spoke back in Cape Town.

"Come," he shouts from under the spill, sounding like he's in a fishbowl. I am jolted from my thoughts. My eye catches an excuse to prolongue the inevitable agony, the convenience-store packet with the extra tubs of ice cream and the Kinder Surprise egg which I chose as my goodnight surprise. A good night surprise always reminds me of the safety of my childhood. My mother often used to put a Kinder Surprise egg under our pillow for us to find when we went to bed at night.

"I'm just putting the ice cream into the freezer. It's all I have to show after losing the bet," I shout over the blaring soccer match and its fans watching me.

"Don't worry, you will have a smile on your face when I'm done with you, now hurry," he gurgles back through the water.

I cringe and my stomach flips. Taking one last cheer from the lamp on the desk that bends in applause with its big shiny head, I imagine it as the famous hopping desk lamp, the unforgettable trademark of Miramax! For the love of film, that's why I have to do this. That's why I am here.

I step across the line between smooth tile and pebbled tile. The oversized square showerhead pours over us like a rain forest. The mirrors are more misted in here. Good, I don't have to see.

I am not turned on. There is no burning desire between my legs. I am not attracted to him in the least. I'm also stone cold sober, so no hazy inebriation helping me along. A little 'Dutch courage' would be really helpful at this point in time. Standing in this five-star hotel in the exotic setting of Asia's Kuala Lumpur, I am so scared even though I know this has to happen. We have to get it out of the way so that my adventure in this new land can begin. My arms clutch criss-cross over my chest, hiding my naked breasts. I've got as far as removing everything, but my full cotton panties. I am dying of embarrassment and fear. I am not Sharon Stone in *Basic Instinct*; I have no sexy moves, but he clearly does.

Standing in that shower, I feel like he is living his erotic fantasy. A voluptuous white woman half his age, standing naked under the misty waterfall. I am all his to devour, I will be his brag tag at the next party he attends. I am the American fucking dream that has infected Asian society with its fantasy of 'white skin'.

"Come on, baby, what you waiting for? Are you trying to tease me?"

He grips hard into my arse and begins to peel my now wet and transparent panties down my legs. I fold forward holding my breasts with one hand and resist with the other. I know I can't cry, I will blow my chances, instead, I laugh. Folded forward, my head is now in line with his crotch. His thighs loom like furry tree trunks in front of me. He pushes my head into the direction of his erect penis. I splutter and choke under the downpour of water.

"I can't, I can't breath like this." This is so much harder than I thought it would be.

He pulls me onto my feet. My eyes meet his. His tight lips and serpentine tongue sponge their way around my face, sucking and pushing repeatedly, flooding my mouth with water, and together we choke. "This is not working, turn around," he says excitedly. I stiffen. His thickset fingers are frantically trying to pry my thighs apart. I can't, I just can't, but I must. My eyes squeeze shut as I face the tiled wall and my fingers curl tightly inwards; they have nothing to grip. All that I have to cling onto for support is an icy cold slippery shower wall. My fingers repeatedly grasp against the wet flatness of nothing. I fold into myself like the "easy 2-step fold-up bed" from infomercials. I move my mind away from what is happening so that my body unclenches slightly. The quicker he penetrates, the quicker it will all be over.

He is inside me now. Fuck no condom! To suppress my panic I think of my Kinder Surprise egg waiting for me; I wonder what little toy is hiding inside. I'm about to think of my mother with her surprises, but I block it fast; I can't, it will make me weak. God, if she knew what I was doing right now.

As he moves behind me, thrusting back and forth, the shivers running up and down my spine have become so intense that I am becoming numb all over. He comes. Whether it's infected or not, I do not know, it's too late now anyway.

If I die of Aids at least I die, because this is fucking crazy, all for a little taste of Tinsel Town. I have removed my mind so far away from the situation that I almost feel like I'm watching someone else perform these unspeakable acts, while I look on, telling my clone how stupid she is for allowing all this, especially the no condom part. For god's sakes, Gené!

He has a 'just-come smile' plastered across his large cakehole. "Aaa, that feels so much better, shall we move to the bedroom?"

He hands me a plush white robe, gesturing to the matching slippers near the door.

"You can have my pair, my feet are too big for these small Asian sizes."

I can't bring myself to say anything.

"Come, let's eat the ice cream. It's your reward for losing the bet."

We sit on the bed, sharing the tub, and I'm so relieved that it's all over.

"Are you taking protection?"

"Well, no, I was trying to …"

"What, are you crazy? Where are you in your cycle?"

"I'm safe for the moment, but I thought you would use protection and, well … I didn't know this was going to happen so quickly."

"Come on? Don't play dumb, you knew exactly where this was going. I'm a clean man. I don't have diseases, what are you trying to imply here? I am allergic to latex, that's why I don't use condoms. My dick will fall off, then what will I please you with, hey?"

I feel small and reprimanded so I apologise for insulting his Aids-free status. I can only hope this is true.

"We will get you on the pill as soon as we are back in India. Now come here, I want you to ride me."

What? I thought I was done?

"But it's so late."

"It's never too late sweets. Besides it's just past 2am – you only have to be up at five."

I am too shy to take the gown off. I'm feeling the same way all over again, no matter how hard I pretend. I mount him as he asks and move to his desired speed until he comes, again. I'm so not there. I'm nowhere in particular this time. It's done for now and that is all I care about.

I move off him and tighten the robe. I glance back into the demisted mirror just before I enter the bathroom. Reflecting back at me are two truncated legs, sprawled limply to their sides, the anaconda is spent.

When I return, he has lit a cigar. Now he really is living out the American dream. The after-sex cigar.

"You better get back to your room before anyone sees. I don't want the client or agency to know."

I feel insulted. The idea of him wanting me and being proud of me would be far more flattering than him bringing me all the way here to be the silent fuck.

"Yeah sure, of course, see you later."

I'm actually too tired to care. At least I won't have to worry about another round. I dress and leave with the slippers on. In my room I turn the 'Miramax hopping lamp' on, placing my Kinder Surprise egg under its glow.

I really need to take a hot bath and listen to some angry music.

I empty all four bottles of hotel cosmetics into the bath water. Shampoo, foam bath, shower gel and body lotion. I soak for almost an hour. My thoughts puncture a small hole into my canvas. It was blank until now. The colours of thought saturate it until there is no quiet white area left. It's busy and chaotic.

I cry. Why am I so upset?

I wrap myself into yet another plush robe, climb onto my bed with its 500-thread duck-down duvet and reach for my CD player and my Kinder Surprise egg …

Finally. My little reward for being brave.

Dawn is breaking behind the two monumental Petronas Towers that are lit internally. Their halogen glow reminds me of … I want to say something clever, but again all I see is penis!

It's too late, but at the same time, too early to get any sleep.

I am over the initial shock of the sex with him. I accept that I am going to have to satisfy his needs for the duration of my stay. It's a two-way street and as long as I am getting what I want then so should he. It doesn't even take that much of a mind shift.

Whatever 'India' wants me to be, I will be and give it my all. One thing I know is that this opportunity is not coming around twice.

The phone rings. I am jolted from my thoughts. A sweet and gentle automated voice recording with an Asian accent bids me 'good morning'.

It's 5am. I dress and get ready to take part in my first location recce ever!

It's not what you know, it's who you know

The first commercial we shoot here in Kuala Lumpur is for a skin-lightening cream with a Croatian model. We 'cheat' her for being Indian. This way the audience will truly believe that the cream really does work. Her skin is paler than any Indian I have seen. Skin-lightening cream has a huge market in India – the paler you are the better you are, class-wise. The director, Kiran Cooper, is the same director that was in Cape Town for the Pickle Perfect bread spread commercial. Although we did not speak in Cape Town it is undoubtably him. He wears a pirate's eye patch. In Cape Town it was black, but today it is white with a Hello Kitty sticker staring back at me. I can't help smiling, very amused. He grunts, smiling back at me, revealing two huge dimples set perfectly on either cheek. His exposed eye expresses his surprise to see me. He is extremely tall with a mop of thick black shiny curls that cascade onto his shoulders covering two sizeable ears. He has a thick black moustache framing his voluptuous lips. He looks menacing, but his looks deceive him – he obviously has a fantastic sense of humour; I refrain from asking about the eye patch.

"You likc it?" he says, pointing at the patch.

"Yes, sir, it's very cool."

"Aa ... my eight-year-old daughter, aa ... stuck it on before I left, she found it in a chewing gum wrapper."

"Hello Kitty's definitely the way to go, sir, it's all the rage these days."

"Everything made in China's the rage these days, my dear."

"Guess so, sir."

Kiran Cooper lives in Chennai; he arrived this morning.

Everyone is extremely conscious of his presence. There is a sense of awe and immense respect toward him. He is in his early forties, but has obviously already made a huge impression on Bollywood. When he speaks, he mumbles slightly. He seems very intimidating with his eye and grand stature, but his tone is gentle and subdued.

He is kind and patient with me. He obviously understands that I am here to please The Producer in the bedroom, picking up on my inexperience on set. I have never assisted a director, and only been on a set three times as a camera assistant. It's different to anything I have done. I am the only 'crew member' from Luna Films on this shoot. I guess The Producer feels it's a small enough shoot for one person to handle. The problem is, not someone with absolutely no fucking clue. Kiran Cooper guides me through most of it. I am costume department, props department and assistant director. I'm spinning! I have really been thrown into the deep end and I am in over my head. The Producer does not want me to show him up in front of the client. He keeps saying, "She's joined us from South Africa, she's been doing this for years."

Behind closed doors he freaks out at me.

"You do not have to be a fucking genius to figure it out, just get it fucking right. Do you need a whack from me or wot?"

On top of all this, I am summonsed to his room every night and then sent back to mine in the early hours of the morning. I am exhausted.

One morning, after very little sleep, I forget the model's shirt that she is meant to wear. Luckily we have not left the hotel yet. We are all sitting at the breakfast table, Kiran Cooper, the client and the agency. I am on my third coffee, my eyelids are being held open with invisible matchsticks.

The Producer walks straight up to me. Hands on hips, shoulders hunched forward, he towers over me.

"Where's the shirt?"

He begins to flick his finger at me. "Where the fuck is the shirt Gené?"

I had to get the hotel to iron it for me the night before. We were such a small unit that even getting the clothes ironed for the model was my responsibility. The hotel delivered it to The Producer's room because I was 'tending to his needs' at the time. I forgot it there. He did not remind me when I dutifully left his room, so I guess this is a test.

"Do you need to be fucking spoonfed or wot? Did you think the shirt would bring itself down here? You must learn to fucking think for yourself. Go get it! Fast!"

I wonder if all these staring people know that I was fucking this man in his hotel room less than four hours ago. Everyone looks away as I leave the table, hanging my head in shame. The creative director takes a picture of the scene on my camera. I find it two days later.

We move on to do a luggage commercial. Again Kiran Cooper directs. This time there is a younger man assisting from the Luna office, Kush.

Kush was also in Cape Town assisting Kiran Cooper. He is in his late thirties and I feel his disapproval towards me. I wonder if he is threatened by the new addition to the crew. His looks are stereotypically those of a very handsome Indian male. He is tall and has strong features; a strong jaw line, perfectly shaped nose and dark-set eyes – making him the perfect character to play Aladdin in *Ali Baba and the Forty Thieves*. He has a beard with flecks of grey; he has matured early, his facial hair making him look a little older. Although not with me, he laughs easily. He is not traditional in any sense and speaks about his creative ideas in a very up-beat European style resonating his talent. Kiran Cooper takes his advice and welcomes his assistance with great fondness. Although they are from different cities they clearly know each other well, having worked together often on Luna Film's commercials. I watch Kush take control of the Malaysian crew. He is confident in his manner and does not lack experience. He is very comfortable with the responsibility of running The Producer's set. I watch him take orders from Kiran Cooper and The Producer without hesition or ego. I wonder why a man his age is still assisting if he is as good as he seems.

Everything is organised as they were already prepping in Kuala Lumpur while I was on the skin-lightening cream shoot. Kush has got it all under control. He is not interested in my help and so I am put in charge of the stills photography. This is right up my alley. I know exactly what to do. The problem is I am not getting any sleep with long hours on set followed by long hours in The Producer's room at night.

Barely a week later, we land back in Mumbai, India. The Producer queues separately to me as he's an Indian citizen. He hands me his passport when we join up again.

"Put this safely in your bag."

He walks ahead. I glimpse at the first page. Date of birth, 12 July 1953. Exactly twice my age.

It's barely been a week and I'm back here dealing with my favourite little trolleys again. I have double the luggage. The Producer has spoilt me. I have kept my end of the deal, but so has he. In fact, more than his fair share of it. After the shoots he took me shopping at the Petronas Towers. I did get a pair of Campers in the end. I got two bottles of perfume, Bulgaria Omnia and a Ralph Lauren. Nowadays the Omnia always reminds me of Kuala Lumpur. Its heaviness and intensity always hits the spot that makes my insides turn and twist like a pretzel. He buys me an upbeat orange Prada handbag and some name-branded clothing. I am not allowed to choose any of it. He selects five tops and two pairs of jeans, one Levi's, one Diesel.

"This should tide you over until your weight drops."

He then proceeds to buy an array of glitzy items with a lot of sequins. A tube top, a dress and some very beautiful Guess slacks. They are a size 6, two sizes too small.

"But these clothes are not my size? If I try them on, they will not fit."

"You're not going to try them on. You're going to lose some weight first."

"I'm not fat."

"Yes, you are, fatsy. Look at your arms."

He pinches the top of my arm hard; it burns and leaves a mark.

I wonder if poor Nisha's waistline is bruised too.

I am no longer a rolling stone. I must stop and begin to fit into this land. Be present and attentive, start learning names, get to know people and make an effort. Everything has happened so fast, it's time to get to know my new home. The light hangs dirty yellow in the smoggy sky. It smudges across everything in its wake. It's a Sunday morning, but the hustle and bustle of the people is in full swing. I don't think it ever slows down. Bombay never sleeps.

There are hawkers and tuk-tuks, taxis and cars, buses, elephants, cows, dogs and beggars. Prehistoric fruit carts, wagons and mobile stalls get hauled in criss-cross directions. The honking and shouting is relentless. Motorbikes and bicycles weave in and out, left to right. There is such a fine line between life and death with the chaotic comings and goings, but nothing ever seems to collide, everything flows in this apparent chaos.

We head straight to Film City for another shoot which The Producer's business partner Alisha has been prepping while we were away. Their first day of shoot is today. Film City is where Bollywood's main studios are. I imagine Universal Studios L.A.

To my surprise we enter what appears to be a jungle, and eventually a clearing, which looks like an accumulation of scrapyards pieced together by dense jungle and bending palm trees that are trying to escape the suffocating weeds. Large mud-crusted hogs rummage through rotting rubbish; crows flutter and squawk above them with attitude. There are stray yellow dogs everywhere. Some are too weak to stand upright. Most of them pass their days sleeping. Flies accumulate around their wet parts – wounds, eyes, noses and assholes. Their ribs, spines and hips protrude at angles. Their joints catch as they slink around. Starving puppies try to attach themselves to dehydrated teats. They are frenzied, gnawing at the mother with their needle-sharp teeth. She is raw and infected. Too weak to care, she lies there, eyes closed, waiting for death to take her away. This Tinsel Town is so goddamned depressing. I follow The Producer into one of these colossal warehouses. The shift from bright light to pitch dark blinds me momentarily. I stumble on the gravel floor. Again I am eyeballed from all directions.

The air conditioning must be blasting at full force. It is ice cold inside here. There is a stage in the middle of the room with a pink Tuscan-style apartment built on top of it. A pebble-stoned courtyard stretches out, with a Vespa parked before the front door. Pretty little plant boxes filled with real-looking plastic flowers hang below each window. Shutters are painted to look real against the pre-fab walling. Italy in India. Each warehouse holds a secret 'cheat land' behind its closed roller door, in and among filth and jungle. Today my land is in Tuscany.

I think everything is going wrong. Over time I learn that this is completely normal. If it's not like this then something is very wrong.

Cables criss-cross along the floor without warning. Avoiding a detrimental trip becomes top priority in the dark. The live wires run straight out of the generator and are just pushed into sockets. There is no earthing. Everyone is talking, one on top of the other. The word 'silence' gets shouted out, then repeated by each and every man standing on the set. Silence takes over ten minutes to achieve and only lasts for ten seconds before the noise escalates again until the next 'silence' is shouted and this cycle gets repeated over and over again.

The director is a Chinese woman from Australia. She looks like she is in hell. Holding her head in her hands, she shakes it in desperation and frustration. I think she is crying at one point. A soft-spoken Indian woman reassures her. She looks calm and in control. This must be Alisha. Everyone is running around aimlessly, or acting as human sandbags staring vacantly as they hang onto poles. Labour is so cheap that there is an overpopulation of crew, causing confusion rather than being productive. I learn that compared to anywhere else in the world, it takes twice as long to achieve anything here, but costs a quarter of the price.

Dark men linger high above us in the shadows, balancing massive film lights on flimsy bamboo riggings meant to be their scaffolding. If something goes wrong, they slip and fall, the bamboo breaks ... a very heavy cradle shall fall. The only other woman besides Alisha and the director is Nisha. She's handling the costume with a very enthusiastic man my age, Sashi.

There is a distinct hierarchy of cast involved in the positions people take on set. The *peons* are on the lowest rank, the assistant directors on the next rank, and the director, cameraman and cast are on the highest rank with The Producer. Sashi is between the *peons* and us, the assistant directors. He is a very proud 'dressman'. His role entails ironing the costumes, making sure they are hung properly in the casts' trailers. Once they are taken off he makes sure they get washed for the next day or, if there is no next day, they are washed and returned intact to production. Sashi speaks very good English and he carries his title on set with much pride. He introduces himself.

"Good day, Madam Jimmy, my good name is Sashi. I am hearing many good vibrations from the people about you. I am happy to work with such a nice *firang*."

"Thank you, Sashi. I look forward to working with you too."

Sashi has a mountain of clothes to iron. As Nisha picks the outfits from the suitcases, he grabs, irons and folds. He works fast, but is very particular. He is wearing a bright pink bandana. Thick black curls escape along the sides, framing his baby face. He has a gold hooped earring in his right ear. A small headphone hangs from his left ear; he is plugged into his mobile phone. Hindi songs blare from the little speaker, which crackles from over use.

"This mobile is my best friend, madam, what mobile madam is having?'

"I don't have one yet, but when I get mine I will show you. Do you only work for Luna?"

"No, madam, I am freelance dressman. I am sometimes working for other companies on feature film, but Luna is always calling. I am going to Cape Town last year for feature film, with other company, it is very beautiful."

Sashi's smile is contagious. His apple cheeks blossom and glow with sweat droplets. He wipes the droplets off, batting his long lashes as the back of his hand moves across his face in an effeminate manner. He wears a white running vest and a braided gold chain hangs around his neck. His exposed biceps glisten with perspiration, catching the fluorescent light as they flex in motion. He moves the steaming iron across the board with a swagger and a swirl, enhancing his metrosexual appearance.

Tradition plays an important role during the first take on any set. On the first day of a shoot, after the first take has been shot, a coconut is smashed, signifying good will and fortune for the film or commercial. Dhiraj the spot boy cuts the coconut into pieces and sprinkles it with sugar. The plate is passed around and we are all expected to eat a piece. I join the chaos and move in waves of extreme hard labour to extreme boredom. The means of communication are so frustrating. The director and I do not speak Hindi and the crew do not speak any English except for The Producer's immediate production team, Alisha, Nisha and Sashi. There is no experienced first assistant director for the director. Kush is wrapping up Kuala Lumpur. Alisha communicates with the Hindi crew and I assist the director as much as I can. I like to feel needed and useful. At times I irritate Alisha as I try to do too much, stepping on her managerial toes. I will learn to get to know her and find a balance. I hope to earn her trust as she is extremely likeable.

If I thought that the bathroom at the Luna office was a hideous experience, this is abominable. It looks exactly like the bog in *Train Spotting*, except that it's a hole and not a bowl. The room resembles a slaughterhouse for goats. Old rust-coloured *paan* is splattered across the walls and floor. It's obviously the spittoon area as well. Globules of snot wobble on the floor hacked out from the back of someone's throat. I am so haunted by the bog that I sneak into the jungle. The Indians would be appalled if they knew a white girl was squatting, naked ass in the air, but I can't help it. I would rather deal with wet and uncomfortable nickers from the hasty 'drip-dry' technique and have the piece of mind that the piss on my frayed jean bottoms is mine.

We are shooting another skin-lightening product. The director decides to put me into this commercial. This time the lead is Indian, a pale one. We do not stop until midnight. The Producer sends his driver to fetch me. He did not stay for the shoot – once he saw Alisha had it under control he went home. When I arrive home he is on the bed watching another soccer match.

"Do you want *khānā*?"

"No thanks, Alisha ordered pizza for the crew."

"Why are you still awake? I'm exhausted, I would be sleeping if I were you."

"I slept for a few hours earlier this afternoon."

"Go get some sleep; you have another long day ahead of you tomorrow. I have organised for Alisha to pick you up on her way to set – she lives close by here and passes us to get to Film City."

"Okay, where are you going?"

"To the office. Now go; the servants will wake you at five."

Fitting in

I am exhausted. We roll from one shoot to the next without a day's rest. The Producer spends most of his time popping onto set, but then going off to secure the next job at the office or at the agency itself. The Producer has four *peons* who remain at the office running for whatever is needed there. The head *peon* of the office is Dhiraj. He speaks a little English. He is my age and always wanting to please. "Dhiraj diet cola, Dhiraj chai, Dhiraj …" and it's done with so much pride. We prep the job and work on it while The Producer lines the following one up, one after another.

Alisha manages the prep work and on-set coordination. Dhiraj comes to set as the tea boy and runner. He adores me and I him. On set his title is 'spot boy' and not *peon*.

We shoot mostly in Film City or at the warehouse that I first went to when I arrived, which I thought were the official offices of Luna. When I return from Kuala Lumpur I learn that the Luna offices are next door to this warehouse. The offices were being renovated and so everyone was working on tin *pettis* (trunks) and plastic garden furniture as a temporary solution. The offices are ultra modern: very hip and fresh in design. Giant clocks hang against bright yellow walls, each one depicting a different time zone. Sydney, New York, Hong Kong and, of course, India. A proper casting room, encased in glass and chrome, is built in the middle of the office space with a professional handy cam set up for auditions. This room is surrounded by an open-plan set up with twenty bright orange desks that all face forward. They each have comfortable blue-and-yellow chairs.

Alisha also sits among us even though she is The Producer's partner in business.

There is only one enclosed office, The Producer's 'cabin': 52" flatscreen TV, bar fridge, surround sound, massive marble-and-leather desk and, low and behold, a bright red studded velvet casting couch. No one can see into this room, it's completely private. The Producer is extremely superstitious and I am told that the 'cabin' has been designed to face Mecca. The rest of the office faces Mecca too. Everybody in the office must face forward, according to The Producer. If you face toward the cabin you are opposing him and his flow of business and this is not allowed.

Downstairs is a music studio and the bathrooms. They are in much better condition now than before.

I sit among the 'kids' in the open-plan area. I choose a desk just in front of Nisha and Kush. Except for Alisha and Kush, we are all in our early twenties. The Producer hires fresh new kids who are willing to work for very little money, get the experience and then move on and study further. Most of these kids are from very wealthy families. A few of them are in casting and production, but Kush seems to be the only on-set assistant director. He is the driving force behind The Producer. The Producer takes him all over the world. He wants to leave soon and study Directing at NYU in New York. It does not take me long to know that I want to do what he does, assistant directing. It is hands-on and immediate.

Alisha picks me up on a regular basis in the mornings and I work closely with her and Kush on set. Alisha tells me that she was married and has twins, a girl and a boy. She got married very young and had her children very young; their education is everything to her. She carries herself beautifully. She wears hip Western clothing and has a beautiful soft face. Her long black curls cascade all the way down her back to her waistline. She is a widower. Her husband passed away almost ten years ago.

Nisha has taken me in unconditionally. She showers me with love and affection. She buys me little gifts and checks in with the servants, making sure I have everything I need. She teases me and calls me her stepmom because I am dating the man who saved her from the dumpster on the beach. She takes me drinking with her friends and fiancé. They all make me feel included, speaking English even though I'm the only *firang*.

Her fiancé, Arin, however, gives me the creeps from the moment we meet. He is sly. I doubt his intentions. He seems obsessed with The Producer, bragging to his friends that he is marrying into The Producer's family. Is that why he is marrying her? He continually asks me what it's like to be the girlfriend of such a famous producer.

I am looked after and cared for by everyone around me. The caring *peons* in the office always have a constant supply of cigarettes for me. After all, I am The Producer's 'girlfriend'. Everyone is always making sure that my needs are taken care of.

The Producer hates the fact that I smoke. He makes it so clear that I hide it from him now, although he has started smoking again. He smokes forty filter cigarettes a day. He blames me, saying it started with the cigar in Kuala Lumpur. Before I arrived he had given up for almost a year. Nisha and I joke around a lot. We get 'merry' on rum at a bar called Rain and smoke our fake Marlboros. 'They' say that the cigarettes in India are bought off the grey market and are not the real deal. They do taste different. The Producer gets his from duty free, so does Alisha. Sometimes we light them at the wrong end due to our intoxication. They explode in our faces. Nisha roars with laughter, throwing her drink over me to 'extinguish' the fire. This starts a rip-roaring episode. I throw my drink back at her. We laugh until she wets her pants.

Sometimes I feel uncomfortable because I cannot pay for anything; Nisha pays for it all. She reassures me that The Producer has taken care of it, but I have my doubts. I have not spoken to The Producer about a possible salary – I don't know how, it's such a tricky subject.

The Producer's servants run my life like clockwork. I have hardly been there and have only got to know the tall young one, Sai. Sai is in charge of getting me up in the mornings with his divine coffee. There is always the knock on the door to wake me so that I can compose and cover myself.

"Come in," I shout once I gather myself.

The door then moves slowly, allowing light to slice the darkness of my cool blocked-out room. He quietly pads across the room, placing the coffee beside my bed. It is always in the same opulent leopard-print mug. He gently puts the side lamp on, beaming at me with a crocodile smile.

"Good morning, madam. Today you me Hindi speaking?"

"Sorry, me only English speaking, but again today we try, okay?"

"No problem, madam, me small English speaking, you me teach Hindi and English teach you me. Remember, madam, my good name Sai. Saying Hindi, *Mera naam Sai' ho.*"

"This is you telling, my good name Madam Jimmy. *Mera naam Madam Jimmy ho.*"

"Okay, Madam Jimmy very good. My coffee is good tasting?"

"Yes, my Sai, so good tasting."

He swings his arms out, totally chuffed with himself, then lets them flop like rag dolls at his sides. His crocodile smile exposes the gaps between his teeth. You could stick a new R5.00 coin between them.

"Madam, you me friends making?"

His eyes sparkle with glee.

"Boss telling *jaldi* (quickly) making!"

He goes straight to the mirrored cupboards and holds up various jeans and tops, pointing for me to choose. Whatever I give the thumbs up to, he puts onto a hanger and hooks onto the doorknob.

"Today this *kapadā* (clothes) wearing, very nice."

He flips the switch to the geyser for the shower as he passes the bathroom door.

This is our morning ritual. I am a whale, he is my barnacle, symbiotically our love for one another grows.

At night I eat food that is made by the 'invisible' cook I am yet to meet. He is also responsible for the lunches at the office when we are not on set. My clothes are washed, ironed and put back very neatly into the mirrored cupboard with newspaper between them. I learn that Kutty dutifully does this with love and pride. He is also responsible for making my bed and cleaning the house. He is the poor fucker who scratched his balls while serving The Producer's rice. I still have not officially met him either. I get driven by a mute driver whom I learn is named Balkran.

Lepracy on wheels

We finally have a day off. It is a Sunday. This is my first full day at home since I arrived in India, one full month earlier. We have shot twenty-one commercials in the space of thirty days.

"Madam Jimmy, boss calling."

I enter The Producer's room. It is arctic-like, his air conditioner blasting past the back of my neck; I shiver. A cricket match drags green and white up and down the almost 2.5-metre television he had flown in with us from Kuala Lumpur. A giant clock with roman numerals hangs next to a stepping machine that poses its very unused alternate arms towards the window overlooking the terrace. The Producer is slumped sideways reading his morning paper, his rolling hairy torso exposed. A massive red, black and white painting hangs above his bed. A portrait of himself. It functions as the headboard. Glasses on his nose, he looks up.

"Levi's has opened in Linking Road. I think we should check it out before lunch. I also want to take you to FabIndia and Cotton World to get some more tops for set, fatsy."

This must be payment for the month's work.

He pulls his giraffe-print duvet open. He is completely naked. "Come."

Linking Road is the 'shopping centre' of the suburbs.

It is a very long road running through Bandra with stalls and shops, one after another. The street is cramped and almost closed-in overhead due to the jam-packed giant hoardings – mostly movie ads with very striking-looking actors.

On our return, I sit in a ray of sunlight that hits the back seat of the car. Avoiding the chill, I slip my new Levi's jacket on. There is a thud on the window in line with my face. A flat hand pushes hard against the glass, but no one is there. It appears to be coming up from below the side of the car. I look down. A legless man moves below me on a makeshift skateboard. He has stopped, looking up into my eyes. His face is young, his eyes are hungry, needy and desperate. As he throws his hand toward my face I notice there are only three-and-a-half mangled fingers. The palm is thick, calloused and cracked. Old blood is crusted around the outer padding where the gravel from the ground has not stuck. He moves on to Balkran's window and makes the same gesture. Balkran opens the window just enough to toss a twenty-Rupee note down toward him. It floats to the ground. He picks it up and pops the cruddy note into his mouth. His two arms begin to turn like bicycle pedals pushing off against the car. He negotiates himself between the traffic. His hands slap down hard onto the ground, propelling him forward. A bicycle swerves out from behind the gleaming gold BMW, trying to weave forward. As he passes the passenger side of our car the skateboarding leper shoots across his pathway from the front of our BMW. There is an accident. He is so low to the ground already that he does not fall far before hitting it. The cyclist ramps into the leper's rotting flesh leaving tyre tracks across the grimy, once-white strips of rag that hold the poor leper together. He falls on top of the unravelling leper, breaking his fall. He gets up instantly, grabs the wailing leper under the arms, plonks him on his board and pushes him from behind back across the road in front of our car and onto the pavement. The impact of the board hitting the concrete smacks the poor leper back off his board. The cyclist is two cars ahead, weaving his way yet again through the heavy Sunday traffic. His handlebars and front wheel wobble, they are no longer aligned. Balkran manoeuvres around the startled leper, who is now dragging his body onto the pavement. Nobody even notices the poor sod. The silence is loud, as if nothing has happened.

Fish out of curry

The Producer rings the tinny bell. Standing with my hands full of shopping bags, I am aware that the servants are taking longer than usual to open up for us. It's so strange that The Producer does not even have keys to his own house. At the age of nearly fifty, everything is still done for him.

The door is finally opened. Sai is hesitant. He holds onto it, not wanting to let us pass. He begins talking to The Producer. Even though I do not understand a word, I can tell that he is nervous, his voice is shaky. The Producer pushes past him, his voice getting louder; I follow. The Producer stops in his tracks. So do I.

The pungent smell of fish mixed with bleach hits my nostrils before my eyes begin to take in what I see. The Producer's home has been re-painted with fish curry. Ball-scratching Kutty is on his hands and knees; three buckets, two bottles of bleach and many rags surround him. A young woman in a candy-pink sari is also moving frantically across the floor with a rag, she sways from side to side with it, dipping, wringing, wiping, dipping, wringing, wiping. Her long ponytail flicks across her bare back as she moves. Nobody looks up; they keep their heads down and work frantically. Sai pads across the floor like a guilty dog. He begins to unzip the ribbed-suede cream couch covers. They are ruined. What once was a blank canvas is now a Jackson Pollock lookalike. Rusty red sauce has been flicked in various directions across them. Some areas of the house have been splattered in dollops; blobs of fish give the work of art a three-dimensional feel. Sauce drips from the ceiling, directly below are pieces of fish, bone still intact. What was a very large oil painting of a naked woman seductively sprawled on a bed now looks like a murder scene. The big black-and-white sculpture of the intertwined couple just needs a wipe.

Balkran arrives. For the first time I see The Producer and him speak, their voices are low, deep and angry. I head for my bedroom to find a safe place to put my shopping bags down. Sai stops me.

"Madam Jimmy, you not going here, you home theatre going."

"Sweets, he got into your room too, just go to the home theatre until they clean this shit up."

"Okay, who is he?"

"Cook, my bloody cook, he's fucking drunk again. Fucking asshole needs a tight slap."

"I want to see how bad my room is." I take a peak, as does The Producer.

My bed is bathed in 'blood'. The slippery blue silk sheets wrapped around rusty red sauce and chunks of fish represent an outspoken installation piece, fit for the Tate Modern. It speaks to me, "When love begins to stink of fish, drown it in a silken sea of destruction."

There is a loud crash from the kitchen. We all run towards the kitchen door. Balkran pushes the heavy door forward. A rock has been catapulted through the large window above the sink. It lands next to Roti, who is making his way along the skirting of the floor with his large tongue. His eyes water from the spicy sauce that his tongue cannot resist slurping up. His flapping jowls wrap around the bits of fish. He gulps and slobbers, spluttering as his nose runs. His mouth must be on fire. This is war, we are being invaded, the canon has spoken! Down below on the ground floor is the 'invisible cook'. Cook is a very thin, sinewy, grey-haired old man. He hops in circles in his *dhoti* that wraps around his bandy matchstick legs, through his crotch, like a nappy. His sleeveless white vest is painted too. His index fingers point up to the sky, moving alternately with his knees, he looks like a puppet on a string as he dances, singing a repetition of obscenities. "*Bhenchod, makichod, madarchod.*"

Balkran and Sai race downstairs to catch him; they try to corner him as he bolts around the BMW. They come for him from either side. He is light on his feet and very fast for his age; it must be the alcohol giving him super powers. He dashes across the courtyard and down the street. He is gone.

"We are going to have to order a take out, are you happy with pizza?"

"That sounds great, thank you."

"I have also called for a new series for us to watch, it's called *24*. They say it's outstanding. Come, let's go to the home theatre."

The home theatre is dark, tucked away at the end of the apartment. It becomes my hideaway haven. This room is The Producer's inspiration cabin – keeping up with the latest and greatest releases, studying his competition as well as viewing his work in progress.

I ask about the woman in pink who was mopping the floor.

"That's Cook's wife."

There are two A3-size photographs that have been block mounted onto wood hanging on the wall above this vast DVD collection. The boy in the first photograph has a face like an angel, soft and approachable. He has gentle black curls cascading off his shoulders, his cheeks are full and pinchable. The boy in the second photograph looks like a clone of The Producer; his arms are stubbornly folded, he has deep dimples embedded into his cheeks, a large nose and full lips.

I ask the question I have been waiting to ask.

"Are these your sons?"

"Yes, the one on top is sixteen now, a real softy like his mom. The bottom one is nine years old, he is me, through and through."

"Where are they?"

"They live in Delhi with their grandmother."

"And their mother?"

"Upstairs. Cook's wife actually works for her."

Oh my God, his wife is upstairs. How could I not ask about his family? Why did I not think he had one? Now what?

The Producer can see I'm worried.

"It's okay, we are divorced."

Nothing more is said about the fish curry incident or his wife and sons. We watch DVDs and eat pizza while The Producer's staff run around tending to our needs and cleaning up their drunken colleague's demonstrative mess.

No one ever disrespects The Producer like this. Cook is the only man to ever have dared such defiance.

I smell a rat

The Producer leaves for Delhi just after 4am. We say goodbye with a hug behind closed doors. I ask to go back to sleep.

Sai wakes me just after seven. Something is wrong. My eyes are prickly, my skin feels like it's on fire. I am dizzy, my head pounds. As I sit up I look down, my thighs are full of dark red spots. Oh my god, he has finally infected me with something.

I look in the mirror. My face, arms, chest and stomach are covered with these spots. I panic. The Producer has already left for Delhi. I need to call him, but I don't have a phone. I fly into the kitchen. Roti is eating his breakfast; he yanks at his chain, thrusting his hips at me, his pink lipstick pushing out with excitement.

I ignore him. Sai is making food to send to the office with me; he is following a recipe book. He looks up, surprised.

"Sai boss calling, please, *jaldi* making *yaar.*"

The Producer's phone is off, of course, he is on a plane.

Now what? Alisha, the only other person I trust. I am so scared, and she's an adult, she will know what to do. Am I contagious? Is it an STD?

"Sai, Madam Alisha calling, please."

As he dials I remember what The Producer said about not speaking about our private life. What will I say? We shagged all day yesterday and now I'm sick. Fuck it, no!

"No Sai, put it down, me boss waiting. You keep trying, when boss answer you telling Madam Jimmy sick and me you calling. Okay?"

"*Arrey*, madam, this is problem *yaar*."

Yep my friend, you bet it's a fucking problem. I have fucked myself ill. I'm so angry with myself. All this for a trip to India, Kuala Lumpur and a few clothes. I am doomed for life, hopefully this STD will kill me, I don't want to be labelled and shunned for an STD. I go back to my room and scrub hard in the shower. This makes everything worse. I am itchy, the inside of my mouth is laced with spots that tingle and pull tight over my tongue.

Eventually Sai gets hold of The Producer.

"Hey, what's up?"

"Um, I don't actually know, but I woke up feeling really strange and I'm covered in red spots."

I don't have the nerve to ask if he has it too or if he thinks it's a sexual thing.

He can hear I want to cry.

"Well, don't panic, I will call my doc to come to the house and see you."

It's after 11am when the doctor arrives. He introduces himself as Dr Bollywood. He is tall with a bald pip. Two pitch-black tufts of hair sprout on either side of his ears. On top of his bald pip are whisps of hair that grow upright. He has a big round tummy that protrudes forward. His arms and legs seem way too thin for the stature of his body. He wears big square tinted glasses, almost like he is trapped in the seventies. He is carrying an old leather doctor's bag, the ones you see the doctors carry on the TCM channel. He has a light blue shirt on and dark blue nylon slacks, like Balkran except with a stethoscope around his neck. He is in his fifties.

He seems excited to see me. He gestures for me to lie on my bed. He presses my neck to check my glands. He puts his stethoscope on and moves his hands down to my chest. My top is in the way, he asks me to take my bra off. I remove it and put my top back on. As I sit upright to breath, he slips his hand under my top again to listen to my breathing. He tells me to lie again and pops the thermometer under my tongue. He presses my stomach.

"Does it hurt?"

"No."

"Are you regular?"

"Yes."

"And menstruation, where are you in this cycle of life?"

"I am about to start."

"The Producer wants you on contraceptive, I will write script to give servant."

"Thank you."

"You begin taking this medicine when you start cycle. Do not skip."

"Yes, I know how it works."

He slips both hands under my T-shirt again without the stethoscope. He begins to handle my breast, pressing lightly, around the sides and underneath under the fold, a breast examination.

"You are having many coffee daily?"

"Maybe three a day, four when we shoot long hours."

"And smoking?"

"Yes, doctor."

"You are lumpy because of coffee and smoking."

He starts to stroke my breast gently now, his fingers circle and dabble across my nipples with their tips. I am sure this is not normal. His head is thrown back, eyes closed. I smell a rat.

I sit up pretending I want to show him the rash. He opens his eyes and looks at me. Before I can say anything about the rash he bends back into his bag.

"This you are having is from Germany. It has common name meaning measles."

"Really, are you sure? Well, that's great news."

"I will take blood sample to be sure, results will come tomorrow, I am calling The Producer Sir."

Like chicken pox, I have never had measles as a child either.

He pulls out an old leather belt, and a little opaque bottle that is empty. The glass is scratched and murky, it has a little cork stuck into it. It has been used several times. The needle and syringe are sealed and unused; I am so relieved. He tells me to sit and ties the belt tight around the top of my arm.

"You must be pumping your hand please, madam."

He is not wearing gloves.

Home is where ...

It's confirmed. I have German measles!

I am not allowed to watch television, and I am told that I must stay in a dark room. I catch up on a lot of sleep. I read a little and pass the rest of the time in the kitchen getting to know Sai and Kutty. Kutty sits on the floor near Roti, peeling a mountain of garlic. Roti is chained. Sprawled out on a mattress like a king he begins to tug on the chain when I come closer. I stop him before he can pull his lipstick trick on me again.

Roti gets a three-quarter mattress while Sai and Kutty sleep next to him on the hard marble floor on a thin grass mat. They are not allowed to sleep anywhere else. They must be at The Producer's beck and call 24/7. The kitchen is their bedroom. Kutty does not speak a single word of English, but he rattles on in Hindi. His gentle face tells me he wants to take care of me and he does. Kutty brings in my freshly washed clothing daily and packs it neatly in the cupboard. He makes me coffee throughout the day. He crawls around on his hands and knees around my bed with a bucket and rag cleaning my space. He pauses between his duties to hold my hand, bob his head and talk to me in Hindi. We have long conversations just looking at each other. With Sai's help I learn that Kutty is in his fifties and is from Kerala. He has two daughters who he recently married off. They are twins. His wife is in Kerala too. He only gets to go home once a year to see them.

Sai is unmarried. He is my age exactly, a 1978 baby. He comes from Madras and only goes home once a year.

The tinny doorbell never stops going. The Producer's household staff run a tight ship. The *istri* (laundry) gets returned daily. The newspaper is delivered before 7am. The milkman comes with fresh *paneer* and milk. Fresh vegetables and rice arrive daily. The Producer's supply list is extreme for one man who lives on his own.

I really need tampons, but there is no way I can explain what they are. I decide to wait for Nisha to visit. Nisha and Alisha have called every day to check on me.

Kutty cleans our house, gets our clothes to the *dhobi*, irons the intimate wear that he has washed, undies and bras, and he then spends the remainder of his day with 'Mummy'. 'Mummy' is The Producer's mother who lives in the building next door with Nisha and her nephew Spy, The Producer's cousin. I believe there is nothing easy about her. She works Kutty to the bone. She loves Kutty, that's why The Producer did not fire him over the rice incident. Like Kutty, she does not speak a word of English. The Producer's father lives upstairs on the fifth floor with The Producer's ex-wife. How strange.

I am grateful for this week. I have got to know and understand the people that run my life in my new home.

I don't see Balkran, he is off duty. Nisha joins me for dinner and we laugh and joke. When I ask her about tampons, she is shocked.

"Gené, we don't get those here, this is India. Girls cannot put things up there. My darling you must be happy with the pads. I will get Sai to pick some up for you."

"God, Nisha, please don't! Can you imagine what he will think? Can't I go to the store?"

"It's a market Gené, when they see your white skin they will rip you off so badly. Anyway, what you going to say? You going to have to show them, no one speaks English in the medical stall. Okay, I will get them for you. When you are abroad you can pick up some tampons for me too, I also prefer them *yaar*."

Nisha is hungry to be white, it comes naturally to her, in her dress, her mannerism and her open mind.

"Tomorrow we will call for Balkran, he will take us to Nail Bar in Bandra. It is the best beauty parlour in town, you gonna love it. You need to look good for The Producer when he returns. I will organise with Balkran, so be ready for 10am."

The big wax

Nail Bar is clearly designed for Barbie dolls. It's done up in hot pinks, reminding me of strawberry margharitas and candyfloss. You feel pretty and girlie just being there. It makes you want to gossip. The beauticians are all dressed in pink with candy-stripe aprons, their coconut-oiled thick black hair done up in long high sleek ponytails. The selection of 'art' on the nails is flabbergasting. Diamante, glitter, stripes, dots and other glamour motifs can be applied. It's way over the top for me. I just want my nails filed, short and square with a natural French manicure. Nisha wants to go all out. She has already chosen her extremely long nails with little diamante stars and slanted stripes on each. I am not going to get away lightly.

"The Producer says you must go lighter with your hair. He wants you to be Barbie blonde."

Nisha wants my eyebrows threaded and my whole body bleached, my hair dyed blonde and a full body wax.

"Have you ever had 'down there' clean, clean?"

"You mean a bikini wax, Nish?"

"Yeah, but completely clean *yaar*, both front side and backside."

"What? No man, can I just have a normal wax?"

"Gené, my love, it's Diwali – you must start the New Year completely clean."

"And we will even bleach the inside there okay?" She's pointing to my backside.

"Nish, what the fuck is this bleaching business?"

"Don't worry my love, you gonna love it *yaar*, just trust me, okay?"

"Yeah, but what is it?"

"It's to lighten your skin and the fine, fine hairs on your face and parts of the body that are not going through waxing. The dark hole must also be light *yaar*."

"Jesus Nisha, this is fucking crazy."

I have never set foot in a parlour before, and now I am suddenly being bleached, my 'rusty sheriff's badge' included.

"Just be trusting me. Go with this lady, her name it Radhika, she will be with you, I will be out here having my sexy hot nails put on."

I wonder if The Producer requested the waxing and bleaching of the rusty sheriff's badge. Can you imagine him telling Nisha that his girlfriend needs to lighten her asshole? I'm sure he did not.

I follow Radhika into a wooden booth with a sliding door. It's an open top. This is great, now the whole parlour can hear what's going on, conversation and instructions.

"Open wide the bum cheeks, please madam."

I'm dreading it.

"Coffee, madam?"

She's bobbing her head from side to side. She is in her element.

"Yes, please."

"I have never worked on white girl before madam, what is your good name?"

"Gené."

"*Achcha*! You are from Cape Town coming?"

This is not going to be a relaxing experience: twenty questions, forced conversations open to the public and my body immersed in bleach.

"Madam, we starting with waxing, then moving on for the bleaching. Okay?"

Fuck, the waxing, I did not even think about the waxing.

I shout from the booth, "Nish, what's wrong with a razor blade?"

The parlour is not full. Only one other client, and anyway everyone's going to hear everything. I've already been asked whether I'm married and if I have children. Her reaction to my response was shock and horror. "Madam, you is getting old *na*? There must be arranging happening, *jaldi, jaldi.*"

She points at my uterus.

"Radhika, how old are you?"

"I am sixteen, madam, having arranged marriage and two *bachchas* (children) already."

Radhika begins with my legs. She smears the hot wax on with a doctor's stick, the one he makes you go 'aaaa ...' with when looking at your throat. Some other orifices are going to have to go 'aaaa ...' soon. She then tears strips of rags and the experience begins. I am torn apart; I can feel the roots rip out from under my skin. I feel raw, I cannot scream, it would be so wrong. Instead my eyes water. She moves on to my arms and then my underarms. She makes me take the armless towelled wrap off, and my knickers. I cannot believe I am 'starkers' with a woman I have never met. Do all women go through this?

"Madam, this leg bending please." She makes me open up like a spatchcock chicken; I can feel a breeze.

Holy shit, WTF! I am so embarrassed. I can't.

She bends down, her head between my legs.

"Madam, I am never seeing white one like this, very full, very beautiful."

I have nowhere to look. I squeeze my eyes shut, the bed has swallowed me.

When she's done mutilating me, she flips me over.

"Madam, this is pulling both side of cheek and holding, one moment please."

I'm finished! I have never ... She sprinkles baby powder into the tender crack; I feel like a baby having its nappy changed.

She cleans up around her and begins to whip the bleach, it is purple in tone – it is fucking peroxide! The pungent fumes burn my eyes.

"Nisha, I'm gonna kill you when I get out of here."

"No, you won't, you gonna love me. Madam, why are you not married and all *yaar*? You must be having at least twenty babies by now ... Madam, you are so old," she teases.

Her laugh is so contagious that I can't help laughing at the whole situation I find myself in. It's all too much. This is what a film producer's shag has to put up with, all in the name of beauty.

"Madam, I am starting with this side so you are pulling one side, one side and keeping open." Yep, it's all about the bum hole today, isn't it?

She smears it in the nape of my lower back and down into the crack. It burns like a motherfucker!

Radhika finishes off on my face. She smears the bleach from the side burns down, along the sides of my jaw and under my chin. I am on fire.

'Madam, you will be fair and lovely very soon. All hair on face is being bleaching."

I am already fair and I have no facial hair, but I leave her to it.

It's finally time to wipe the peroxide off my body, between the crack and off my face. My skin is hot, red and blistering. What a demented thing to have agreed to do. Radhika reassures me that it will settle. She creams me down with aloe cooling gel.

I hear a high-pitched voice enter the pink parlour. It commands attention. There seems to be a lot of fuss happening behind the pre-fab walling of my little booth. The voice, female, is rattling off in '*Hinglish*' (a mixture of Hindi and English slang). I only understand bits of it. She wants coffee, she wants biscuits, she wants a foot massage, and the rest is all in Hindi.

I dress and am led out of my booth and placed facing a mirror. Nisha faces the mirror behind me. We talk into the mirror communicating with each other's reflection. Nisha's nails are almost done. They are long and gaudy, but she is very chuffed. She holds them up to my reflection. It laughs back at her. I shoot her my middle finger.

"Only you, Nish – stars and stripes, the American dream."

I am watching the newcomer in the mirror. She is my age,

very fair, petite and very pretty, but her beauty is marred by the permanent sour look of dissatisfaction on her face. Her feet are soaking in a footbath; she blows into her coffee cup mumbling and pointing down. There are three beauticians working around her: one is combing and separating her long locks, which are highlighted extensions; the second is preparing her pedi; and the third trying to file the nail on the demanding finger she keeps pointing. Nisha is moved next to me. As she sits down her reflection meets with the sour girl's reflection; they acknowledge each other with a fake smile and a swirly finger wave.

I lean sideways into Nisha. "You know her?"

She leans in to whisper. The gossip is on.

"She's The Producer's ex."

"Ex what? She's too young to be his wife?"

"Ex-girlfriend. She wanted to be an actress so she got with The Producer."

"The Producer had an ex before me?"

"Well, yeah, he's had a few."

"Oh, that's great news. I guess this means I'm not going to last very long then?"

"Don't be stupid Gené, of course you will, you're very different to her."

"She's behaving like she's very famous. Is she?"

"No, she got as far as modelling. The Producer put her in a few commercials, but she never made it big. Her claim to fame now is that she's dating a very famous cricket player. You know, here in India cricket players are like gods to us."

Now that Nisha is talking to me, I catch the sour girl glaring at me with slit eyes. Fuck her, what's her problem anyway? I can also be a bitch. I have reason to be – my asshole is on fire.

Radhika has now started painting bleach into my hair. She wraps segments of it in foil. I begin to look like someone who is trying to make contact with Mars. Nisha's beautician does the same to her.

I speak an octave higher than before. I get dramatic. My

reflection bounces loud expressions across the room into the direction of the 'ex'.

"My darling, The Producer is coming home tomorrow, I've missed him so much. My heart aches to see him, hold him, kiss and caress him. Oh, it's been such a nightmare without him. I'm lost and incomplete when he's not around."

I put my hand up to my foiled head. Nisha puts hers up to her mouth, hiding her giggles.

"Thank god for Sai and Balkran. Even Roti has been a doll. He follows me everywhere and snuggles up to me at night, keeping me safe until his master returns."

I snivel. My eyes, closed against my hand, flick open to the screams of the sour bitch and the scattering of beauticians. She has kicked the bucket. Water swishes and slops onto the floor. She storms out, shouting and pointing at me in Hindi.

"Don't ask, she called you some really bad names."

"Well, I asked for it, didn't I?"

"Yeah, the good thing is that you can handle these Indian bitches, Gené. I think you gonna last longer than six months, my love. You can't go anywhere, you're like my stepmom now."

I have met an ex-girlfriend. I have still not met the ex-wife who lives four storeys above me. I can't resist, I have to ask Nisha about her.

"Oh, you didn't know he had a wife? Gaya Aunty is more gentle and all, *yaar*. I lived with her and The Producer before they separated; she was very kind to me."

"Why did they get divorced?"

Nisha moves in, her foils rustle against my foils.

"She went with another man. The Producer caught them in bed in another apartment he owns across town. She moved in with this guy, but it never worked out. She came back, but you know how it goes."

"There are always two sides to a story. Do you think The Producer was messing around before that, and that's what made her do it?"

"You know The Producer, Gené, what you see is what you get. Please, don't tell him what I've told you, he will kill me *yaar*."

While waiting for the bleach to lighten my hair, Radhika makes me throw my head back and hold my eyelid down with one hand and pull the brow up with the other. She puts one end of a long cotton thread between her teeth and pulls along my eyebrows with the other. The hairs get caught between the twist of cotton from her teeth and hands and they rip out from the root. My nose burns and my eyes water, my eyebrows are incredibly thick and bushy. She shapes them into beautiful bows, framing my face and making my eyes look bigger. Threading is painful, but so worth it. My eyebrows have never looked this good. The contrast between the black brows and blonde hair is overpowering, but striking.

I wonder how many girlfriends The Producer has had before and after his divorce.

"Am I the first *firangi* girlfriend The Producer has ever had?"

"I think so. Maybe he had a girl or two while travelling abroad, but he has never had a white girl in India, that's for sure. Anyways I don't see too many *firangs* around, only in Goa on holiday."

"Who ended the relationship with this model that was just here?"

"She cheated on him. He caught them in bed together."

"What?"

"Yep, just like what happened with his wife."

"You're kidding right?"

"No, I don't kid when it comes to gossiping about The Producer."

We finally leave our pink parlour six hours later. Balkran is waiting patiently in the gold BMW. He's having a nap. When we pull the car doors open he wakes with a start. I am expecting a grumpy silent driver, but not today. I see a whole new side to the mute man. His voice, which I hear for the first time, is high pitched and excited.

He speaks to Nisha in Hindi, throwing in the phrase, "no pruuublim *yaar*". He turns the CD player up full blast. Holding up a CD cover, an overdressed girl in a sari with bells in her nose poses seductively. The title reads "Sweet Honey Mix". A Hindu version of Shaggy's "Sexy lady" song throbs through the car; the speakers vibrate with the bass.

"Madam, this is my whole car, favourite car. This is nice my car? This is BMW. This is no tension, CD this is listen, madam. Boss *ekdam*. Okay, no problem? Lunch going? Sai coming?"

Hands free

The Producer returns from Delhi. It's Sunday morning, and Diwali. The boredom is broken. Being alone in his home with nothing to do was getting tedious. Going where he goes, working in his office and on his sets has become my life. It's all I have here.

"Come, we need to get to office to do the *puja* (Hindu prayers)."

Diwali is the festival of lights. It symbolises the victory of good over evil. Mumbai has come alive. Fireworks and crackers explode continually.

The car is enveloped in a frozen stream of air-conditioned air, The Producer's cigarette smoke and the overpowering loudness of silence. Balkran stares ahead, his face dead pan. It's hard to believe I saw a totally different side to him just the day before.

I break the silence.

"Your driver reminds me of your elephant god, Ganesh."

"Actually you are right, it suits him; it's his fat stomach that makes him so similar." The Producer slaps Balkran hard across the guts. Balkran flinches, but stares ahead.

"By the way, fatsy, talking about big stomachs, I have arranged for my personal trainer to come and see you later. I assume you are over the measles. We need to get you into shape, it's a new year and I don't like being with fat girls."

"But I am not fat. Maybe I could lose two or three kilograms, but what's wrong with how I am?"

"Look at your stomach. I want to see a flat stomach. Look at the tops of your arms – at least 10 kilograms, fatsy, at least!"

He leans back and pinches the top of my arm hard. It leaves a mark, again. As we drive through the over-crowded streets, his large body wobbles like jelly in the car seat as Balkran manoeuvres us slowly over the bumps. And he calls me fat.

"Why are you so tired? Did you not sleep well this week?"

"No, I gambled last night, *na*. It's what we do the night of Diwali. We stay up all night to gamble."

"Oh, in Delhi?"

"Ya, where else Gené?"

"With who?"

"With Gaya's family."

I know by his tone not to ask any more questions. His ex-wife's family lives in Delhi. I wonder if she was there too.

We are stopped at a signal light. There is a soft rapping on my window. Big soft eyes in a square face smile back at me. Immediately The Producer nudges Balkran without looking. He pulls out a 1 000-Rupee note and winds down the window. He places the note between two stumps. The man has no arms from the elbows down. I have never been touched by such a gentle smile.

"That was so kind of you," I say to The Producer.

"I have been giving to him for years. He is the one beggar I will support. Poor bastard, can you imagine not being able to scratch your balls or give yourself a hand job when things get itchy and your balls go blue."

All the Luna staff sit in a circle on the floor in the casting room.

Alisha is dressed exquisitely. It's the first time I have ever seen her in traditional clothing. She is wearing a turquoise silk sari, chandelier-like jewelled earrings and a red dot is planted on her forehead. She has bangles going right up to her elbows. Her hair is straightened – she must have also done 'parlour duty'.

There are two men I do not recognise, the *pujari* (priest) and 'Spy', the man who lives with Nisha. He is The Producer's cousin and spy, and oversees the film side of The Producer's production company. At the moment Luna Films is in the middle of shooting a feature film with Samson Night. It's a copy of the American film *Stolen Hearts*. The Producer often goes to his film set without me. I have only been introduced to the commercial side of his company so far. Spy looks like a compressed version of The Producer, with thick square glasses that double-up his eyes. He has the same moustache. When I ask Nisha if this is a coincidence, she explains that it's done on purpose.

The *pujari* has placed palm leaves along the wall and sets out rice, money, nuts, bananas and marigolds around statues of gods on a white sheet. We sit in this circle for almost three hours, the *pujari's* voice drones on and on in Hindu prayer. Most of us drift in and out of sleep. We come to every time the *pujari* rings a little brass bell. After the ceremony we feed each other *barfi* (triangular marzipan sweets with silver-leaf). Everybody goes home. We have the rest of the day off.

The Producer and I stop off in Linking Road at the new Nike store. I am bought proper running shoes and some running pants with matching tops.

I have never run on a treadmill before in my life.

The steps leading to The Producer's apartment are decorated with little candles. Coloured rice powder is sprinkled on the floor in pretty stencilled designs called *rangoli*. The servants have gone all out to create a festive atmosphere. Sai invites me into the kitchen to see the extra effort they have made with their little shrine. Candles burn along the counter and the floor is decorated with the same rice-powder-stencilled designs of flowers, peacocks, suns and mythological figures. The elephant god statue and a framed photograph of a dark-looking deity are dowsed in marigolds and incense burns sickly sweet and exotic. A halved coconut, cooked food and bananas surround the shrine. The skinny drunken grey-haired cook is back. He is cooking up a Diwali storm. The kitchen is hot and steamy, sweat beads form on all our foreheads. The air conditioner is off.

"Sai, why aircon not using?"

"Boss telling, no *yaar*. Only when Roti sick."

I take photos of them around their shrine. It's the first time I have picked up my camera since I got here. They love the attention. Even Balkran comes to join in. Roti gets his photo taken too. He is sprawled out on his mattress, his colossal head glaring straight into the lens. I swear I see him wink at me with his big bulbous brown eyes.

The Producer and I sit alone at our festive table. The rest of Mumbai celebrate in huge crowds of families over long dinner tables of food, drink and 'merriment'.

The Producer does not encourage drinking. In fact, like smoking, he is totally against me doing either. He does, however, smoke like a chimney now.

"Enjoy, fatsy, this is going to be your last high-calorie supper."

Ironically I stare at Jesus Christ in a silver sculpted picture of the Christian 'The Last Supper' that hangs above the dinner table. My last supper. The Producer seems to like the Christian icon. He also has a huge gold-foiled painting of a faceless Jesus Christ in his lounge.

Little bit jelly ... Turkish delight!

I am woken just before five. Kutty wakes me for a change.

"Black coffee, madam."

No more sugar-whipped mocha-frothed mug of buzz.

He sets it beside me. He heads for the cupboard, removes my new gym pants and a top. He pulls the bottom of my silken duvet up exposing my feet. He starts putting on my socks. I don't want to get up; it's so dark outside, the crows have not even begun their morning forum.

I rebel with a moan, squeezing my eyes shut tightly. I flop back, making his job harder.

I am introduced to my new personal trainer, Trainer. He takes my measurements with a tape measure, tripping twice as he delicately tries not to touch. He makes me take my own bust and thigh measurements. He does my waistline.

"Are my measurements very much over the norm for my height, Trainer?"

"No not too over, madam, just the belly you are having."

"How bad is my belly?"

He chooses his words very carefully.

"Aa ... it's a little bit jelly ... Turkish delight. But madam, we will be showing The Producer Sir results. No less than twenty minutes on treadmill then I will be making you pushing the weights and all. Lunges and crunches are of most importance too. Results we must be having madam, every day we must be training harder than hard. I will not be resting until results are showing on your body."

He stands beside me while I run. He turns up the speed. He stops at speed nine. I sweat after the first five minutes. He tells me all about his brother, the famous trainer behind a famous actor called Samson Night.

I laugh.

"Like the luggage?"

"No, madam, this is his stage naming. Samson because he is strong like lion and has very long hair up until his waist which he has bleached golden like a lion's mane. People are saying that all his strength is coming from his hair. He is doing many shampoo ads and all. He is very serious about his body and his hair. That is what is making him so famous, like a money machine."

"Is he a Christian?"

"No, Muslim."

"So where does the Night part come from?"

"Night because he does not sleep and is always having big parties in the night. Like the lion he is 'hunting' at night. He comes alive at night. Everybody in Bombay wants to be him. Young boys are having cut-outs of him in their wallets. All gyms use him for publicity and all the women want to be his girlfriend. People of Bombay are calling him 'The Lion'. He is having a tattoo of a lion on his left wrist, his fans are also having tattoos on their wrists in his honour. Even my brother is having one."

Trainer has a dense shadow, swollen dark around him. It belongs to his brother. He finds himself living in it. I am sorry for him. He is not the brother that trains The Lion. He is just the other. One of life's conundrums, you want the trainer that gave results to the famous man, then you too will look like him.

"Trainer, I will try to be famous one day, just for you."

"Madam, we will work hard so that you can be on front page of *Bombay Times*."

We methodically grind through his programme.

"Madam, have you be meeting The Lion?"

"Me? Why would I have met him? I don't even know of his fame."

"Madam, you did not know? He is The Producer Sir's good friend. He is acting in The Producer's last film and is acting in The Producer's new film that they now shooting only. You are very lucky, the people of India are worshipping him. You will be meeting him, this is my full guarantee."

The Producer walks in half asleep. He stands in his boxers, with his legs apart and his hands on his hips. Turkish delight, defied by the laws of gravity.

"Time to weigh you, fatsy. Come, the scale is in my bathroom."

I follow The Producer. Trainer follows me. The three fucking blind mice.

"Take off your shoes and get on, let's see what it says."

Trainer has become mute in The Producer's presence. When The Producer obviously discusses me to him in Hindi, his response vibrates under a faint crush of vocal chords.

I have not stood on a scale since I was a teenager. I never want to be challenged by a number again. I enter a blinding space. I don't look down.

It's my 14th birthday and the tears are tearing through my father. We are standing in a musky wood-panelled office in a psychiatric hospital in Johannesburg. I am skeletal. A fine baby-like fluff covers my hanging skin in a desperate attempt to keep me warm. My hands are icy, my fingernails are purple, brittle. The doctor passes a form to my mother to sign. My father can't look up; his face is sodden with tears.

"This is to certify her to the state."

I stand speechless behind my seated father, wriggling my teeth with my tongue. They are so loose I can bend them so far forward that they lie horizontally against my tongue. It's a miracle they don't dislodge from the gum and bone. My breath smells like a rotting rat trapped beneath the floorboards. I am too empty inside, too weak to care about the pain I am causing.

Anorexia Nervosa is my new title. I arrive at Saint Mary's DSG in the January of 1992. I am weighed and poked with a stick by the gym teacher. We are lined up and told how fat we are and made to swim and run and squat and told that ladies do not pig out on weekends. I recoil inwards and begin to self-destruct.

We are Italian. Food is what rocks us in unison and keeps us bound together. Every precious moment we share as a family revolves around food.

It does not take me very long to become skeletal. By 28 July 1992, on my 14th birthday, I am admitted. This is the one thing I can control and in turn it's the bull's-eye to my Italian family's heart. I am cruel and heartlessly stubborn.

At the hospital you get twenty minutes to eat your three-course meal five times a day. If you don't complete it all in twenty minutes then you get strapped to the bed, a tube rammed down your throat and a nutritional shake pumped into that shrunken stomach of yours. They regularly scrape my throat with the stained pipe that's been down other loony throats. I lie on a bed as my stomach is over pumped; I begin to feel like a stretched balloon. Before I die there I manage to escape.

For the next four harrowing years I fight the fight and my family fights with me. I change schools. I go into heart failure at Roedean, my new school. The psychiatric hospital will not take me back. I go to Morningside Clinic. They cannot manage my addiction. I am sent home to die. I am moved around until my grandmother takes me in. She is a constant. She is patient, my golden rod. She keeps me upright and she takes me forward, one step at a time. Together we build a tightrope of trust and understanding.

At 17 I finally bid my eating demon farewell and I vow never to stand on a scale again. Fuck Anorexia Nervosa, I'm done! I am moving on to a new land on top of my magic faraway tree of life.

And now, six years later, it feels like The Producer and Trainer have become my very own psychiatric hospital weight monsters. They lean over me to see the number I represent, each extending a curious head over my shoulder.

"Sixty-six-point-three, fatsy," The Producer's voice bellows, eager with discontent. I still don't look down. I concentrate on the toilet that has got such a fright from The Producer's sudden need to shout out my weight. Its closed lid separates slightly from its bowl, showing its toothless mouth. After a moment, it settles flush with the seat again.

"Sir, we will be showing you positive results by next week. This is my true promise to you. We will be making many hard attempts on this matter concerning Madam Jimmy. How much weight will Sir be wishing for her loss?"

He's putty in 'Sir's' hands. The Producer wags his extended finger in Trainer's face.

"You will be making sure the stomach and arms go first, at least eight kilograms, Trainer. No mucking about, make it happen. Fast. I want her fitting in a size 6 at least. We will weigh her every Monday morning until I am happy."

I am everybody, and no different to anybody, and nobody. I am unable to say 'no' to The Producer's demands. It's his body now.

Waiting

I am exhausted and weak. If Atkins was alive, he would be getting hate mail from me. I am only allowed to eat protein and green vegetables. I run five kilometres a day followed by an hour of deadly lunges, crunches and weight lifting.

Sometimes The Producer makes me run at night when we get home. By the following Monday I am three kilos down. I am not allowed a day off.

My muscles burn with stiffness. My whole body aches.

"Madam, you are tired, you must be taking massage."

I don't know what he thinks I do with my day, but The Producer most certainly does not allow for time to relax and have massages. Wherever The Producer goes, whatever The Producer does, I'm expected to be at his side, waiting. The Producer's a workaholic, strangling in his own mission to be the biggest producer in town. I am expected to accompany him everywhere; it feels like I am always waiting. Why can't The Producer let me go and explore Mumbai, go home and find things of interest to do or spend time with Nisha who lives one block away from us? I could even do my workout in the evening so that I can get a proper night's sleep. But he will allow none of it. I must wait.

"I brought you here for work, not for a holiday."

"I know, but there is nothing for me to do at the moment."

"You are learning, by observing."

"But I don't even know what you are saying."

"Don't come with your shit, Gené, just do as I say and stop trying to be clever."

I am no better off than his servants waiting on him. We are expected not to think. The boredom burrows holes in my head. I must keep my brain working before it withers. So, I begin a scrapbook to record my time in Bollywood. I decide I need pictures in my scrapbook. I will find occupation in my photography.

The office is very quiet. We are not shooting any commercials and Kush is as bored as I am. He is researching film schools in New York on his laptop. He speaks to me a lot more than before and when I take my camera into the office he shows great interest. We have found a common playground. He is impressed with my knowledge of photography and the equipment I hold in my bag. I ask how he got into film and if he has always been an assistant.

Kush opens up and tells me that he was actually a creative director at a very big advertising firm. Unfortunately his wife at the time also worked there and when their marriage ended so did his career. He could not work in the same space as her and decided to move on. He had always wanted to get into the film industry and this was his chance. He knew The Producer through the agency and asked for a job. He's been here ever since and only now does he feel ready to move on and get to film school to secure his position as a director before he's too old. He seems hell bent on following this dream.

"Was your marriage arranged Kush?"

"Totally, I had no idea what she looked like, up until I lifted the veil on the day."

"Crazy."

"It is and that's why it never worked, but unfortunately our tradition has a different take on the idea. Mixing such ancient traditions in such a fast-moving modern world gets tricky."

We convince The Producer to let us go out to take pictures.

Kush knows the city well and we explore on foot. He begins by taking me to the little pavement community that lives opposite our office. I hold back, not wanting to offend those who have so little with my grotesque lens and my morbid curiosity to record their misfortune.

Kush walks straight into their slum. The invisible wall of 'us and them' falls away quickly as he engages with the little ones. Their little hands reach up to him with smiles. Their parents look on approvingly. I cross the road and join him. The children are in awe of the colour of my skin and who I am. They circle me, touching, grabbing my white skin. They try to smear the 'milkiness' off as if I may be dark underneath, laughing and smiling in amazement when nothing changes. A little girl with big brown sparkling eyes, curly hair and huge dimples slips her hand in mine. She pulls me to the door of her home, gesturing for me to sit on the step. She enters the tin shack and returns with sweet smelling marigolds on a string. She places the garland gently over my head letting it fall around my neck. All the while Kush is snapping away on my Canon Ds 1. They do not speak a word of English except for one word which they repeat as they refer to me with overwhelmed excitement, "Aunty, Aunty, Aunty!"

Kush speaks gently to them, asking them to pose and do things for the camera. This creates hysteria. They jump and shout and laugh and claw and fight to be the centre of attention, each one trying to outdo the other with poses and actions. They huddle together and wave. If it was dark, their smiles would light up Bombay's polluted skies. They are like little Christmas trees. I fall in love with the concept of shooting street children. Kush hands the camera to me. He says something to them using the word 'Aunty' in the midst of the excitement. The attention is on me again because I have the camera. They invade the camera lens with gusto. "Aunty, Aunty," they squeal as their smiles warm my heart. I can't get enough of them. We use five rolls of 36 exposures in less than an hour.

The favourite *peon* from the office, Dhiraj, has joined us. He arrives with a bag full of packets of 'Good-Day' biscuits which he has purchased from the *biscuit wallah*, the cart next to the *chai wallah*.

He hands them to me.

"Madam, you must be thanking the *bachcha*s and be giving gift."

The children are so happy to see the biscuits. They clap and sing, clinging onto their biscuits for dear life.

"You see, Gené, this is how you do it. Don't be scared, they will not hurt you. You can get pictures of the real India by just giving them something small in return. For them it's a big thing. Let's go to the lab and see if we got some good ones."

Dhiraj returns to the office. He smiles at me before he goes.

"Madam, you are very helping, me I am your duty, I am taking you for photo if Kush Sir busy."

He likes the fact that I have noticed the people that deserve to be taken notice of. He has taught me something today: to give back after I have taken.

The office leaves early again. I ask Nisha, Alisha and Kush what they are doing with their evening. It's a Friday, we will work all weekend but still, a Friday is a Friday after all. Back home Fridays feel like the day of relief, accomplishment and the beginning of a party waiting to happen. They all have plans. Kush is playing poker with his mates, Nisha is going to movies and Alisha is going out to a party. They all kindly ask if I want to join them, but I dare not ask The Producer. I am here to work, only.

Back seat

I lie down in the dark on the cold leather back seat, thinking I will get more sleep on the way home. It's after 11pm. The Producer is surprisingly interested and encouraging about my day. He wants to talk while he plays chess on his phone. He usually never talks when he's playing.

"Did you take nice photos, fatsy?"

"I did."

"What pics did you take?"

"We took beautiful pictures of the street children. We gave them biscuits in return for letting us photograph them."

"That's very good, you must keep up you photography while you are here and take as many pics as you can. When god created India, he gifted us the rainbow. Look at the endless spectrum of colour that moves around us. I am happy you are doing something constructive with your time, fatsy. I want to read your scrapbooks. When are you going to show me what you have done?"

I don't like the idea that I will have to sensor my diaries because The Producer insists on reading them. I change the subject.

"Kush handed in the rolls of film and bought new rolls on your account at the lab next to the office. I know the expense is mine, but I don't have any money."

"That's okay. I will cover it for you as long as you keep shooting."

We wind through the suburb of Bandra. We drive along a promenade. I see that we are on Carter Road. This is not the way home; this is near Nail Bar, where most of the film stars live and most of the hip restaurants and bars are.

"Where are we going?"

"I need to meet with my actor friend. It won't take long. Wait here."

His actor? It must be Samson Night, The Lion, that Trainer was telling me about.

There is no 'come' instead it's a 'wait here'.

I lay back on the cool leather. I look up through the window. I look for the moon, I have never looked up at the sky in Mumbai. I realise that there is no moon and no stars – there never is as Mumbai is too polluted for such lavishness. It does not take long before I begin to sweat and stick to the leather seat. The night is hot and muggy. Balkran puts his head back and closes his eyes. He is in a mood. The car is turned off. We have no air conditioner to cool us down. We are forced to keep the windows open. The mosquitoes begin to carry our vital fluid away in their swollen bellies. Their wings struggle, they move slowly, battling to stay afloat. Balkran swats his face. I choke at the idea of swallowing the vibrating blood suckers that hone in on me. I sit up and complain. What if I swallow someone else's blood in the belly of the blood sucker?

"Please Balkran, *do* minute of aircon *yaar*?"

"Boss telling no engine putting, this is diesel *khatam*!"

I can hear very loud music coming from the apartment block that The Producer entered. Has he gone to a party? Is he eating and drinking and dancing, while I itch all over? I scratch hard into my skin, leaving long red fingernail lines across my white skin that glows under the streetlights. I'm too irritable and hungry to sleep. I get out and walk along the pavement that separates land and sea. It stinks. I sit on the promenade wall and light a cigarette. I am eyeballed from every direction. I feel awkward, but not unsafe.

I walk some more to avoid being sucked dry. I light another cigarette and move its burning hot cherry near the battlefield of bites I have accumulated, trying to relieve the itch.

I notice an array of 'penis extension' cars coming and going from the apartment block that The Producer entered. Who has a meeting after 11pm with pumping music? Whoever lives there must be very rich and very famous. There's a press van with a satellite dish on its roof, parked adjacent to our BMW which seems dull in the light of all these flashy cars.

It's been more than two hours of waiting. It's almost 2am. This is starting to feel like a cruel joke. I have this overwhelming need to walk towards The Lion's building. I must find the apartment that The Producer went into and knock on its door. My head knows better: I can't, I was not invited. I did not get asked to 'come'.

I go back to the car. Balkran is snoring. I plug into my CD player and curl as much of my torso and head into the shelter of my Levi's jacket as I can.

My oh my, tis the smallest mosquito net I ever did see.
As I lay my weary body down, I suddenly need a pee.
My skin transmits an electric itch at least not from a flea.
Shall I do a Virginia Wolf and drown myself in the fucking sea?

I dose off, my bladder throbs – it's so full that my eyeballs float.

Balkran and I rise to attention as The Producer opens the front passenger door.

"Sorry about that, it took longer than I thought."

The Producer flips his phone open and begins to play chess again. My angry eyes bore into the back of his head, it's five past three. Is that all he has to say? He glances back with a smile. Oh wait, there's more.

"Why aren't you sleeping? You have to be up in two hours to train, fatsy?"

My words are dry and chafe the back of my throat as they come out.

"I didn't think you would be away so long. The mosquitoes almost carried me away."

"Well, aren't you lucky they didn't? Are you hungry? Shall I get Sai to prepare you something?"

"What about you?"

"I had something in my meeting."

"No thank you, I'm fine. It's probably good for my weight if I don't eat." I hate what I'm saying. I'm being a martyr.

"Do I have to train today? I am so tired."

"Of course you do. Anyways it's too late to cancel now."

If he knew he was coming here why didn't he give me the option earlier?

"We weigh you again in two days, fatsy. Don't you want to see results?"

He leans forward into the foot well. I notice a box and a packet at his feet that were not there before. He passes them back to me.

"My actor friend sent you gifts."

I hold my gift on my lap, unimpressed. Protein shake powder and two bottles of shampoo.

Kutty wakes me. I … am … fucked … My body screams, my head says no and my legs won't move. Kutty pulls me up and holds the mug near my nose. He wraps my hands around it. He says something soft and soothing. He throws his hand open, gesturing a question. I pull down the duvet. A deviant smile pushes my dopey eye-lids upward. I am already fully dressed in my gym wear. I got into them before I went to sleep two hours earlier.

Kutty claps his hands with delight. He fetches my shoes. He slips my socks on, then the shoes and ties the laces while I finish my coffee.

Trainer is waiting. The servants have already shown him my gifts.

"Madam, this is best gift ever! Samson Night is a legend and he is gifting you protein shake and shampoo. This is very big occasion."

"No, it's not! I'm fucked. Please let's just get this session over with, with as little talking as possible, please?"

"Madam, what is troubling you?"

"I have not slept and I'm grumpy, that's all."

"Madam, you must be getting proper sleep for training, you are having big party with Samson Night? He is a Muslim, he is celebrating Eid. Today is Eid. The Lion is having big party every year, it will be appearing tomorrow in newspaper. What he is saying to you when you are meeting? How is he looking off screen? Was party good?"

"I have not met him and I did not go to any party, I had to wait in the car until three this morning while The Producer was apparently having a meeting with him."

We say no more and Trainer lets me get away with just a few stomach reps and a run. While I run, he goes off to the kitchen to show Sai how to make the precious shake. Trainer, Sai, Kutty and Roti enviously watch me suck the cherished liquid through the straw until it is all finished. They are in awe; this is Samson Night's shake – will I look like him in a few hours? Sai takes the glass and pours the last few drops down his throat without letting the glass touch his lips. He flexes his biceps.

"This is very good look *yaar*, like Samson Night."

"Trainer, can you get this shake here?"

"Of course, madam, there is sports shop in Bandra near to The Lion's house only."

"So why are you all making such a fuss?"

"Because, madam, Samson Night is gifting, it is very special more than the one in the shop you are getting."

I shower and wait on the veranda for The Producer. He is late. He was lucky enough to sleep in. I'm irritated, I could have had at least an extra hour's sleep. I wish we could have pushed my training to later. It's so tricky – The Producer is paying for the service and so I don't have much say in the matter. Maybe I should try and get a nap in, but with all the coffee I have pumped myself with, I doubt I will be able to. Sai comes out of The Producer's room.

"Where is boss?"

"Shower."

I move outside to the verandah with the *Bombay Times*. I light a cigarette and look for the horoscope section.

> *Leo July 22–August 21 You are dealing with difficult circumstances, unfair and very bamboozling ... You cannot avoid them, learn as much as you're able to about the people and the situations involved. Once you do, you will discover that they prove to be an interesting challenge with many rewards.*

A murder of crows caws loudly. They are relentless in their conversations. They squawk at each other with violent affliction. They are busy. They scavenge the verandah, hopping across the bannister, picking at everything in sight. Their intensions are brash.

I read the headline news, "Rapist wins Rs 60 Crore Lotto jackpot".

"Morning, fatsy, did you have a good workout? How was your shake?"

"Morning. My workout was hard due to my sleep depravation. The shake was good thanks."

"Stop whining, the challenge will make you stronger. You're looking thinner by the way. I like it. Did you use the shampoo?"

"Yes, it smells good."

"We'll pick up more of that shake for you, Samson Night says it's the best thing to be on while training. I'm heading off to my mom next door for a quick visit. Wait here, I will send for you when I'm ready to leave for the office."

I wait. Again. I smoke a few more cigarettes and read my book, *The Virgin Suicides*. There is still no Internet or computers in the house. The Producer has a desktop at work, so does Alisha. The rest of us do without. Kush has his own laptop that he brings to work. I still don't have a mobile phone. Apparently it is being delivered today. The Producer chose it. He says it's a surprise.

When The Producer calls for me to come downstairs, it's almost eleven. I get to the office refreshed. I sleep all the way to work. My music pumps hard into my ears blocking out the 'honky tonk' of Bombay's busy streets.

G is for goat

Kush needs to submit a short 20-minute film on 16mm to NYU. They will consider his application based on the merits of the film submitted. He holds up a 16mm film camera.

"You wanna come with me and help shoot it? You can take stills while I take footage. A film shot in these streets will definitely give me a different edge compared to all the Americans applying."

The children from the dwelling across the road surround us again, laughing and touching. "Aunty ... Aunty."

I am caught in my own thoughts. This world belongs to a different time. There are certain aspects like their IT and accessibility to the latest technology that seems to be in time with the rest of the world, but everything else around me is still frozen in time. They live and operate as if it were two hundred years back.

We stop in a street where two boys play enthusiastically with a handmade kite. A goat watches them with interest. The goat is dressed in an old red knitted jersey. It's falling apart with holes. His front legs are in the arms, the neck line hangs neatly around his neck. It's a perfect fit. He almost looks human. He is eating out of a bucket in front of him.

Before I can ask, Kush replies, "Today is Eid. This poor fucker will be slaughtered later and made into *biryani*. They dress them to keep them warm and feed them a lot to fatten them up for today's slaughter. You see *yaar*, it's all about making the goat the best he can be for Allah."

"It's not cold?"

"It is in the mornings. Winter is almost here."

"If this is your winter, I'm not complaining."

I go down on my haunches to get a shot of this peculiar setting: goat in the foreground, the boys enthralled and occupied with their kite in the background. After a few shots, the goat moves forward, glaring at me with his arrogant yellow-green Satan eyes. He tries to buck me.

"He does not want his picture taken. Come."

The slaughtering has begun and watered-down blood runs through the makeshift drainage system of the streets. The air smells heavy. Iron mixed with dampened flesh.

There is an apartment block adjacent to us, across the road, slightly offset from the slum that I always go into to photograph, with a blue door and my sunshine boy. I call him that because he loves my camera. He has become my muse. A goat bleats loudly from a top-floor balcony; he is wearing a green jersey.

Dhiraj arrives to tell us lunch is ready. Kush makes him stand in front of the camera to be interviewed.

"What are you asking him to do?"

"I'm asking of him to be telling us of this very important day for Muslims and to be giving us story of significance of this 'goatly' animal."

"But he's not Muslim."

"No, but he is funny."

Kush drops down to the ground so that he can shoot upward, fitting Dhiraj and the goat high up on the balcony of the building behind him into his frame.

"Okay rolling ... and action."

Balkran is standing behind me, teasing Dhiraj as he gets camera shy. He recoils, laughing, and covers his mouth. Kush says something encouraging. Dhiraj manages to pull himself together and begins an animated interview.

The goat's bleating has become ear-piercing. It is so loud that you can hear it over the noise in the street. Dhiraj points up to the balcony, continuing to talk.

Kush pans into the goat. The goat is throwing his head from side to side. His nostrils flare, absorbing whatever smells are intoxicating his mind. He stomps his front hoof repeatedly. He is frantic. Kush moves in on another goat that has had his jersey taken away. He is being held between a man's legs. This man is in white Muslim attire, but it is very bloody from the misfortune of many goats before this one. He is the slaughterer. Another man dressed in crisp white Muslim attire with only a few splats of blood stands alongside the slaughterer sharpening a very shiny knife with a stone. The scraping creates hysteria with the goats lined up behind the one about to be slaughtered.

Kush explains that according to the Muslim slaughtering rules, not only must the blade be sharp, but it must also be free of any nicks to ensure a swift and efficient death.

The goat between the man's legs sends a haunting bleat upward to the goat on the balcony.

Kush pans up, they are talking to each other.

The goat on the balcony gives out one last long bleat and jumps. The fall is quick. The sound when the goat hits the ground is disturbing: cracking of bones, splitting of skull, the splattering of encased organs that hold weight with their contents.

Kush pushes forward and across the street.

"I must get in there *yaar*! This is award-winning stuff."

I cannot go. The children from the dwelling are there, exploding with excitement. They also want to be filmed with the suicide goat. The goat between the man's legs struggles for his life. The slaughterer raises his arm high, the blade catching the light. I turn away and put my hands over my ears.

I enter the office. Lunch time.

We have tomorrow off. It's a Sunday and still no new shoots have come in.

Ex-citement

Nisha wants me to go clubbing with her tonight. I am exhausted from the previous night's wait, but I could do with a party.

"The city will be buzzing Gené, it's Eid."

"I'm too scared to ask The Producer. You ask."

She enters The Producer's cabin and exits moments later.

"He says you can come as long as you are home by three."

"So now I have a curfew?"

"It's better than nothing, I'll pick you up by ten?"

"Where's this club?"

"In Juhu only, it's called Sins, in the JW Marriot hotel."

We get home early from the office. It's just gone nine.

"Eat your *khānā* before you get dressed."

The Producer seems annoyed. He did not say a word to me all the way home.

"Are you okay? Is it okay if I go out with Nisha?"

"As long as you behave. No more than two drinks and be home by three."

"Okay."

"Come show me what you are wearing before you leave."

I have lived alone and taken responsibility for myself since the day I left school. Italy, Durban, Cape Town, booze, drugs, parties and I went to live with a man double my age whom I did not know, in India ... now he wants to tell me how to behave?

He does not eat. He goes to his room. I eat alone. My reflection in the wall-to-wall mirrors keeps me company.

The club is packed. It's loud and the music pumps. Everyone is dressed in bling. The disco lights catch the sequins on the garments as these flashy 'pieces' move. It's a very elegant club. It has to be if it's in such a prestigious hotel.

The hotel is beautiful. There are huge koi pools running through the gardens with an infinity pool practically on the beach.

Nisha leads me to the bar. We shoot back a flaming Lamborghini each and order a second drink. Rum for her, vodka for me.

I am highlighted in the crowd by the ultraviolet light. I am the only white person there. I am also the most underdressed. All the girls sport short glamorous dresses, including Nisha. I am wearing my Levi's and a white shirt. This does not deter the boys. They begin to surround us. Nisha steps in, but it's not long and we are all dancing, smoking and drinking together. People can't stop staring. I love to dance and it shows. I have not had a drink since I first went out with Nisha when I arrived. We drink far more than two drinks. The boys are buying all our shots. They cheer me on. I relish the attention and entertain them with my dance moves. I teach them 'big box ... little box ... post it ... post it', 'fly fishing' and 'starting up a lawn mower'. I let rip. So do my jeans. At some point in my hyped-up drunken state, I do a funky move going down on my haunches and my jeans rip in the crotch, all the way up my arse. I have a G-string on. My bum cheek glows in the ultraviolet light. It's time to go home. When we check the time it's past 4am. Shit!

There's a knock on the door. This time the door does not wait for my consent. It opens.

The Producer's stern voice and a harsh beam of light slip through the holes in my head.

My ears conduct a sonic landscape of reverberating base through my skull. My brain bulges, gasping for oxygen, trying to process where I am and how I got here. Am I still on the dance floor? The incessant loud squawking of crows gives it away. I am back home.

"Do you plan to sleep all day, fatsy? Come. Gaya wants to meet you."

I cannot digest what he has just said to me. It's too much for this hanging body. I'm saturated in alcohol. I can't lift my head.

"Your wife Gaya?"

"No, the cat's mother."

"What? Now?"

"Yes, now. She's been here for over an hour waiting for you to move your lazy bones. You obviously ignored what I asked of you. Too much to drink? What time did you get home?"

I figure this is a trap. He knows the truth. If he asked the servants they would not dare lie to him.

"At four o'clock. Sorry."

He turns his slumped shoulders on me and leaves.

"Get out here, Gaya is waiting."

My eyes are gunged up. I fell asleep with my contacts in and now the 'crusties' have moved in. I pry my lids open. The lenses stick dry and crispy to my eyeballs. They scratch and burn. My body fights me. I feel sick. My head hurts. My stomach heaves forward as I sit up, I must get to that toilet.

I have someone waiting. I vomit on their watch. My teeth are growing a fur farm. My oesophagus feels like a gravel road shooting acidic stones as I drive the sick back down to my stomach. My voice is hoarse from all the smoking. I quickly rinse my mouth. I sweat, white and pale, the alcohol is seeping through my pores. I wash my face, brush my teeth and spray some perfume. I look a mess. My hair is maxed out in different directions. My eyes are blood shot. Fuck it! I grab my jeans and pull them over my pyjama bottoms. I grab the first T-shirt from the cupboard, 'Little Miss Naughty'. I'm not thinking.

I walk through a downpour of dread. I am ashamed. Who am

I? Where did I come from? What have I been doing with her ex-husband? Why do I look like this?

The two oversized cream couches face each other. Gaya sits on one facing The Producer who is sitting on the other one. I sit next to The Producer. He gets up.

"Right, I'm off to shower." He is still in his boxers and a T-shirt.

I shift, conscious of how I look, smell and taste.

Gaya is dressed in a beautiful white dress, Western style. She holds a navy Gucci bag on her lap. Her hair is short and folds around her face like Betty Boop. She is fair skinned and very pretty.

I want to tell her that I come from a good home with parents that have incredibly strong values in place and that this looks worse than it is.

As a child growing up I am afforded many privileges for my imagination to run wild. In the late afternoons I like to sit on the high wall that surrounds our house where the angle of the sun casts my shadow onto the flat cream wall that holds the domes on the roof. I point my toes and imagine I am doing 'flick flacks' in the sky. I am a trapeze artist cartwheeling through the sky, a princess in this palace. I believe in the *Magic Faraway Tree* and will live my life changing lands just like Enid Blyton allowed Jo, Bessie and Fanny to do.

Every Friday my mother takes us on an adventure and every season change we are taken to the big Woolworths in Sandton City for a new set of 'jammies' and holiday clothes. My mother spends valuable quality time with us.

My father is the most generous man I know. We are driven to art classes in Pretoria every Tuesday and on our way back we get to buy a 'prezzie' from the CNA in Menlyn Park.

Our house is plush and extravagant. It is personalised to our Italian lifestyle. It stands out, huge and exotic in the middle of nowhere on an empty plot and people from around call it 'the Taj Mahal'. My mother is incredibly house-proud. We have underfloor heating and a massive Gaggenau kitchen. A massive walk-in pantry and 24-carat-gold plated taps and bidets in every bathroom, just like a 'real' Italian family. My bedroom has wallpaper on the ceiling which my mother took me to Biggie Best to choose. I chose soft fluffy clouds in blue, purple and violet hues. When I lie on my bed and look up, I'm in heaven.

I pride myself on my Italian heritage and constantly wish I was in Italy and not here.

I love Sundays. My father makes gnocchi and we all get a chore in the process. We always have people over and sit from twelve noon, only ever getting up from the table after dark when my mother has made sure that lunch has run into dinner. My parents are not strict or demanding, they do not expect us to be overachievers either. We are 'free to be'.

We are close, yes, we are close and we are fortunate.

Thank god for those constant years. Here in India they remind me where I came from.

Gaya speaks. Her voice is soft and gentle like her face.

"I believe you are from Cape Town, Gené?"

She knows my name. I know hers.

"Yes, Gaya, have you been?"

"No, but I have had dealings with people from there. I believe it's very beautiful?"

"It is."

"Do you like India? Are you enjoying the work?"

"Yes, very much, thank you."

Silence.

Gaya breaks the uncomfortable situation first.

I am without armour. I look like shit, I feel like shit. I was not prepared for this. She is so beautiful.

"I am going to the Marriot for a swim with my sons. You are welcome to come with."

"Thank you for your kind invite, but I have some work to finish. Maybe next time."

Gaya stands to shake my hand. I stand. Then it dawns on me. My jeans are torn right across my arse. I put a hand behind my back to feel. My arse, covered in pink pyjama pants, is exposed.

I must not go first. I must hang back and not let my back show.

I stand in one place and wave her off as she exits the front door.

The day plays out as it always does on a Sunday. After The Producer has showered, he returns to his couch to play chess and ponder his next strategy for the week that lies ahead.

The Producer hands me an orange Sony Ericsson box. The phone inside is a silver-and-orange Walkman phone. It comes with great headphones and specialises in playing music.

"This is perfect, thank you."

I hug him tightly and give him a kiss. He reciprocates with satisfaction.

"I thought you would like it, it's so you, now you can listen to the music you are always listening to on here."

He takes it from me, and inserts the battery and the sim card.

"Now you can call your family whenever you want. It has roaming."

"Thank you so much."

"Come, let's eat."

We sit at our large round table; servants tiptoe around us serving Cook's famous fish curry. Things are back to normal. Cook is back and Kutty serves the rice minus the scratching. The fish curry is rusty red, spicy and full of flavour. It is the best thing I've had in the past three weeks.

The Producer calls for dessert. A bowl of *kheer* arrives. It's a rice pudding that is sweet like condensed milk and rich like clotted cream. Delicious! He serves me up a bowl.

"Today you can cheat, you've done well, fatsy."

Weigh day Monday

After my workout with Trainer, The Producer summons us to his bathroom.

"Sixty-two-point-four, fatsy. *Achcha!* Very good."

"Fatsy, if you carry on like this, I will be able to take you to a party soon."

"Is that why you left me waiting outside Samson Night's house the other night? Are you ashamed of me?"

"No, I would not put it that way. I just don't want Samson Night to think that the only woman I can get is a fat cow."

"But … I'm not …"

"I want him to see you at your best. He always has very beautiful women and I want my white girlfriend to match up to his …"

He is smug. I'm offended.

I look down at the number on the scale. I've done it. I have seen the number and I will beat it. Fifty-seven, here I come! I feel a wave of adamant defiance rise up through my neck and into my cheeks. They glow red with determination. I need to channel it positively, and not let it become an obsession again.

As we stumble through the tightly packed streets in our gleaming golden frozen cocoon-on-wheels, I feel triumphant. Although The Producer has insisted on the weight-loss and the stringent exercise regime, I feel better for it. The exercise has motivated me, giving me far more energy than I had before and I feel far more confident in my skin. I am running six kilometres a day, which I never thought I could have done before. I have perfectly pedicured nails, highlighted hair, a smooth hairless body and Hollywood white teeth. Although I have a full mouth of good-looking teeth, The Producer sent me to the Bollywood stars' dentist to have my teeth whitened. He has given me a gift. I am learning to respect and love my body. Thanks to him I am starting to look my best.

We arrive at the office. Everyone is on top form. We finally have work again. It's a very small low-budget commercial for a kitchen appliance telesales show combined with a game show called, *Get richin' your kitchin.* It will feature a senior actor that, in the fickle eyes of Bollywood, fell from grace years ago. The chosen director for this commercial is Kiran Cooper again. India's best. There is a series of seven commercials, all set on an aeroplane with different scenarios.

Kiran Cooper arrives from Chennai. Everyone in the office is extremely conscious of his presence again. There is a sense of awe and immense respect towards him. He gives Alisha a huge hug, she laughs with him as they share common ground – they are both from the south. He follows The Producer into the cabin.

I go and sit in between Kush and Nisha. I want Kush to load some music from his laptop onto my new mobile phone. We huddle together.

"Kush, if Kiran Cooper is so big, why did The Producer choose him for such a small job?"

Kush whispers.

"Because the actor we will be working with is ... how can I put it? Complicated and tricky. We need someone that can handle Bly Avibath and work really fast. We have seven commercials to shoot in three days, only Kiran Cooper Sir can pull something like that off *yaar.*"

Nisha cuts in.

"Kiran Cooper Sir has won many awards, all his films have been super hits and he is in the *Guinness Book of Records* for the director who has shot the most films in the world. He is only in his forties."

Kush adds to the suspense of the hushed conversation.

"He works with a great team. His art director is also the best in India. His name is Harvey Sydnam. Together they can shoot a feature film in five weeks. They have been known to split a studio in four. Harvey builds four different sets for four completely different films. Kiran then shoots on them simultaneously, jumping from one set to the other, flipping his brain into each completely different story. Kiran hardly ever takes more than one take. He always knows exactly what he needs to cut a film. That's why he can work so quickly."

"Wow, that's amazing."

"He is the master of comedy."

"Why does he wear an eye patch?" I whisper.

"He was hit in the eye with a cricket ball as a child and lost it due to complications," Kush replies.

Kiran Cooper leaves The Producer's cabin and comes to talk to us. When he speaks he mumbles slightly.

"Gené aa ... *yaar* ... would you ... aa ... like to come with me to meet our aa ... sort of star, Bly Avibath?"

Nisha pinches me.

"Gené, you better go, it's such an honour that he wants you to assist him."

"Thank you, Kiran Sir. It would be an honour to accompany you."

"Of course aa ... you do realise *yaar*, aa ... the honour is mine, my dear."

His smile flashes a pair of gorgeous deep-set dimples at me and I am immediately put at ease.

"Great then, sir, let's go."

I whisper to Kush before I leave.

"Why did he choose me?"

"He likes you and you're gonna be his assistant for this job."

"Why? Where you going?"

"I'm going to Australia for a holiday with my sister on Friday. I won't be here for the shoot."

"But, I can't assist without you."

"Of course you can, you're ready *yaar*. Look how good you've got."

We drive toward Film City. Kiran Cooper sits at the back next to me; his driver stares ahead. He offers me a cigarette. We light up.

"I have never had a white girl as an assistant. I like the idea and I can bet you that Mr Bly Avibath is going to enjoy you too."

"Why do you have such an English surname, sir?"

"Well it's actually a stage name. My surname is actually Kuppuswamy, like every other filmy person's in this town, so I changed it to Cooper, the closest match I could come up with and I love the Mini Cooper car. I imported one from London; it's at home in Chennai."

"What colour?"

"Sunflower yellow and all."

"What's the actor's name that we're about meet? I keep forgetting it."

"Bly Avibath."

"What does he look like?"

"I will point him out when I see a hoarding with him on it. That is if I can find one these days aa … he is not very popular ... He has not done a film in years. Landing this game show will hopefully help to bring his popularity ranking up again, I think the poor man really needs the work. Aa … that's why we are going to meet him at Film City, he's on set at the moment shooting the actual game show, we are just doing the commercial for it."

"Sir, did you study film?"

"No actually, I studied to be a psychologist aa … I love people and the reasons behind their behaviour, then by chance I became an editor."

"And now you're a director?"

"Yes, well, the one led to the other aa … If you understand the editing process you can see each shot and what is needed before you start directing. That way you don't waste time re-taking shots. I seldom need more than one take."

We pull into Film City and park in front of a dilapidated trailer. There's a satellite dish hanging off its bracket on the roof.

We are led to the trailor door. A dark-skinned man with navy slacks and a white shirt opens it for us. He looks like Homer Simpson's boss: short, squat-faced with a sharp nose. His eyes are fixed on us like a crow that's just seen something shiny. We step up into the icy air-conditioned trailer. Kiran Cooper beckons me to go first. There is a strong scent of sandalwood incense burning. As I pull myself up onto the first stair, my eyes are at floor level so that I see his feet first. They are in steel calipers; I'm surprised. I take another step. He is standing in long cream cotton trousers that drop in folds around his heavy thick-soled shoes. His shirt is also cream and long with a high collar and a long powder blue and navy paisley silk scarf that falls along either side of him catching on a pair of crutches in either hand. He holds himself up, balancing easily on one crutch to free his right hand and shake mine.

He reaches out to me. I am on his floor level now. My hand is in his hand and all I can do for the first few seconds is stare deep and long, long and deep. He is hunched, but tall and very striking. I look down disturbed. His electrifying, crocodile-green eyes are not a common feature in Indian men. I force myself to look up again at his penetrating gaze; the strong contrast of green against brown skin makes me uncomfortable, but I'm transfixed by their demand for attention. Black rings outline his irises, giving him a wild look like the photograph of the Afghan girl taken by Steve McCurry.

He is neither Asian-looking nor European, but a subtle combination of the two. His eminence wraps around me like a fuzzy blanket on a stormy day. Kiran Cooper is behind me. He leans past my frozen form to shake Bly's hand.

"Good Morning, Bly, it's been a while hasn't it?"

"Too long, Mr Cooper. I think time for you and I to make a feature film together."

Bly's eyes come straight back to mine.

"And you, madam, to whom do I owe the pleasure?"

His voice is deep and seductive.

I fumble.

"Do you speak English Ma'am?"

"Aaa ... Sorry, yes, Sir, um ...Bly ... Avi ... bbb."

Fuck, this name!

"This is Gené, Bly, she will be my assistant on this job."

Kiran Cooper squeezes my shoulders, steadying me from behind. I am immobilised.

I have never felt like this before, about anyone. What is wrong with me? He gestures for me and Kiran Cooper to sit on his tattered sofa, yellowing sponge escaping bulbously where the fabric has worn thin. His clothes and this trailer are remnants of a past enriched with plenty of money. All that is left of it is here in front of me, bleached by a scorching sun. I sit quickly. My legs are jelly. He lowers himself with his crutches on the sofa opposite me. We stare at each other. His face seems unnaturally bloated. Maybe it's the medication, Cortizone for pain or a bad lifestyle, alcohol and pills? Coke bloat even?

"And where do you come from, Gené?"

"South Africa."

"That's a very nice place. I have been, often. Are you from Cape Town, Gené?"

"Yes I am."

"*Achcha*! Mind blowing! That's fantastic news *yaar*."

He slaps his knee and smiles, twisting his head closer in my direction. His stare drills deeper. He is smiling. His voice is strong and animated now. He does not break his stare as he leans into me. His silver-grey eyebrows arch menacingly as he investigates my thoughts.

"So, Kiran Cooper Sir, let's talk about these seven scripts, I need to get back to set soon."

Kiran Cooper begins to explain. Bly turns to Kiran Cooper occasionally to ask questions, but returns to our fixed gaze every time. I am transported away.

I am in Vincent van Gogh's "Starry Night" painting. I am a little girl standing on top of the white cathedral rooftop. I am wearing an electric purple dress and a matching purple fascinator.

I have my arms stretched upward to the starry sky. The sky whirls and weaves inside and outside of me. In, out, in, out. My heart expands, making space for this enormity. My whole body tingles. It lifts me to a place of exceptional heights. I feel drugged. I am an enchanted being. I can fly. I twist and turn in the starry sky.

"Well, that's that then. Mind blowing *yaar*! I shall see you both in three days' time. I look forward to working with you Miss Gené."

My hand is shaking as I step down the stairs of the trailer. I notice an armoured Jeep with four guards in purple uniforms standing stiffly with machine guns mounted across their chests positioned next to the shabby trailer.

"Why are they here, sir?"

"Aa ... on top of all his troubles, Bly suffers from agoraphobia."

"How can he afford armoured guards if he has no money?"

"Subsidised by the government. He took the press to court and won the case saying that social media had caused his trauma. He gets them 'on the house'."

Soon we are driving and Kiran Cooper is speaking, but I am still flying.

"He's had a big effect on you, aa ... hasn't he?"

I blink hard, my heart is still racing. I swallow hard. The magic goes down to my stomach and flutters gently, keeping me electrified and buzzing. He reads my thoughts.

"He is a real forgotten star, Gené. That's what it feels like to be in the presence of a real star."

"Sir, his effect on me makes no sense. I have never seen or heard of him before. My stars are people that I have followed from Hollywood, George Clooney, Brad Pitt, not this balding, crippled old man whom I never knew even existed."

"I know what you are trying to say, aa ... even the people of India have forgotten what a real actor should be. Today everyone thinks that a super star is a bulging muscled gangster with zero acting talent and silicone gells stuffed into any sagging part of his anatomy that may reveal signs of ageing. You see, my dear, he is the true meaning of forgotten talent. All because his polio has got the better of him. Just because his legs don't work so good no more does not mean he cannot aa ... act, but here in Bollywood aa ... you see my dear it's all about the dance and not the act."

"What happened to him?"

"So many things aa ... his first big problems started aa ... many years back. He contracted polio as a child. When Jonas Salk's polio vaccine was introduced to India there was this aa ... frightening concept among our people that the polio drops were part of a conspiracy to sterilise their children and they aa ... refused to let them be vaccinated. Sadly, Bly was one of the children who got the virus. He was lucky and did not get it as bad as some children. It only left him with a severe limp. He did not let his disability get to him *yaar*, he aa ... became a fantastic dancer and started acting. He was good and his life was good. He married and had two beautiful children. But one day his luck turned in a very sad way aa ... he was visiting a friend with his two-year-old son and three-year-old daughter. The friend had a big swimming pool. The children were outside playing on their tricycles. You know those tricycles where you aa ... strap the kids' feet in so they can't fall off?"

"Yes."

"Well, Bly went into the house for a split second with his friend and the kids were gone."

"Gone where?"

"Aa ... they both rode straight, aa ... into the swimming pool one after the other, poor things. Aa ... they sank, silently drowning at the bottom of the pool, their feet strapped to the pedals, their tricycles holding them down."

"Oh my god and then?"

"Aa ... By the time Bly found them it was too late."

"That's the most horrific ..."

"It is my dear, aa ... and after that Bly could not cope. His marriage ended and he entered a very dark place, a place that you do not wish on anyone. He adopted a lifestyle of self pity and self-destruction, a reliance to alcohol and bad things, very bad things. His career has never recovered. He is too consumed with sorrow and cannot come to terms with the loss of his kids or his wife. It's as if he's waiting to die. I am hoping this show will give him what he needs to turn what's left of his career around. Sadly, aa ... with age and a very bad lifestyle he suffers from a condition called post-polio syndrome."

"What is it?"

"Aa ... it's a condition that affects polio survivors years after the initial attack. In his case, from much neglect he is experiencing severe muscle weakness in new areas of his body. That is why he has gone from just being left with a limp to now, aa ... having to rely completely on crutches. There are days when he has to remain in a wheel chair, especially when he gets tired. Hence the loss of work. No one wants to see a cripple dancing in the Swiss Alps or against the skyline of Manhattan. His current state is aa ...just not condusive to the genre of Bollywood film."

We return to the office to prepare for the shoot. The Producer calls me into his cabin.

"I believe you've met our actor."

"I did."

"And? Did he scare you? They say he's gone completely mad in his old age?"

"'No, he made such an impression on me."

"That forgotten old man? Are you smoking something I don't know about?"

"No. No one has ever made me feel the way I did today. I became numb and jelly-like. His crocodile-green eyes pierced right through me. I was in a painting reaching for the stars, my body became electric all over."

He looks surprised.

"Really, did I not have the same effect on you in Cape Town?"

He is in a good mood and has taken it for what it is. If I had said that about any other man, I would know all about it. He gestures to me to sit across from him. I pull out a chair. I glance at the red velvet casting couch, my eyes scan for potential 'hotspots'. I wonder if it's been used yet. I am getting very attached to the life The Producer has to offer. My feelings toward him are growing and suddenly the idea of having to share him makes me jealous. I am becoming reliant and dependent on him.

"Here, sweets, I got you something to help improve your picture taking."

The Producer pulls a long Canon box from his desk drawer and places it in front of me. A new zoom lens. I've never been able to afford a lens like this. I'm gobsmacked. I walk around and hug him.

"Thank you, thank you, thank you."

Later that night, I am in my element as we drive home. I lie on the back seat staring at the sky through my new lens. Even though there is too much pollution to see a star, I have my starry night canvas inside my soul and it sparks, glistens and glows, igniting me forward.

Get richin' your kitchin

There seems to be a lot of fuss around the costumes for Bly Avibath. Nisha and 'dressman' Sashi are handling it. Due to his disabilities there is only one designer that can tailor the right cut for Bly's crippled body. The designer arrives at the office with twelve suit bags and a very stern face, wearing one of his own immaculate suits. He is weedy with small cat-eye spectacles on his nose. A tape measure hangs around his neck. Four of his own assistants accompany him. I'm not sure why he needs four, exactly. He wags his index finger at Nisha and Sashi who take strict washing, ironing, hanging and transportation instructions.

Shoot day has arrived.

Harvey Sydnam, the art director, has outshone any quality of set that I have seen so far in Bollywood. His work is impeccably neat, clean and realistic. I feel like I am standing on a real plane. The commercials will be shot in the business-class section. The seats are wide and comfortable, navy blue with white napkins hanging over the head rests.

The plane has an open top, enabling the crew to light and shoot from above. Men work frantically from bamboo scaffolding, adjusting more lights that loom above. They are double-checking their knots between the supporting bamboo and the ropes that hold the lights in place. Their director is way too important to have a two-tonne light fall on top of him.

Harvey comes to introduce himself to me. The man looking at me has a soft smile and bright apple-green eyes. He is fair skinned with a beard and looks Portuguese.

"Hello, I am Harvey, Kiran's art director."

Now he reminds me of Bilbo Baggins. I cannot resist. I lean over and hug him.

"Hello Harvey, I have heard so much about you."

Our connection is instant. He feels like home.

He originally comes from Goa, where most of the population is Catholic. Besides his European looks, he wears a gold wedding band on his left hand. He must be Christian. He smells like Calvin Klein, but unmixed with spice. He rolls his words like Kiran, but in a much clearer way. He offers me a long cigarette. We have a cigarette together and I know we are going to become good friends on this job.

Alisha helps me position the extras into their seats. They are in awe of Kiran Cooper and sit quietly, listening attentively to my instructions.

I have been asked to play the role of an air hostess in one of the commercials that will be shot on day three. The additional artists that are playing roles with Bly are put through makeup and then through costume with Nisha. We are organised and on time.

Sashi is only taking care of Bly's clothes. He is in a state. Dhiraj, my favourite on-set *peon,* beckons me to follow him, Sashi is calling. I am led to a tiny backroom behind the set. The smell of sewage wafts through the narrow passageway. Sashi dances over an ironing board, dipping his fingertips lightly into the fabric of Bly's first costume change, a cream *kurta* (long shirt). His vest is drenched in sweat. His pink bandana seems to be sopping. He looks like a rabbit caught in the headlights.

"Madam Jimmy, I am waking all night making this *kapadā* perfect, but again I must do it, I see a line and look these ones also are having new lines appearing when I am coming this morning."

He points with the steaming iron to the hanging garments; they look perfect. His arm flops across his face like a windscreen wiper trying to get the dripping sweat out of his oversized eyes, steaming iron still gripped in his hand.

"Sashi, you are going to drive yourself mad. These are perfect. Stop fussing. Put this into its bag, let's go and hang it in Bly's trailer."

"You madam, you taking, not me. I am scared. This actor is very angry man."

"No mister, you're coming with."

Once he has put the costume into its suit bag I take his hand. He pulls it away immediately.

"Madam, this is very bad *yaar*, if The Producer Sir ..."

"Okay sorry, come let's get this done."

"Madam, I am not believing you are taking my hand in romantic song, what I am telling my wife?"

My 'gaydar' has never been so out.

"You have a wife?"

"Yes, and one *bachcha* girl. I am taking one picture of you. This is for showing my wife. I am every day talking of you. She is very jealous, madam."

He holds up his phone and begins to click at my face as we walk.

The portly doorman stands at Bly's trailer door.

"Good morning, sir, my name is Gené, this is Sashi. Please can you hang this in Bly's trailer? It's his first costume for the day."

He scans me with narrowed eyes. All I see is Homer Simpson's boss. He holds out his hand without a smile. He says something to Sashi in Hindi, Sashi replies. He is clinging onto the suit bag for dear life. He strokes it twice like a much-loved pet, then reluctantly passes it to me.

The trailer door swings open. The doorman points.

"You must put it in there."

I climb the stairs. Sashi holds his hands under the bag, just in case. He is neurotic. The door shuts immediately behind me. They are obviously trying to keep the air-conditioned air in. I smell him. His scent is everywhere, but he is not here yet. I begin to float towards his non-existing embrace. My head begins to paint along the yellow twirls of the starry sky. STOP! HANG! LEAVE!

Sashi takes my picture against the trailer. The Producer comes towards us. Sashi scuttles away, disappearing behind the van. The Producer looks at his watch impatiently. He says something to the doorman. The doorman shrugs his shoulders, mumbles something back in Hindi. The Producer does not intimidate him.

"Have you set the costume?"

"Yes, I have."

"Is everything else ready?"

"Yes, just need our star."

"Our star is three hours late, on my clock, my money."

The doorman narrows his eyes toward The Producer.

"The time he takes is the time he takes. He is not far."

"Gené, call me when he arrives. Kiran Cooper and I need to see him first."

The Producer walks off. I go and look for Sashi. I want to smoke. He is behind the trailer with Dhiraj, who is making tea and coffee on order for the crew over a bunsen burner. Dhiraj digs in the supplies *petti*. He pulls out a box of cigarettes and bobs his head, smiling from ear to ear. Sashi translates.

"He is getting this brand specially for you."

He hands them to me with a cup of black coffee. I can smell the fumes of alcohol seeping through his pores. His eyes are glazed over. I love him. Sashi rolls what looks like a white chalky paste between his palms, he adds a little tobacco then turns his back to me and pushes it between his bottom lip and his gum.

"What is that?"

"This is my cigarette."

"What is your cigarette?"

"It is lime and tobacco mixed ... better than smoking."

"Why do you turn your back?"

"Respect, madam."

Everybody around me stops in their tracks. Bly has arrived,

slowly emerging from the dust. He is in a tuk-tuk, the armoured jeep snailing behind him.

I move toward the front of his trailer. The doorman nods at me.

"You happy now? Go tell your boss."

I hover first. I want a glimpse.

Before I know what's happened, he is being led in a circular formation towards his trailer door by four men in purple. Indian government offers good service. I can just see a striped beanie moving up the stairs. The door shuts behind him, the four men remain around the door area.

The Producer and Kiran Cooper walk together toward the trailer. They are ever so self-important. The Producer's fists are clenched at either side of his body. I notice that they are strutting in unison. I look on with Alisha, remaining at the entrance of the studio.

"Did you say hello to your new love?"

"Not yet, he moved too quickly, all I saw was his beanie moving in the middle of his four guards."

"Oh, he had a beanie on? Means he still has to put his hair on. That's gonna take some time, we might as well have a coffee. Dhiraj ... *coffee de na*."

The trailer door swings open, The Producer and Kiran Cooper are walking out. They've been in there for less than a minute. And now? They both point at me curling their index fingers toward themselves.

"He wants you."

They both say it.

"What?"

Kiran Cooper puts his hand on my shoulder and speaks calmly and gently.

"Aa ... He wants you to show him his first costume, he wants you to tell him which script we shooting first and aa ... he only wants to deal with you."

"Really?"

"Your dream is coming true, my dear. Go sit with him."

He points at my clipboard.

"Remember we are shooting this fourth one first so the cream *kurta* is first."

"Yes, sir, it's all set."

The Producer smiles.

"Don't fuck it up."

I walk towards the doorman. I look back. Everyone is watching me. Alisha gives me a thumbs up. The Producer and Kiran Cooper stand cross-armed with spread-eagled legs. They smile, macho macho. The most important men on set, and he wants me.

A man stands at Bly's dresser, he is laying out cosmetics and brushing an auburn wig.

"Good morning, Miss Gené."

"Good morning, Mr Avibath."

He shakes my hand. His hands are small, delicate and bony. His skin is silky thin.

"How are you today? Are we running on schedule?"

"Yes, Mr Avibath."

"Yes, what? Yes, we are on time, yes ... what? Show me what you have planned for today, tell me about my costume changes and tell me about the script and my lines. You are the assitant director, aren't you?"

"Yes, Mr Avibath."

"Bly, please call me Bly from now on."

He carefully uses his crutches to manoeuvre himself onto the tattered sofa and pats the space next to him. I sit next to him, our shoulders touching. My veins pump overtime pushing all the blood to my face. My cheeks glow red. He puts some reading specs on, leans down close into my clipboard and becomes animated. His head is in my lap, when he looks up he is in my face.

"*Achcha*, mind blowing! Three lines in total? Very good. Now Gené the assistant, tell me what to wear."

I open his suit bag.

"Cream? I like it, cream is a good colour on me Gené, what do you think?"

He holds it up against himself. I think I love it when he says my name. I think I love him. I want to banter back. He must see my sense of humour too.

"I think it would look better without the beanie."

"*Achcha*, very good. Are you going to stand there and watch me dress?"

I leave. As I get to the bottom of the stairs the doorman smiles at me for the first time. His eyes narrow even more.

"My boss likes you. We are going to work well together."

I look up and everyone is standing at the studio entrance watching me. They all want to know. I tell them. I am excited. I am in charge.

The set is quiet and controlled when Bly is on it. My world is divided in two. Him and me, then them. Kiran Cooper works quickly. Today he wears a yellow eye patch with an acid smiley face on it. Bly bates Kiran Cooper jokingly. Kiran Cooper does not buckle under the intimidation.

"*Arrey*, Kiran Cooper, this script is mind-blasting, shall we turn it into an award-winning film? I heard you can direct?"

His strong voice fills the studio and he makes everyone laugh as he takes the mickey out of us while we work around him.

"*Arrey*, which idiot wrote these mind-blasting lines that I have to deliver? Whomever it was should go for some script writing lessons *yaar*."

He is king, he has come to life under these lights, no longer a fallen forgotten soul. Even though Kiran Cooper is director, Bly dictates.

He does not acknowledge The Producer.

After the first take, we traditionally break the coconut. Bly takes a piece from the plate and eats with us. When we are resetting shots, he sits in a corner. He calls me over and asks me questions about my family and my home. He shares his peanut brittle with me. He asks how I got here. I tell him I work for Luna. He looks at me long and hard. Does he know? I wrap a piece of peanut brittle in my call sheet and hide it in my pocket for later.

We get two commercials in the bag in less than three hours. The set relaxes. The noise escalates. The room inhales deeply, followed by a long exhale of relief. Crew members' shoulders sink lower, people become shorter.

Two down, five to go. I go and find Sashi. We want to lay his three changes for tomorrow, tonight. He is in his little ironing room finishing off the last outfit, his mobile phone crackling out some Shaggy tune sung in Hindi. It is as if he is delicately playing the piano along the stitching of each seam. He is methodical and precise. He does not see me standing there until I throw the two outfits that Bly wore earlier at him. They are scrunched up in a ball, that's how they were left, ripped off as fast as possible, inside out. Sashi scrambles to catch them. I have given him a fright.

"*Arrey*, madam, this is respect *yaar*. Not throwing and treating like old shoes."

"Why don't you wear one while you pack away? They gonna get washed anyway. I dare you Sashi."

Nisha walks in and joins in on the dare. We spur Sashi on.

"Come, mister, I will take a pic for you, then you can say you wore the clothes of the scariest actor in Bollywood."

"Nobody cares *yaar*, madam, he is forgotten by all."

"Not to me, I can still smell his perfume. Smell it, it still smells like power."

We help him pull it over his sweaty vest and tie-dyed jeans. He takes his pink bandana off. He stands stiff, but proud.

"It is having a very important smelling."

I dig into my pocket. I unwrap the brittle.

"I saved some *chikki* (peanut brittle) for you. It was Bly's; he shared it with me."

He holds it up and puts it to his nose, closing his eyes as he inhales its rich burnt-caramel scent. He bites into it, keeping his eyes closed. He chews slowly, savouring each bite.

I take a picture.

Sashi opens his eye to look at the picture I have taken.

"I did not change into him. I am still looking like me."

On the second day, we shoot three commercials in four hours. I know my role. I am ready to answer all Bly's questions with more than a 'yes'.

Kiran Cooper pushes me to push Bly. I nag him to hurry by repeatedly knocking at his door. "How much longer, Bly? How much time do you need, Bly? We are ready, Bly."

On our last day I am up before five. Trainer is a proud trainer. His client is appearing in a commercial today. His client is also showing results: I weigh sixty kilograms.

My phone rings. Other than Nisha it's the first call I have received on this phone. I never get calls. I don't recognise the number, but I take the call.

"Good morning Gené, this is Bly."

I laugh.

"Yeah right, and I am the queen of England. Who's this?"

"It's Bly Avibath."

"No, it's not. Stop messing around, come on, who's this."

"Gené, it's me, Bly. I am calling to notify you that I will be late for our shoot today."

"Um ... oh my god, I'm so sorry I really did not think it ... it really is you."

"Yes it is, but you are not the queen of England are you? So the reason I am calling is to say I may be a little late."

"Thank you for letting me know, I will notify everyone."

Film City has press everywhere. A huge film set burnt down. The Producer stops at the site – a smouldering set with a huge gaping black hole in its roof. I stay in the car. He walks to a group of important-looking people who stand devastated. He pats each one on the shoulder and then he leaves. We drive two warehouses down to our set.

"That set had an original Picasso in it. Gone, all gone. It was said that this set was the most expensive set ever built in the history of Bollywood."

I think of all the live wires criss-crossing the floor from the night before, their bare ends stuck into sockets like hardened spaghetti sticking out around a crusty old pot. Why am I not surprised?

We get through our last day free sailing. I get to be the airhostess that serves Bly in the commercial. He is always sitting and all shots are taken from his torso up. He never has to move on his crutches or get up. My makeup is pancaked thick and bright. I look like a Chinese doll.

It's a wrap. Kiran Cooper pats me on the back. He holds my neck between his fingers from behind.

"One day I want you to aa ... do a film with me."

He laughs. He looks scary, but must be the kindest man I have met in India so far.

I go one last time to Bly's trailer. I want to say goodbye to the man who has made me believe in the magic of stardom. I only have four months left of my six-month stay. I won't see him again. The doorman stands patiently at the door. He offers his hand.

"It was good working with you, madam."

"Thank you, you too. I would like to say goodbye to Bly."

He knocks for me. There is no answer.

"Is he in here?"

"Of course, look his guards are still here, you think he is a magician?"

"Almost."

"Go, he is probably on a call."

The doorman swings the door open and pushes me forward.

"Bly?"

As I move up the stairs he is balancing on his crutches, pants around his ankles, he is tucking a vest into his boxers. My eyes roll up his very long, thin rickety legs; thin silk skin falling in folds, purple veins protruding. I turn and crouch down onto the bottom stair banging for the doorman to open. I put my hands over my eyes.

"Sorry, Bly, so sorry, really I am so sorry. Sorry. Sorry."

The door opens from the outside. Click. Bly shouts something in Hindi, it shuts again immediately. Click.

In a flash he is doing up the zip and bending over me, "It's okay, Gené. I'm human just like you. I have legs and all ... you've come to say goodbye?"

"Yes, and thank you for all your help. It was a magical experience working for you and you are my favourite actor by far and I really like you and ..."

I feel like a race car scrambling for the finish line.

"You are going to make a fine assistant, Miss Gené. Take care."

"You too."

I move in to hug his tall body. He hugs me back, quickly. I turn and leave. I look back one last time. He is on the phone. Goodbye magic man.

Bollywood bizarre

Christmas is a month away. Although everyone around me is either Hindu or Muslim, the Bombay party scene begins to heat up. Luna will not close completely. The *Stolen Hearts* feature film that The Producer is shooting with Samson Night is still being shot and everyone will still be expected to come into office every day except for Christmas and New Year's Day.

Parties are happening all over town and The Producer calls me to his cabin. I scan the casting couch again. No hotspots. The damn thing was chasing me in my dreams the other night. Why do I care so much? Am I worried about catching something or have I developed feelings for The Producer that are making me want to be his one and only?

He slides an invite across the table.

"We are attending a huge one tonight. It's the opening of a new club in Juhu called Vie Lounge. Tonight you will get to meet Samson Night. Ask Nisha to take you to Nail Bar, now."

He slides a double wad of hundred-Rupee notes across his desk.

I walk out of Nail Bar feeling like a million dollars.

I arrive home and go to The Producer's room. He is sitting on his bed watching cricket, surrounded by Morgan shopping bags.

"Hi, sweets, I picked something up for you. Morgan just opened in town."

He has bought an array of clothes, all with sequins and glitter. I choose to wear the black dress with a pink sequinned belt, he approves.

"Do you like my hair?"

"Ya. Just don't overdo the makeup, and no eyeliner, it makes your eyes look smaller."

The Producer sits at the back of the BMW with me, he holds my hand. There is no time for him to play chess; the club is not far from home. There are rows of flashy Bentleys and Ferraris parked at the entrance, which outdo our BMW. Balkran stops in front of a long red carpet; the press are waiting. The Producer gets out. I follow him. He holds me around the waist.

"You're on the red carpet baby, just smile and wave, keep your head up high. Don't slouch. Suck in that stomach, work it."

Cameras flash me from all directions. I am in Bollywood. This is it.

The club is done up with multi-coloured lights, netting, ribbons, balloons, flowers, bamboo and lots of colour. The room is full of elegant people that sweat wealth. It oozes out of their pores. Exotic Indian film music pulsates throughout. Diamond chandeliers hang from ears. Canary yellow and chameleon green silks move and sway. Flamingo pink woven cashmeres, plush brightly coloured leathers parade and prance. A disco ball spins above me, mirroring the glitterati of Bollywood. The scent of expensive perfume lingers, laden heavy with myrrh, bank notes and platinum. Jimmy Choos, Louis Vuittons and other outrageously expensive stilettos shuffle, twist and twirl. Men's pointed crocodile-skin shoes and over-polished Italian leather lace-ups shift around me as I am squeezed through the crowd. The Producer knows them all. Shaking hands as opulent cufflinks size each other up. I feel like I'm in Aladdin's cave, the Gené trapped inside my plain black tube, the only treasure I have to bare is a fake sequin belt holding me together as I try to digest this over-iced cake. I don't need the jewels. I am the gem. I am the only white person. The only blonde. That's all I need to be noticed. The men can't stop themselves. The Producer is protective over me, his white prize. They flutter forward like fornicating pigeons, wings wide open to find out. The Producer pushes out his chest as a warning not to get too close, the dance of dominance.

The women are wary and hold their husbands back, doing the dance of nonchalance: "if you ignore her long enough, she will go away." Long-nailed hand gestures, the flapping of sour lips and fake hellos are passed around the room.

The Producer gets involved in conversation. I need air so I head for the outside deck overlooking the beach. The conversations surrounding me become amplified, and I begin to process what's being said.

"*Achcha*, look who's arrived, that bitch with her new fake boobs."

"The job was done in Dubai, not bad *yaar*."

"I hear that the job is serving her well, she's landed a film with an American actor, naked scene with him in the shower."

"Who operated?"

"A doc in Dubai."

"She's too cheap for my liking. I don't see what all the men see in her, drooling like dogs."

As I pass the bar, a man is ordering a drink.

"I want two pegs of your best whisky, hold the cubes."

Alisha is standing on the packed terrace, she has straightened her hair, she looks younger and even more striking in her flowing evening wear. She waves toward the dance floor. Gaya and four overdressed women are glaring at us in a disapproving manner.

"They don't look too happy to see you," I say.

"It's because I'm speaking to you, she probably feels betrayed."

"That's pretty stupid, we see each other every day and work together. It's not your fault."

The women approach us. I fall over myself to be nice.

"Hello Gaya, you look beautiful tonight."

Gaya greets Alisha with kisses then slips her arm through

Alisha's and leads her away. The four women flash me with their 'cobra eyes'. One of them speaks.

"So you're the white girl living with Gaya's husband?"

I have nothing to say. I walk away. I fume towards the dance floor, looking for The Producer. I want to go. Why did they say Gaya's husband? Aren't they divorced? The Producer is standing with his ex-girlfriend from the beauty parlour, Nail Bar. They see me approaching and it's registered too late, I cannot avoid the encounter.

"Gené, meet ..."

She curls her lip at me.

"We've already met."

"Hi, we did not actually speak the other day. I'm Gené. You are very beautiful, I believe you're a model?"

Snapping forward, she screeches in disgust.

"I'm not a model! I'm an actress! Get your facts straight!"

She storms off, leaving The Producer with a smile of satisfaction smeared across his face.

"What's the smile for? That was not funny."

"I love a catfight between my women. So you've met her before? Where?"

"At Nail Bar, the day Nisha took me, just before Diwali."

A young man approaches us. He has been overfed as a child. His stomach hangs heavy over his belt.

"How much for the night?" He points at me.

The Producer grabs the guy by his collar and sneers at him in Hindi. His forefinger waves fiercely between the man's wide eyes. The Producer lets go, pushing him backwards. He spills his drink over himself and quickly staggers away. The Producer brushes the front of his shirt off.

"He thought you were a 'pro'."

"I gathered that."

"Come, let's introduce you to Samson Night."

"Really? Are you sure I'm thin enough for the great Samson Night?"

"Don't get clever. Come, before I change my mind."

Samson Night is surrounded by a flock of doting people. He stands in the middle of all the attention, a glass in one hand, a cigarette in the other. He is just hitting forty. His oversized arms glisten with oil. His chest is puffed out like a pigeon. His pecs are taut. His T-shirt clings tight around his steroid-built body. His long bleached-blonde hair is tied into a ponytail, swaying across his back as he laughs animatedly, shifting on his feet to the music. He appears to radiate light. He is The Lion.

He is very tall for an Indian male. His Diesel jeans fit snug around two beautifully formed buns. His features are bold, he has a strong Arabic nose, slightly bulging eyes, fair skin and pursed lips that are edible. I can see the Islamic influences in his looks and his hairless body. He is charming and speaks with a strong American twang, resembling the one The Producer puts on when speaking to white people.

"You must be Gené, I've heard so much about you, yeh?"

"Hello Mr Night, and I've heard so much about you."

"All bad I'm sure. Your hair looks in good condition, are you using the shampoo I sent for you?"

"I am, thank you."

"Come what can I organise for you to drink?"

He snaps his fingers at one of his bodyguards.

"Vodka and lime please."

The oversized man obeys and heads for the bar. I notice a tattoo of a lion on The Lion's wrist. When the bodyguard returns with our drinks, I notice he has one too. All the men working for him have one. They have their own little gang going on here.

A very beautiful young woman sits quietly behind The Lion. She is in her early twenties. She wears white and has a soft angelic face. We are introduced.

"Gené this is my girlfriend."

I put my hand out and expect a soft gentle response. I am surprised. She seems aloof and uninterested, she half-heartedly greets me, her words drowned behind her encrusted self-importance, wrapped with arrogance.

I try to engage.

"Are you an actress too?"

She looks past me.

"I'm not from India. My mother is Russian, my father is Indian. I am modelling at the moment, but learning Hindi so that I can act at a later stage."

She gets up, a woman and a bodyguard follow her.

The Lion and The Producer are deep in conversation about the same girl that I heard the women speak about earlier. They are like little boys discussing her rack. The Producer boasts.

"You know she got into film because of me?"

"Really, she was one of yours?"

"Yeh, for a while. She's changed her name."

"How did you all meet?"

"On a plane, she was an airhostess."

"Nice! Well, whatever her name is, she's gonna be the next hottest thing. Did you hear she's landed a film with an American actor and all?"

"Ya, naked scene in the shower. With those tits, she's gonna set the screen alight."

I interrupt.

"Sorry guys, but I thought you were not even allowed to kiss on screen in Bollywood let alone be naked."

Samson Night explains.

"Yeh, but she's different, she's pushing the boundaries in a different league. The film is a foreign film not a Bollywood one."

I have to ask.

"So, she was an airhostess and you got her in. In return she became your girlfriend?"

"Ya, I stole her from a politician friend of mine. She served him on a plane from Delhi and they got talking. He really wanted her and she really wanted to get into film, so he called me up and asked if I could help. I told him to send her to me and then I stole her right out from under his nose."

The Lion looks surprised. He asks The Producer something in Hindi, they laugh.

I need to get some air again. I can't seem to get the timing right in my head. The Producer is recently divorced, but he's had two girlfriends. There must have been some overlapping and cheating from his side too. How else? I catch sight of Kush leaving the dance floor. We sit on a sofa outside where we can hear ourselves think. I ask him about his trip to Australia with his sister, and he asks me about having to be in the same room with The Producer's ex-wife and two of his ex-girlfriends.

I comment on The Lion and he tells me that there are a lot of toxic stories surrounding his reputation.

"Like what?"

"Some very bad things have happened when he's been drunk."

"But he's such a health freak?"

"He drinks way too much. The steroids do most of the work."

"What happened?"

"He was drunk, alone on the water in his monstrous speed boat, there were five fishermen in a little row boat pulling in their nets. He did not see them despite it being broad daylight. He drove right over them. One died, the other four were seriously injured."

"And now?"

"Well, he was jailed, but got bail 'because he is The Lion'. The case is still going on. If you go to Bandra you will still see the broken-up pier on the water that he smashed into after hitting the fishermen."

"Will he go to jail?"

"Probably not. These stars think they can buy immunity for their mistakes because of who they are. People in India give them way too much importance."

"It exists in Hollywood too."

"Of course, that's the industry we work in, mate. Want another drink?"

"For sure, mate."

We move to the bar. Kush orders us mojitos.

"So how was the shoot?"

"Amazing."

I tell him all about Bly and the effect he has on me.

"You know you're not the only one. He has that exact same effect on me. Sometimes I think I'm going mad because I'm the only one who can see the immense talent that that man still has. He deserves a comeback, he has so much talent in him. He would really do Bollywood proud if people just gave him a second chance."

"Kiran Cooper still sees him as a star."

"Well, then I guess that makes three of us against the rest of India," he sighs.

"You are going to make a very good director one day."

"Thank you, Gené. And you? What do you want to be when you grow up?"

"I want to be invited to Bly Avibath's house on a Sunday and sit around with him eating roast chicken and brandy pudding."

Kush laughs. "I actually have this dream to direct my own film one day starring Bly Avibath. I want India to see him again, see him for the talent that he really is. I want to write a script that will compliment his ability to act and not dance, in the hope that he will have a come back."

The Producer joins us. "The day you direct Kush, is the day it snows in Bombay."

I get the bartender's attention and order another two mojitos. They are making it easier to be here. I'm gonna need a few to get through the night.

A is for affection

I am averaging four parties a week. It is getting exhausting. I may be losing weight, but my shoulders are getting broader and my skin is getting thicker.

By my fourth party I'm creaming my way around the over-iced cake. I know who to avoid, who to know by name and have got into the way things swing. Fake greetings, order drinks, bitch about what someone's wearing, have a laugh at their expense, go tell them how good they look. Pose for the tabloids, order another drink, hit the dance floor, find a tray with canapés, eat too many when no one's looking. Order another drink, go to the bathroom, touch up makeup, dance. Drink more, gossip more. Got it? The press are having a field day with me. I appear on page three of the *Bombay Times*, more than once. They refer to me as model Gené. I proudly cut the articles out and stick them into my scrapbooks. I have never appeared in a newspaper before.

There's an apartment two floors above us that The Producer also owns, but rents out to a family of four. The couple have two little girls aged seven and eleven. I hear them on their balcony laughing, joking and loving. I feel sad. I suddenly miss home for the first time. It stabs sharp into my gut. The tears come.

It's time to give my split family a call. I have lost contact with everyone back home. How can I begin to explain what I've been up to? Everything is so different here. I'm so different here. It would all be too complicated to explain.

I call my mother first. She sounds sad. The divorce is taking its toll. She says she does not have any money to call me and that she hopes I call again. I send love to my brother and end the conversation. Her sadness makes me want to cry. I am too far away to deal with it. I hate that they're divorced.

I then call my father. He is pre-occupied and busy. He has a new girlfriend and his new business is gaining ground. He sounds happier than my mother. This makes me sadder. He tells me that he is going to Italy for Christmas to see his family. He is going alone.

The Producer walks onto the verandah as I am saying goodbye. "Were you speaking to your father?"

"Yes. I also called my mom."

"How are they?"

"Okay. My mother makes me sad. My father has a new girlfriend."

A very thin grey old man walks onto the verandah with a walking stick. He is dressed all in white.

"I am The Producer's father, pleased to meet you."

"I am Gené, pleased to meet you too."

Sai is there with a tray and a glass of water. The Producer's father takes it and drinks the entire glass in one go. The Producer and his father hug with emotional distance between them. We sit. He says something in Hindi, The Producer grunts and looks to the floor. The Producer rocks at the edge of his seat; he seems uneasy. He says something, his father grunts; they both still look to the floor.

We sit in silence for a long time. I break it by asking where he stays. He points upward.

"With Gaya, my daughter-in-law."

I smile. "That's nice."

Nothing more is said.

Eventually he stands. The Producer helps him up.

We say goodbye and he leaves.

I go to the home theatre and watch an entire Hindi version of

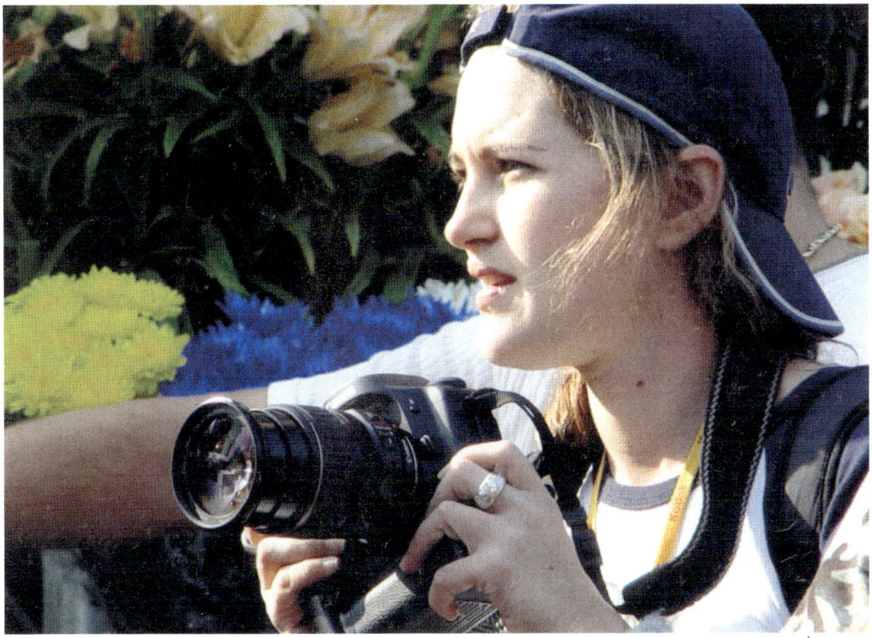

On set in Romania, October 2004

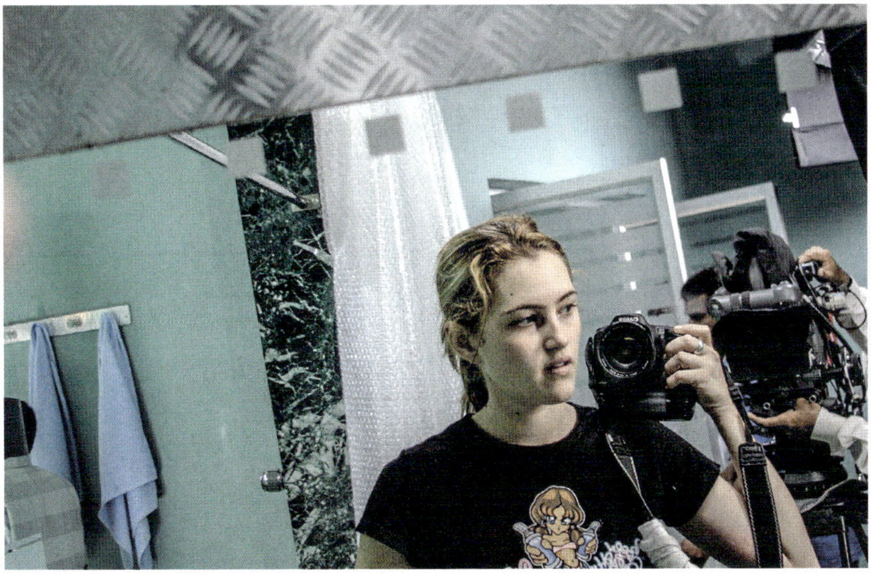

On set in Chennai, December 2004

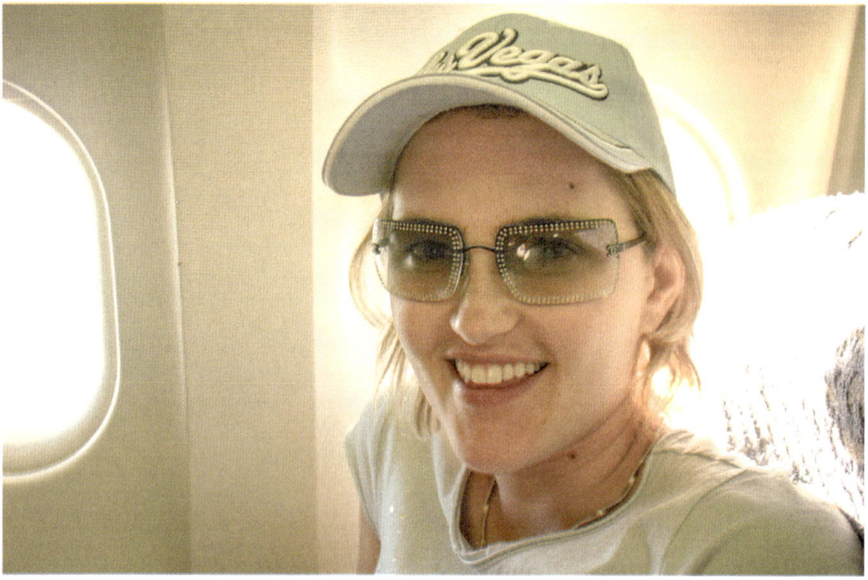

In Las Vegas, December 2005

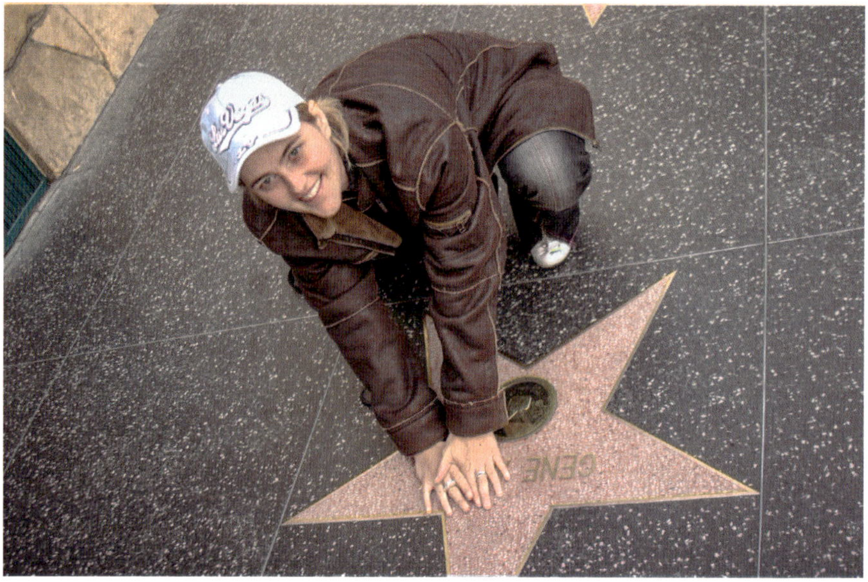

In Los Angeles, January 2006

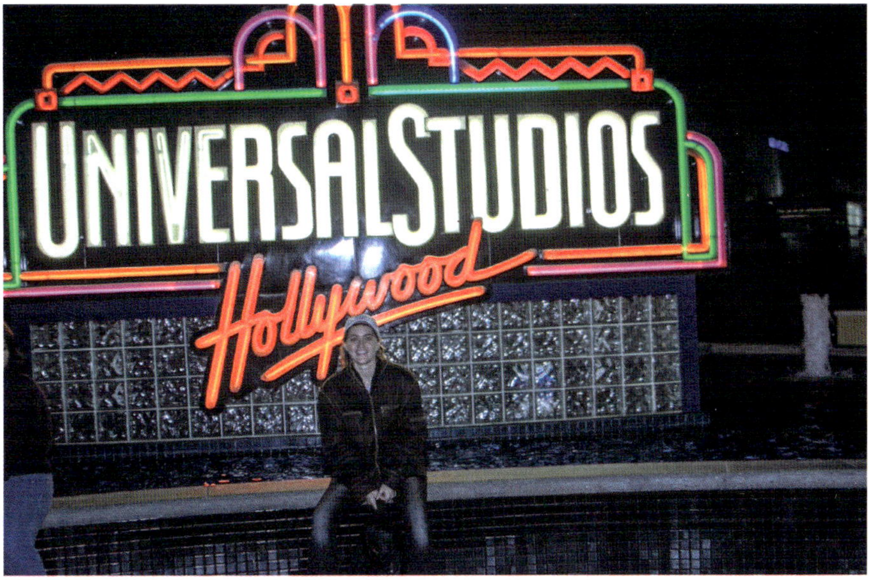

At the 'real' film studio – Universal Studios – December 2005

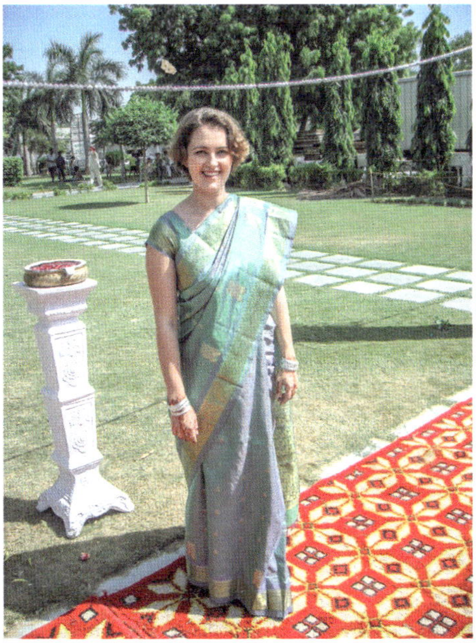

At Nisha's wedding, November 2006

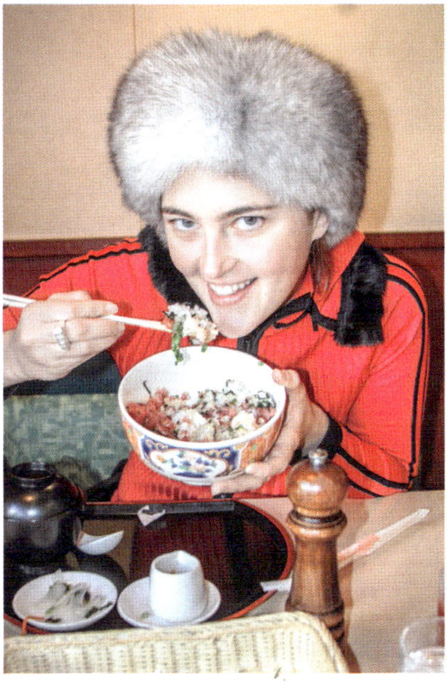

In Japan, January 2009

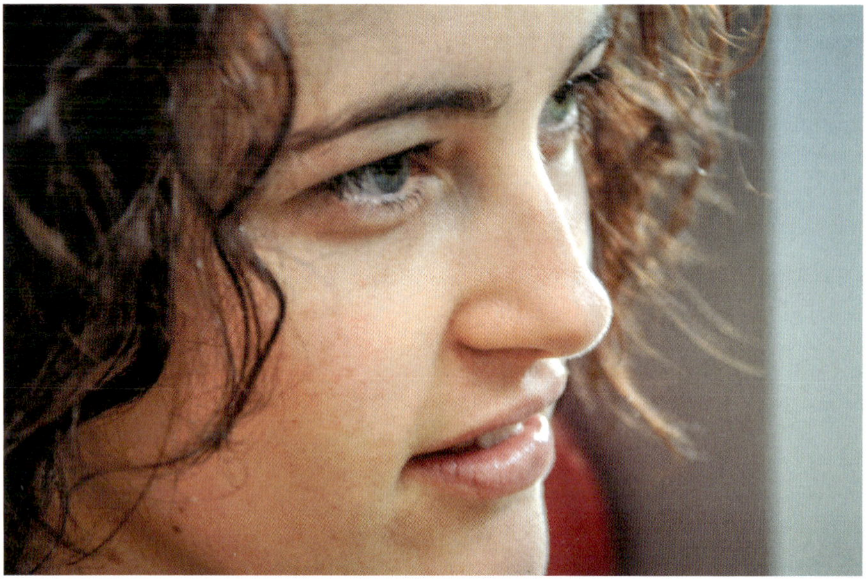

Having a very enlightening chat with Harvey and Kiran Cooper in a café in Romania, October 2004

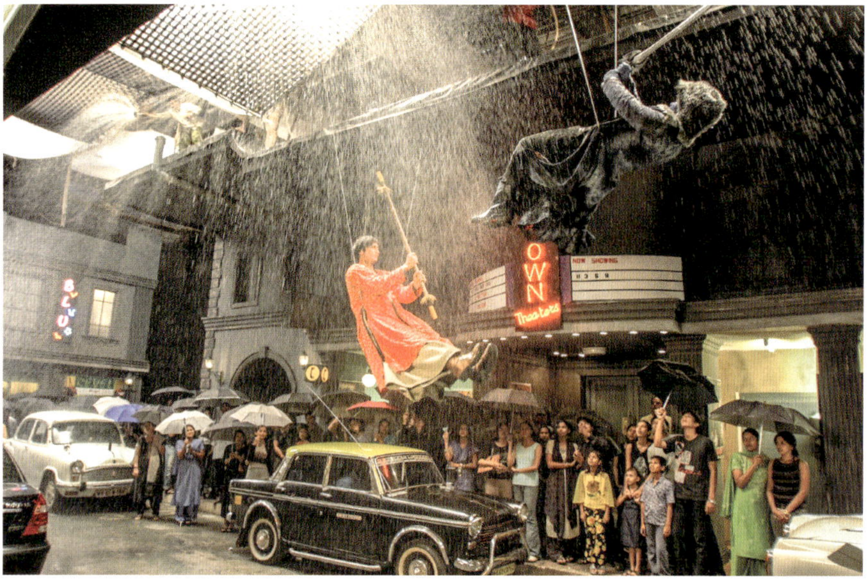

Filming a commercial at Film City, 2004

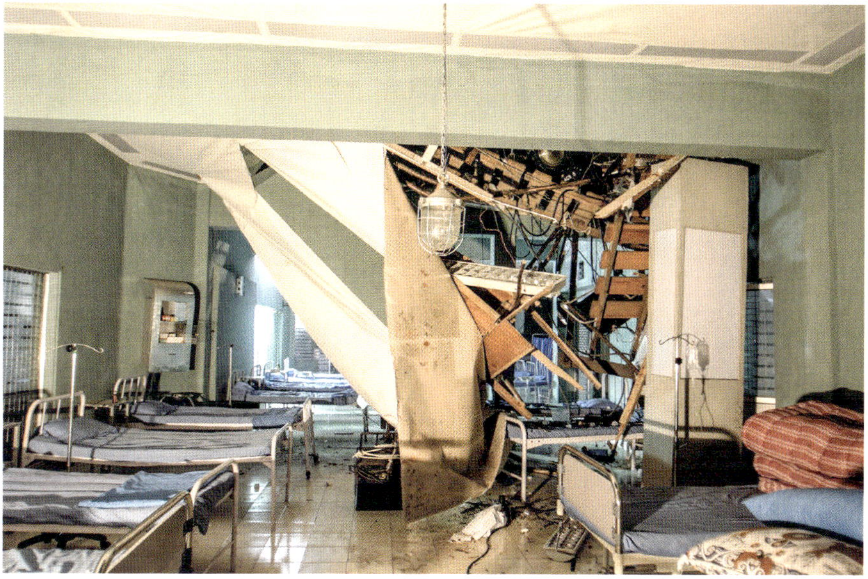

The destruction that the lighting equipment caused when it collapsed over the cuckoo's nest

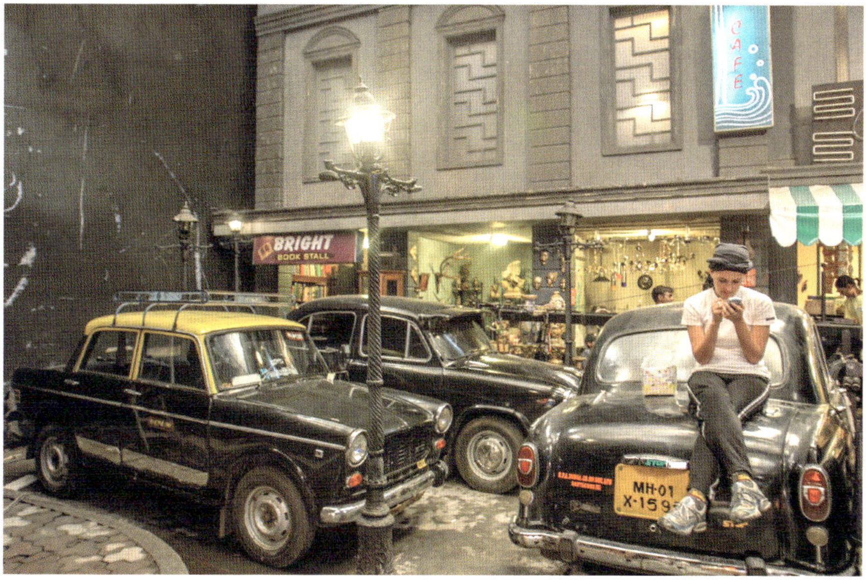

On set at Film City, 2005

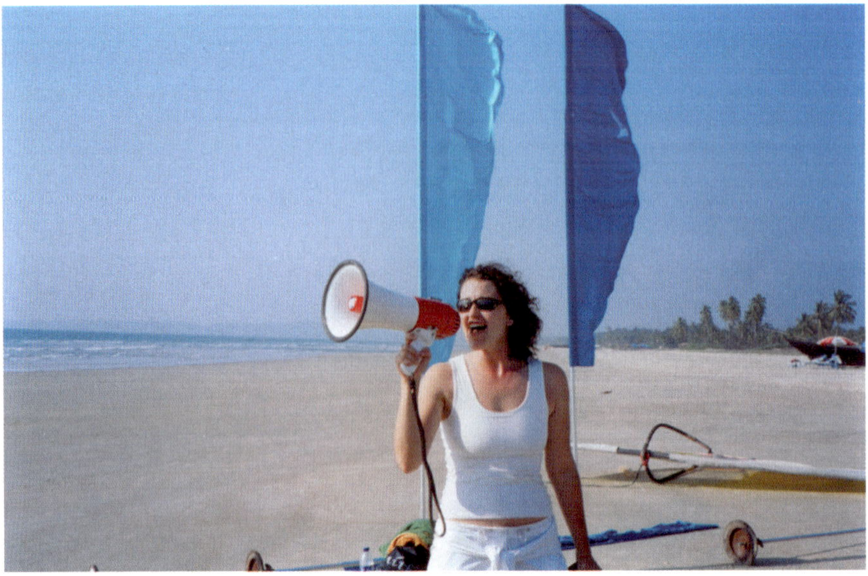

On set in Goa

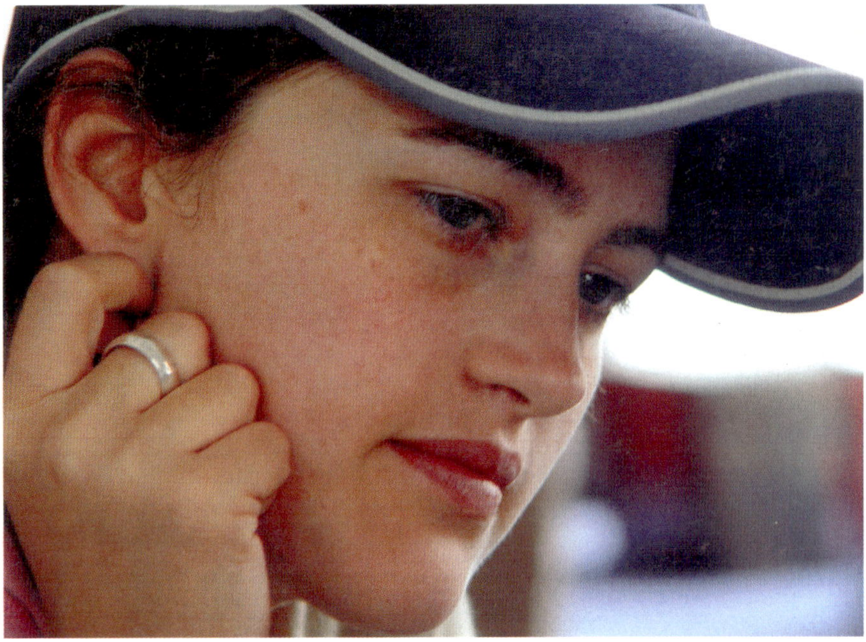

Talking art with Harvey, Romania, 2004

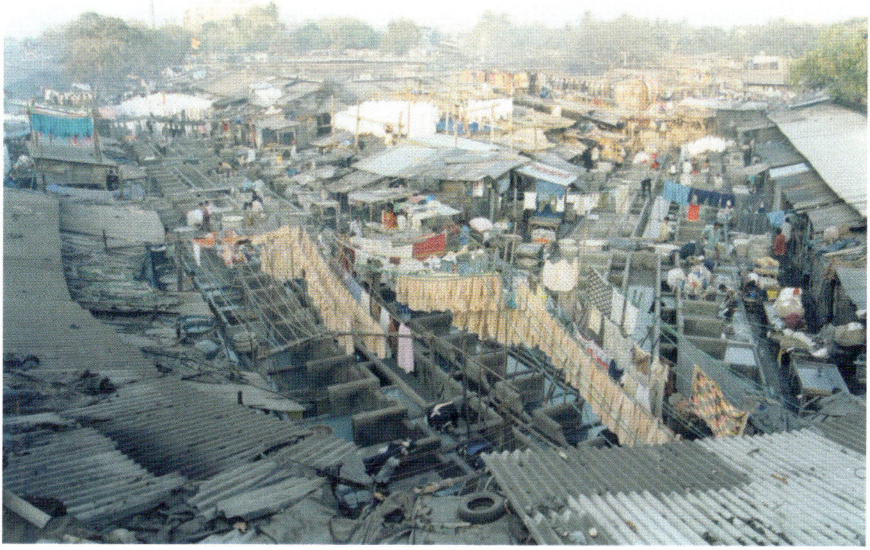

The dhobi ghat

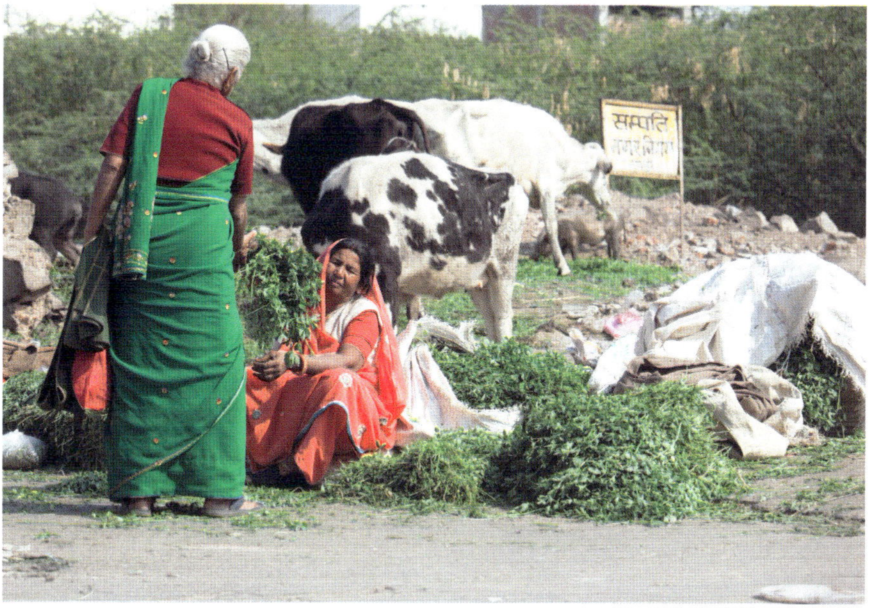

The local grocer, 'Woolies in India'

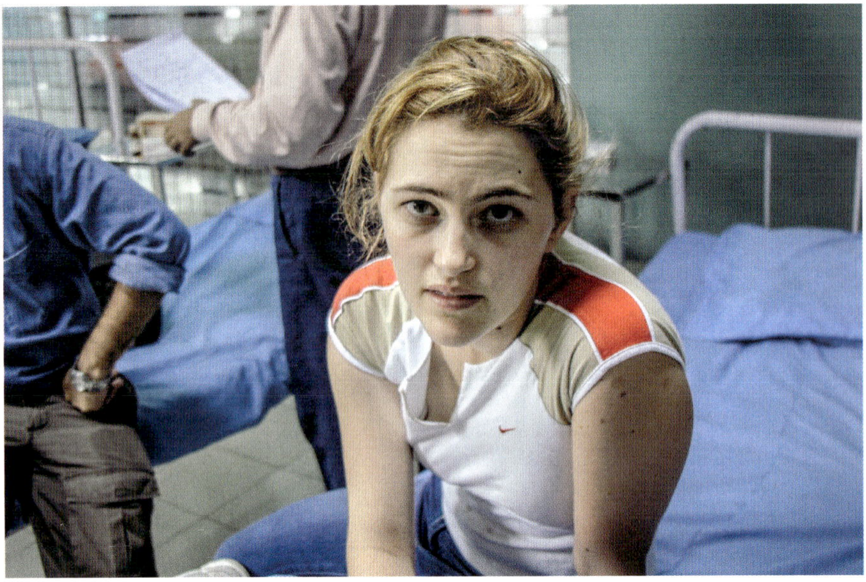

Beauty comes at a price

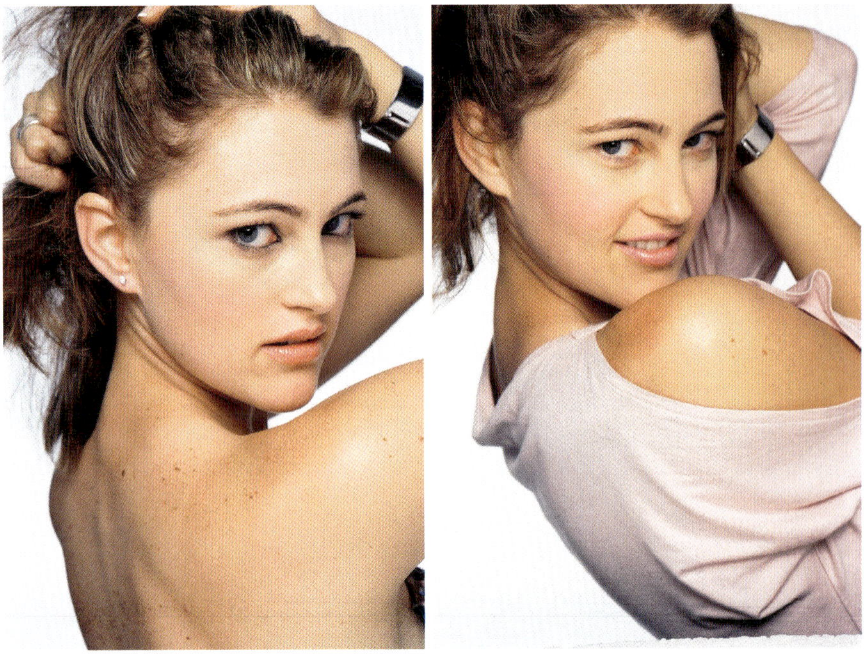

Photoshoot with Bollywood's best photographer, 2005

E.T. It's been copied to the T.

After three-and-a-half hours, it ends. I go and find The Producer who is on his bed, watching cricket.

"Did you enjoy that? It won best film last year."

"How? It's a stolen story."

"Not really."

"Yes it is, it's *E.T.*"

"In a way, only."

"Not in a way, it's a direct copy."

"Well, all films get their ideas from Hollywood."

"From which film did you steal the film that you're shooting at the moment?"

"We did not steal anything, we just based the concept on *Stolen Hearts*."

"Unbelievable."

"Stop being such a 'white woman'. Come, I want to take you out for something special to eat."

The Producer takes me to a place in Bandra. I see the broken-up pier that Kush told me about where Samson Night had his boating accident. An old grey-haired woman in an electric purple sari cooks *chapatis* on an open flame next to the pier. A small wooden sign is knocked into the ground with the words 'bakery' painted on it.

"I heard that Samson Night had a very bad accident over there."

"Who told you?"

"I'm not sure of their names, they were discussing his trial at the party."

"Yeah? Well, best you don't repeat too much of what you hear at these parties."

"Your father seems nice, you guys don't talk much."

"We say a lot more to each other than we have in the past. At one stage we did not say a single word to each other for ten years."

"Oh. Why?"

"It's a very long story."

"How old is he?"

"Eighty-seven."

"Why does he live with Gaya?"

"They get on very well, and he has company and people around to help him up there."

"Oh."

We arrive at an overcrowded shop done up in red and white called Elco. There is a counter, some fridges and a man with a cart. There is no seated area; everyone stands with their little paper bowls lined with foil. This is Indian fast food at its best. We queue in front of the cart. The man running the show has his bare hands in a huge tin pot of liquid. As he swirls his hands under the brown liquid it releases an odour that smells like fart. There are small yellow spongy balls floating on the top of this curious cauldron. There are hollow crispy deep-fried golden balls stacked next to the man. He moves quickly, cracking a hole into the ball with his thumb. He then scoops up some of the liquid into the ball and places it into an outstretched arm holding a paper bowl. The outstretched arm pops it into his mouth and returns his empty bowl to the serving man again and again and again. When the outstretched arm is satisfied it moves on.

"What is this?"

"*Pani puri*, try it. The smell seems offputting, I know, but it actually tastes really good."

"Can't wait."

Eventually we are next. I am given a bowl and I follow what I have seen. The smell makes me gag, but once the crispy ball is in my mouth and the ice-cold liquid and crunch fuse together, it's all worth it. It's a taste that cannot be described – sweet, salty, spicy, acquired and unique.

"You like it?"

"I love it!"

"Please promise me you will only eat from here under my supervision. There are a lot of these *pani puri wallahs* around but the water used is not clean. Some of these guys steal ice from the mortuary to keep the spicy water cool. You can get very sick."

"Okay."

We stand on an island in the middle of the road waiting to cross.

I am overcome by gratitude toward The Producer, and I realise that I am falling in love with him, his culture and his country. I take his hand, turn to face him wrapping my arms around his neck. I hug him.

"Thank you. Thank you so much for everything you have given me."

His reaction is shockingly brash. He pushes me away so fast, and frogmarches me across the road. Before I know what's happened, I am on the backseat, he is in the front seat and Balkran is pulling away slowly, trying to get through the crowded street. I stare out the window. The street has stopped moving, silence. Everyone is staring at our car, at me.

"Don't ever touch me like that in public again."

"Sorry, I'm so ..."

I can't get enough air to finish my sorry.

"This is not South Africa, we do not show affection in public, understand?"

"Yes, sorry, I'm so ..."

"It's okay, just don't do it again."

"Okay, sorry."

Silence.

When we stop at the signal light, Balkran passes me some Rupee notes to hand to the armless man who is smiling and waving at me with his stumps. I roll down the window, maybe he wants my hug?

When we get to the house, I go to my room. I feel empty, hurt and stranded. I want affection and love. I don't want to be the 'beneficial partner' living in another room. Summoned, used, then sent back to my quarters. Get nice clothes every time I lose weight. I want to be held, I want my hair to be stroked. I want my lips to be kissed not just when we are having sex, but twenty times a day just because we can. I want to be looked at in the eyes, in my eyes.

I want love and affection from this older, overweight, different-cultured man. I do, because it's all I have here. It's all I am allowed to have here. Him.

Chalk and cheese

I finish my morning training, shower and wait. The Producer is still sleeping. I drink my shake on the counter. Balkran arrives. Even he is surprised that The Producer is still asleep. I wish he would let me know when he's planning a sleep in, at least I can have a later start too. He wants us all to be waiting on him. It's very tiring.

The bell eventually rings. An hour later he is ready.

"I have to go and see my mother before we leave, you coming?"

"Should I?"

"I think it's time you met."

We walk across to a white building next door. We catch the elevator to the seventh floor. We ring her tinny bell and Kutty opens. He's already started his morning duty with 'mummy', washing her floors. Nisha and The Producer's cousin have already left for work.

A woman comes from the kitchen; she is tall and masculine. Her nose mirrors The Producers nose. Her shoulders hunch as his do. She is a slighter, feminine version of The Producer dressed in a brown sari. Her voice is deep. Her arms are strong. She does not speak a word of English. She slaps me on the back and pushes me to her lounge. The house is furnished simply, dark wood and floral. Various Indian gods are planted around the house. She is a devout Hindu.

We sit. She leaves and returns with deep-fried biscuits and cold buttermilk in steel tumblers.

Her smile is wicked, her eyes sharp. The Producer speaks on her behalf.

"Drink."

Chopped green chillies float on top of the ice-cold buttermilk. The same smell of fart makes my nostrils flare. The buttermilk is salted. It cools me. I enjoy every sip of it. The Producer's mother does not take her eyes off me; her look remains sharp, her smile wicked. She bobs her head from side to side asking me questions. I do not understand a word. She clutches my hand hard between her nails. She wants answers. I look to The Producer.

"What is she asking me?"

"Never mind."

The Producer sits at the edge of his seat again, looking at the floor. He grunts at her questions. Like yesterday with his father, he has nothing to say.

We finish our buttermilk. She pushes the plate of deep fried biscuits into my lap. I shake my head.

"*Shukria*, but no thank you."

She refuses to take no for an answer and begins to feed me.

"Eat or you will offend her."

When the last biscuit is forced into me, The Producer stands.

"Come."

I am still trying to swallow the oily sweet dough in my mouth. I shake her hand. She grips my hand, says something, slaps my shoulder and we leave.

"How long have your parents been divorced?"

"Since I was nine."

We drive to the office in silence. I give my armless man more money at the signal, this time from some money I have left over from my trip to the parlour. It feels good. I wish I earned my own money to do with as I please.

At the end of the day I enter The Producer's cabin. He is with The

Lion discussing a new film. They are talking about some famous politician who is coming to visit The Producer from Delhi tonight. Gaya is throwing a huge party on the rooftop of our building. He will visit The Producer first and then we will all go up and attend the party.

The Producer points to the casting couch.

"Join us, I was just telling Samson about an old friend that is visiting tonight."

"Is that the politician that you two were talking about at the party the other night? The one who sent you the airhostess to get into film?"

"Yes.'"

Samson Night has an entertained smile slapped across his face.

"I wonder what he will say when he sees you with Gené?"

"Fuck, I never thought about that. Now that you mention it, he has a thing for white woman. It's gonna drive him mad. He's gonna want one just like you."

As Balkran negotiates us through Bombay's chaotic streets back home, The Producer decides to play a trick on the important politician.

"Why don't we take his envy even further? To have a white girlfriend in this country is a big thing, but to have a white maid is almost impossible! Why don't we pretend that you are my maid from Italy? We can dress you up and say that I brought you back with me after shooting there. He thinks he has it all, but this will be one thing that he has never had. He will be so envious. If he buys into the trick, we will say you have a sister needing a job. Watch how he jumps at the idea."

I agree to play the maid. We stop at a party shop. We find a classic black-and-white French maid's outfit and some black fish-net stockings. The Producer sends Sai to the market to get me a bright red feather duster. I put my hair into a French roll.

We plan our trick to the very last detail. We have a plan. We are a team, a couple having fun. We share a secret.

The Producer tells Sai and Kutty to leave the apartment for the night. Before they go, Sai sets a tray with red wine and snacks. He is sure that The Politician will drink red wine. He leaves the corkscrew on the counter and shows me where the rest of the liquor is kept, just in case.

The Producer brings him a shirt to iron and we put it on a hanger ready to be worn.

We wait. Eventually the doorbell rings. The Producer goes to his bedroom. I answer the door, my feather duster in hand.

A short stocky man stands in front of me with two armoured guards at either side of him. His bowtie and jacket seem too small for this bulging torso.

Before I can deliver my line, he speaks. He is confused.

"Ah ... um ... Sorry, I must have ... umm ... I'm looking ..."

"Good evening, sir, you have the right house. Please come in, the Master is expecting you."

His eyes are wide with surprise, his head protruding forward. He wipes his eyes and follows me to the couch. His guards remain outside the door.

"Please make yourself comfortable. The Master will be with you in a minute. Can I get you a drink?"

"Red wine ... I want red wine."

He does not look at me. He is looking at my legs in the wiry stockings.

I leave and return with his drink. I leave again, passing him in silence with the freshly ironed shirt. I enter The Producer's bedroom. The Producer is waiting, buckled over in suspense. We are too anxious and excited to speak. We use sign language. He puts the shirt on, goes to the mirror and tries to compose himself. He takes a deep breath and chuckles into his hand. I have never seen him like this. A little boy on Halloween. He walks out. I follow him. Both men begin to greet each other loudly in Hindi. They hug and slap and laugh and talk at the same time. The Politician does not waste any time, he asks about me in Hindi.

"Where the fuck did you get her from?"

"Who? Oh my new maid, Gené?"

"Does she do more than just clean for you?"

"Of course she does, and she's pretty good at it too."

"I have to get myself one of those."

"Her twin sister, Stephanie, is desperate to come and stay with her in India."

"Excellent! How much do you pay?"

"Just a roof over her head and keep her happy in bed."

"Never?"

His mouth hangs open in disbelief.

I go back to the kitchen to fetch The Producer's shoes, the brush and polish. I bend down in front of The Producer. He pulls on his shoes and I begin to brush them with polish.

"I don't fucking believe what I'm seeing. Colonialism in reverse, fantastic!"

The Producer swaps to English, he winks at me before he speaks. This is my cue to play along.

"Gené, isn't your twin sister desperate to come to India?"

"Yes, Master, I am looking for a job for her."

"Can we call her now?"

The Producer comes to the rescue.

"My friend is a very distinguished politician in Delhi. He will take good care of your sister. His home is very big and very comfortable."

I look disappointed. This is my moment to end the charade.

"Delhi sir? Unfortunately that won't work for us. She wants to be close to me. Being twins we find it very hard to be apart."

The Politician begins to panic. He stands and takes my hand.

"Please, I will fly her down every weekend."

The Producer takes over.

"It's time to go upstairs."

The Producer looks at me, gesturing that I change and meet them up there.

"Gené, clean up and call your sister. We will come down later and hear what she says."

The Politician insists pleadingly.

"Take my number. I want to know as soon as you have an

answer. If you need me to talk to her I will, just come find me upstairs."

The men leave and I go to my room to change. I can't wait to see his face when I get up there. I'm sure The Producer has already told him how busted he is. I hope he takes it as a harmless joke. I let my hair down. It falls in curls onto my shoulders. I put on a little makeup and some gloss. I change into a slinky black cat suit. I feel good. I will be on Gaya's turf so I must tread lightly.

The rooftop is packed and, in true Gaya style, the décor tasteful. I squeeze through the same crowd that is at every party, avoiding Gaya and her 'girls' giving me the cobra-eye stare. The Producer is standing with a group of men I have never met. The Politician stands next to him. As I approach the men, The Politician's phone rings, he answers it. The Producer continues to introduce me. I smile politely, making my way around the circle of men with a handshake. They are all from Delhi. When I get to The Politician, he holds up his finger miming, 'one moment'.

He turns his back to me and continues his conversation on his mobile phone. His smile was not one of surprise or recognition. I'm confused. I turn to The Producer.

"Did you tell him?"

"Not yet sweets, we can tell him as soon as he is off the phone."

"I don't think he recognised me."

"Why don't you go and get yourself a drink, meet me back here."

I leave The Producer with his friends and head for the bar. Balkran is the bar man; he is also managing the tandoori oven.

"Madam full drinking. This is my drink what?"

"Vodka *aur limbo aur* soda, please."

"Madam this is 'amazink tandoor tikin'. You try me giving?"

I take a skewer loaded with bright orange charred cubes of chicken. I stand at the bar stuffing the cubes into my mouth. They melt like butter. The exotic flavour of tandoor makes me salivate. I suck, slurp and chew. My cheeks are full. I can't contain my compliments; I speak with my mouth full.

"*Arrey* Balkran, this is best tandoor ..."

I am interrupted by The Politician.

"You know this man?"

I work the cubes down my gullet as fast as I can, wiping my mouth with the back of my hand, I suck on my teeth hoping there are no black bits of 'char' between them.

"Yes, Balkran, The Producer's driver."

"Oh you know The Producer do you ... I am The Politician. And to whom do I owe this pleasure?"

His accent has changed. More British.

I can't believe what I am hearing. He still does not recognise me from downstairs. I cannot resist. Before I know what I am saying, I lie. I just have to see how far I can go with this ridiculous performance.

"Lucy, my name is Lucy."

He laps it up, like a dog that's discovered vomit on the floor.

"Well, pleased to meet you Lucy. If I may ask, how do you know The Producer?"

I am taller than him in my stilettos. My cleavage is at his eye level. He does not lose sight of it.

"I ... I work for him at Luna."

"Aaa ... you do, do you? Lucy, what do you do at Luna?"

"I'm an assistant director."

"Where did you say you were from?"

"South Africa."

"Best wine in the world."

"You've been?"

"Many times, I love ..."

"Cape Town," I interrupt.

He laughs.

"Great minds think alike. I like you, Lucy."

"Sorry, would you excuse me for a moment, I just need to ... sort something out."

I head for The Producer. The Politician shouts after me.

"I will be waiting right here, Lucy. Can I get you another drink?"

"Sure, I'll be back."

I get to The Producer and hiss into his ear, I'm beside myself. I feel like I'm in a movie, I want to push it as far as I can.

"He did not recognise me, so I said my name was Lucy from South Africa and that I work for you. He believed me."

"You're kidding, right?"

"No, you have to tell him."

"No, let's wait a bit. Play along – let's see how stupid he really is. Look he's calling for you, go!"

The men that were standing with The Producer have moved to The Politician. He pulls me into the conversation.

"I was just telling these gentlemen about The Producer's white maid from Italy. Have you met her?"

"Um ... yes, briefly, when attending meetings downstairs."

I can't understand how he does not recognise my voice. I did not even put on an Italian accent. Is he really that stupid?

"She's got gorgeous legs. Splendid tits and an ass that wiggles when she walks. Pity she's not British, we owe them a screw or two!"

The men burst into vulgar fits of laughter. I feel flushed and violated, the joke's on me. I don't hide my annoyance.

"Is she pretty?"

"Very, sexy too and it get's better. She has a twin."

The men laugh disbelievingly.

"No really, I've just confirmed her for myself. The Producer says they fuck for free."

I become arrogant.

"You do realise that the 'Fuck for free' has feelings. We differ in the jobs we do, but we all have the same thought processes and brain functionality. She's probably an intellectual being despite what she does for a living."

"Yes, but it's what she does for a living that degrades who she is, putting her on a lower level to us. It's like chalk and cheese really. She's just a maid and you're a little more than that."

"Is she prettier than me?"

"No, she's much thinner, probably because she's a peasant, not exposed to the good life and all ... fucking sexy though."

He strokes his bulging guts with his bloated hand. He reaches out, clasping his stubby fingers around my wrist pulling close into my right ear. His slurred whisper pushes a spray of spit and hot air into my ear canal.

He makes my teeth curl.

"If you play your cards right, I may just want to take you back to my hotel later. I only stay at the Oberoi. You would like it there."

I am uncomfortable. My game has turned on me. I need saving. I catch The Producer's attention. He makes his way toward us. The Politician pats me on the arse. He turns to The Producer with a smile.

"I was just getting to know your little assistant over here. I see, you're bringing them in from all over the world. I was wondering, can I have her for the night? After all you owe me one after stealing my airhostess. Have you seen how famous she's become? She's had her tits done recently. I hope you did not have to pay for them?"

"I had nothing to do with her tits; that was a long time ago."

The Producer's stare is following The Politician's wandering hand. He pats my arse again and pulls me into his side.

The Producer's fists clench, his jaw stiffens as he grits his teeth.

"Lucy and I have business to discuss downstairs."

He pulls at my arm and leads me towards the lift. The Politician is still holding my other wrist, I'm being pulled in half.

"Why don't I come down with you? Your maid can entertain me while I wait. When you're done with business I can take Lucy with me."

"Our meeting will take some time."

"I'm sure Lucy can make her own decisions."

The lift opens. I'm being held on each side. The Politician does not let go. The Producer pushes G.

We are at The Producer's front door. The Producer wobbles his head, insisting on something in Hindi. He amicably and patronisingly pries my wrist out of The Politician's hand. He rings his tinny bell. Kutty opens the door. He pushes me in, follows and shuts the door in The Politician's face.

"Where's the maid?" I hear The Politician shout.

The Producer shouts back, "You're drunk, go home."

We stand staring at each other. I don't know what to say. I wait for it. The Producer is fuming. I am embarrassed and angry with myself. I did not think about the repercussions. It went too far. I feel cheap. The joke is on me. It's not funny anymore.

"Why did you let it go so far?"

"Because you said we should wait."

"Well, why did you not tell him you were my girlfriend?"

"Because I would look stupid after the fact that he told me that you shag your maid."

If anyone is humiliated it's me. I had to hear the vulgar comments that were being "maid" about me! Excuse the fucking pun!

"You think this is fucking funny? Go! Get out of my face."

He storms off to his room, I storm off to mine. The ball in my chest splits into shame, disappointment and anger. I feel violated by my own doing. The air conditioner chokes with me as it gasps for air. I have manifested my fears of being The Producer's white fuck into reality, twice. I have violated two of me, putting two of me to shame. It was just meant to be a harmless joke. Unfortunately, he did not cotton on in time.

Sticky fingers

I complete my workout and am dressed and ready by the time The Producer wakes up. I am on the kitchen counter with 'my boys', trying to explain with our limited means of communication that some of my clothes and two bottles of perfume are missing. Sai insists that all the clothes from the *dhobi* (laundryman) have been returned. Once Sai has taken care of The Producer's chai and newspaper, all three of us go to my room and search. I cannot believe that one of them has stolen from me and they seem genuinely worried and perplexed. Sai begs me not to say anything.

"Please, madam, boss not telling *yaar*. Tonight you are coming, I am having all items for showing you return."

"So you know where they are?"

"No, madam, this is full day searching. I am returning for finding, but boss not telling. Full tension. I am *dhobi* checking and all house."

They go off in a disturbed huff. Maybe the items will magically reappear and we can forget about it.

I don't know where to put myself. I sit in my room and wait. I am dreading seeing The Producer. While I wait I mull over the mystery of my missing things. If my boys are stealing from me I am going to be so disappointed. I really hope my things are found and there is a logical reason for them having 'walked'. These guys are my friends, my support system. The people I lean on for comfort. The Producer sends Sai to call me. He is waiting in the idling car. We drive to the office in silence. I am in The Producer's bad books. This sulk is going to last for a while. Everyone at the office wants to know how it went last night. The Producer avoids the question by disappearing into his office. I sit with Alisha and tell them about the night and how wrong it all turned out. Alisha is gentle and consoling.

"You need to be careful, baby, The Producer is a very jealous man. As you know from his previous experiences, he has reason to be."

I have little to do. I go and sit between Kush and Nisha who are watching a DVD on Kush's laptop.

Kush consoles me.

"So it all turned to shit last night, mate?"

"Kind of."

"Looks like he's gonna take it out on all of us."

"Sorry."

"Not your fault, mate."

Nisha gets up.

"Kush, can you pause, I need to go to the bathroom."

As Nisha gets up, pushing her soft leather bag under the desk, it gapes open. I spot two bottles of perfume that I recognise. A pink bottle of Gucci Rush with a message written on it in black permanent marker from my mother, 'My darling Peanut...' and a bottle of Dolce and Gabbana Light Blue, still in its velvety powder blue box. They are mine.

I wait for her to leave. I cannot believe my eyes, I am so angry. Without a second thought I pick up her bag and go straight to The Producer's office. I am the last person he wants to see. I explain my story. He just stares at me. The anger rises in his face, his jaw clenches in time with his fists, placed on the desk.

"Call her," he growls.

Nisha is back at her desk. She is looking for her bag.

I am scared and angry and hurt. I hate confrontation.

"Nisha, The Producer wants you in his office, now."

"Now? Why? Did you see …"

There is a wave of panic coming over her. It clicks and she turns white.

"Wait, I can explain everything, it's not what you think."

"Okay, come explain it in here, I'm sorry if I am wrong, okay? I just want my stuff back."

She follows me; now I feel bad.

The Producer sits fuming. He has not unclenched a single muscle since I left. He growls at Nisha.

"Explain."

"I … I … was just … I … The Producer … I am sorry, I … I don't know what I … I was thinking."

She begins to sob.

"Stop that."

He tosses the perfume across the room onto the casting couch.

"Gené, take your stuff and go."

He turns to Nisha.

"Don't let me ever …"

I leave. I really feel bad.

Nisha exits the cabin after a long while, her hands covering her face. She runs past me and down the stairs towards the bathroom. I follow her. The door is locked, but I sit down on the floor and speak gently to her.

"Nisha, I'm sorry, but you are the closest friend I have here, my only support. I can't have you stealing from me. I need to be able to trust you. I'm sorry I went to The Producer. It was really childish of me. I should have confronted you myself. Sorry. Please open the door?"

I hear her come closer on the other side and slide down beside me.

"I don't know what I was thinking, Gené, really I don't. Everything is going wrong for me these days and I just … I just did this stupid …"

"What's going wrong?"

She begins to cry.

"I hate my job. I hate living at The Producer's mother. His cousin kicked me last night because I made him angry. Arin keeps stalling our wedding. He is my only way out. If we marry I won't have to live with them. I'm so sorry, please forgive me?"

"I'm sorry too, Nish."

I begin to sing the Tracy Chapman song "Sorry", replacing the word 'sorry' with 'sari'. I wrap my pashmina around my head, with only my eyes showing.

Nisha opens the door. I've got her laughing through her tears. We hug for a long time. I don't want to lose this friendship. I need her more than she knows.

Common ground

I wake up just after 3am. I am ill, my sheets are soaked in sweat, I am cold, my stomach cramps. I want to vomit and shit at the same time. I sit on the toilet and let it pour out of me. I hold an empty shoebox on my lap. It's getting soggier and soggier with every hurl. I want to lie down, but I can't. It keeps coming out of both ends. Eventually I am too weak to care, I am empty. All that's left are a few bouts of bile coming out the top end. I sit on the floor, lifting up when the bile comes. The toilet cannot flush anymore. I cover each mess with toilet paper. I get my duvet and lie next to the toilet until Kutty comes to wake me.

The cramps are back. I shake uncontrollably. My bones ache and my teeth chatter. I am death warmed up. Kutty holds my hand and wipes the soggy bits of hair that are stuck to my face away from my eyes. He runs a facecloth under the tap and gently wipes my face. It's warm and comforting. He takes the soggy shoebox away. He does not flinch at the smell. I am embarrassed, but too sick to do anything about it. He smiles and whispers gently in Hindi. He leaves and calls The Producer. I don't want The Producer. He is angry with me and has been since The Politician episode. He stands over me.

"What did you eat last night?"

"I might have had a little taste of Nisha's Chinese."

"And?"

"I had a watermelon juice."

"What did I tell you about eating raw foods off the street?"

"I thought ..."

"You must learn to listen, Gené-baba." He softens. He picks me up and carries me to the bed. He sits next to me and calls Dr Bollywood.

The Producer watches while Dr Bollywood examines me. I am relieved we are not alone. My stomach is too close to my breasts.

"*Achcha*! Common case of Delhi belly. She must be having regular sips of electrolites even if it does not stay down. We must be avoiding dehydration. I will give injection. Let her rest. If it is not clearing in next two days we will be putting her on dripping and hospitalisation will take place at soonest convenience. Let us monitor her closely. I am hoping injection and pills I am giving will be sufficient."

Dr Bollywood opens his bag and takes a syringe and needle out, the size they would use on a cow. He places three vials next to the bed. He begins to draw them up. Once mixed, the syringe is full of what looks like a strawberry milkshake. He plunges the needle into my arse. It burns momentarily and then I am gone. I begin to float. The cramps subside, the nausea fades. I am tired, I want to sleep. I hear Dr Bollywood pack up his bag next to me. He speaks to The Producer in Hindi. Everything echoes past me. I am here. I am nowhere ...

Thanks to The Producer's presence I am safe. Dr Bollywood leaves empty-handed; he did not manage to get his little fondle this time.

Everyone goes about their daily chores around me. The tinny bell rings, deliveries are being made, people come and go. I am left to sleep. The floating feeling from the strawberry milkshake is heavenly and it lasts for what seems like forever. Sai comes in and feeds me a couple of teaspoons of Electrol every hour. He continues his teaspooning duty through the night. I am heavy and weak. He holds me up. I swallow and go back to sleep.

The liquid stays down.

Two days pass. I can eventually keep my eyes open. It's almost 9pm. I lie quietly, alone, waiting for something to happen. The tinny bell goes. The Producer is home from the office. The last time I remember seeing him was with Dr Bollywood. He opens my bedroom door.

"The Producer?"

"You're awake, fatsy? How you feeling?"

"Better."

"Good."

He turns on the light, my eyes strain. I've been lying in the dark for much too long. His hands are full of Morgan and Mango shopping bags. He looks pleased.

"I can almost not call you fatsy anymore. You've lost more weight."

He places the bags next to me.

"I took a chance, I thought you may fit into a 26 after this bout of Delhi belly."

I excitedly go through the items of clothing that The Producer has bought me. Each piece is exquisite, laden with sequins and motifs. There are dresses, pants and tops, all size twenty-six. They fit perfectly. The last time I was this small …

I lean over and kiss him. We are alone. He looks at me tenderly, I have not seen him look at me like this before. He strokes my cheek.

"Your eyes are sparkling from all the sleep you've had."

I smile and hug him.

"Thank you so much, you are so kind. I am so sorry for everything, I'm sorry for making you cross and I'm sorry for what happened with The Politician and Nisha and…"

He puts a finger to my lips and hands me an envelope. I open it.

It's a business-class ticket to Italy in two days' time.

"I think it will do you good to spend Christmas in Italy with your father."

I am a little surprised and unsure. I now only have three months left here. I don't want to waste time in a country that I can visit any time. Is he trying to get rid of me? Did I push him too far? I don't want to seem ungrateful so I thank him again with kisses.

"I have to go to Delhi tomorrow and will only be back once you have left for Italy so I'm only going to say this once."

"What?"

He cups my face between his enormous palms and kisses me long and hard like he means it.

"I'm gonna miss you."

I want to be with this man forever. I don't want to go away now, I am finally settling into this new life. I belong here with him. I need him. He is my life. I can be who he wants me to be. We have found common ground.

"When is my return flight?"

"I booked you back for the thirtieth so that we can spend New Year's together."

"That's great, thank you."

"Freshen up and come sleep in my bed tonight. We can have dinner in bed. I got us some new DVDs to watch."

We make love because we both want to and I get to lie in his arms all night. I wake up next to him and Sai brings us breakfast in bed. I feel like I am in a real relationship with a man that I love.

In Italy everything feels awkward. I am trying too hard. I want to be Italian and Indian at the same time.

Surprise after midnight

I land in Mumbai from Italy just after midnight. It was good to have a change in food and see my father. The Producer is waiting for me like he did when I first arrived.

I am careful not to show too much affection in front of Balkran, I squeeze his hand instead of a hug.

"I think I'm becoming an Indian. I could not wait to get back here."

"Good."

We arrive home, and Sai and Kutty carry the bags up to my room. There is a packed suitcase on my bed. I'm confused. I try to ignore what it could mean and busy myself with unpacking the gift I have bought for The Producer.

I place the beautifully wrapped gift on the bed, hoping The Producer will call me to sleep with him again. I want us to carry on from where we left off, closer and in love. I want to make the most of the time I have left. Maybe he feels the same and will keep me longer? I don't want our relationship to be set on a stopwatch anymore. I want more.

The Producer comes in. I give him a belated Christmas gift, an Armani wallet from Milan. He likes it, but seems preoccupied. I want to ask him about the bag and if I can sleep next to him, but I am scared to know the truth so I hold back.

"I also got you a Christmas present."

He hands me an envelope. I open it.

Two business-class tickets to Hong Kong leaving in two hours.

One is in my name, one is in his.

I cannot believe my eyes.

"So? We? We will be in Hong Kong for New Year's?"

"If we hurry, we might just make it."

We get back in the car with newly packed suitcases. It's 2:30am when we get back to the airport. Our flight is at 4am.

Hong Kong is electric. The lights, the buildings and the Christmas decorations are far bigger and better than anything I have ever seen. The streets are packed with people shopping. They all carry bags branded with names I never even knew existed. I am totally overwhelmed and exhausted, but too excited to sleep. We check into the decadent Mandarin Hotel, overlooking the harbour. We share a double bed. Perfect. Everything is perfect. We are a real couple. The age and racial difference does not matter anymore. I love him. Does he feel the same way? He must do. After everything he's given me in the past two weeks.

It's almost 4pm and the street parties are getting ready to explode all over Hong Kong. There is no time to sleep. I want to wrap myself around him and show him how much I've missed him, but we can get back to that later. It is time to celebrate the New Year. The Producer wants to shop. We catch a ferry to Kowloon and enter the biggest cluster of malls I have ever experienced. The Producer does not hold back. He buys me more clothes, a watch and new sneakers. We go to Armani Exchange and Hugo Boss for him. He mainly wears these two brands. We find a great Chinese restaurant with Peking duck and dim sum. Although The Producer is strict about my weight, we share a strong bond of fondness when it comes to food. It is when we enjoy each other most. After dinner we force ourselves to stay awake to see the New Year in. We join in on the street festivities. I buy a princess crown and some glow sticks. The Producer wears a pair of glitter glasses that say 2004. We dance and walk and watch the incredible firework display.

By half past twelve we are back in our room, exhausted. I begin to feel panicked again. It's the New Year and if we are a couple in love we should make love. It's been more than three weeks and I want to make sure The Producer still wants me. I can't understand my insecurity, but I have to act on it. With a little effort The Producer is convinced.

The Producer falls asleep almost immediately, and I begin to panic again. I can't get a grip on myself. At first I felt compelled to have sex. Now it is becoming a necessity for my self-assurance. As if without it I am not part of him or his life. Is it because I am running out of time and I am in love? Or have I just become totally dependant on him and obsessed with the idea of belonging to this different land? How can I make him want me more and for longer? I don't want to go home in two months' time.

A gigantic singing Christmas tree the height of a seven-storey building outside our hotel window wakes us just after 8am. Hello 2004!

The Producer has started making a shopping list. We skip breakfast and head straight back to the shops, this time in Causeway Bay. The streets are packed; New Year is an excuse to shop in Hong Kong. We find an electronics store and buy a Sony Wii and some games for his younger son and a new laptop for his older son. The Producer and I stop at a Starbucks. The Producer takes out his list, checking who else he needs to buy for. Something he says takes the wind out of me.

"We must get to a cosmetic store. Gaya needs a few Lancôme products. I also want to pick up a nice bag for her, maybe a Gucci like the one your father got you."

Before I can stop myself I snap back.

"She has a Gucci, she was wearing it when I met her."

"That's okay, she can have another one."

I stare at my feet, fuming. Why am I so upset? He can buy gifts for whomever he wants. I don't like being so ugly, but there's something about the fact that he's buying gifts for his ex-wife that's getting to me. I don't like seeing this ugly side of myself.

"Is there a problem?"

"No."

I overcompensate with a smile.

"Just a little tired."

"You're in Hong Kong, you can't be tired, come!"

We find everything on Gaya's wishlist including a Gucci bag identical to mine. I am irritated. We find another fantastic restaurant; the idea of good food lightens my mood.

"Excuse me for a minute, I need to make a phone call and check on something."

The Producer makes a call outside. He comes back wearing his work face.

"Tomorrow the camera rental houses will be open. We need to pick up a tilt-and-shift lens for a commercial we will be shooting next week."

"Oh, what commercial?"

"We are shooting a commercial with a French Canadian director Pierre Bordeaux. He is insisting on using a tilt-and-shift lens that you can't get in India, that's why I chose Hong Kong, we killing two birds with one stone."

We spend our last two days in Hong Kong eating, renting the lenses and shopping. I try to enjoy every last drop of attention I am getting from The Producer because as soon as we get on that flight home it will all change. Out of India, we get to share a bed, eat all our meals together and I can show affection towards him in public. His obsession with work is also somewhat in hiding while we are away. We don't have sex again and I try not to get too worried about it. At least we did it once while we were here. Guess it can be considered a normal relationship? But not for long ... We board the plane and The Producer's mobile comes out. He becomes mute and zones into his chess game. I try to hold his hand, but he warns me with a look.

"Get some sleep. When we land we are going straight to set."

I feel emotionally whipped. The first time I sat on a flight with The Producer to Kuala Lumpur, I did not know how I was going to want any of this. Now I want, I want, I want. Love me! Love me! Love me! Pleeeeeaaaaa...se?

Fowl play

We land at 8:30am on Sunday morning, 4 January 2004. Balkran is waiting for us like clockwork. We had to buy extra luggage to get all our shopping on board. He takes the overloaded spastic trolley from my frustrated struggling hands. We drive to Sassoon Docks in Colaba, a pier made up of large concrete cones rising out of the sea. The entire Luna crew is setting up a shot; their balancing skills are being put to the test. A crowd of onlookers are being roped off the quay. I see Sashi and Kush trying to negotiate with a group of eunuchs who are obviously threatening to boycott the shoot unless they get paid off. This is a common demonstration with eunuchs. They are known to invade weddings, shoots, births and other events. I see The Producer hand a wad of notes to Balkran who goes and helps Kush and Sashi bribe the beauties. They are groping their crotches and showing fists. Because they are social outcasts and considered to be unlucky in their own lives they are believed to be lucky for others. Many of them have male genitals and female breasts, but no uterus and grow facial hair due to their hormonal imbalance. They slip under the rope, entering our cornered-off section of cones which is serving as the set. They make a beeline for the only white man in sight. The man can't be missed. He sticks out like a sore thumb. He is tall and striking with curly silver-grey hair cut perfectly. I'm too far to hear what he is saying, but he is very animated. He is instructing the model and the director of photography, both trying very hard to balance on the cones, especially the director of photography with the camera on three legs. He is dressed all in white. His slacks and moccasins are a brilliant white. In India? Not for long ... His white shirt has some bright-coloured Picasso figures on the front. He wears orange-framed designer spectacles and three watches on his left arm, all with matching bright orange straps. He must be Pierre Bordeaux, the director. I watch a little boy with a monkey on his shoulder approach him. They want the white man's money.

The monkey is well trained. He gets Pierre's attention by tugging on the pristine trousers with his grubby hand. He begins to dance. He twirls and somersaults and spins in his little pink tutu. The boy holds up a hoop and the monkey flick flacks through it. Pierre is not in the mood, he has more important things to worry about. He throws the monkey a croissant that he was chewing on. The monkey is unimpressed and throws it straight back at him hitting him on the shoulder. The French-Canadian director begins to howl for Kush.

Kush is in his element. He rushes past me, taking the lenses I have carried from Hong Kong with him.

"Coming, mate, just sorting out a little problem and all."

"I've got a bigger problem over here, mate. The circus has arrived!"

I now understand where the whole 'mate' thing with Kush comes from. Kush adores Pierre, who will not direct in India without Kush at his side. The Producer sees me and waves his hand at me, a lit cigarette between his fingers.

"Go make yourself useful. Introduce yourself to Pierre, I'm sure he will appreciate another white face to keep him company."

I don't want to rain on Kush's parade; he can handle Pierre. I offer help to Sashi who is balancing on the cones closest to the water's edge. He has a cage full of white doves and two plastic buckets.

"Can I help?"

Sashi passes me a bucket that's been squashed to the brim with frantic white doves. He holds his hand over the top, squashing them down as they struggle, passing the bucket to me.

"And now?"

"When Pierre Sir shouts 'and … Action', you throw them up into the sky across the frame of the camera, hit the bottom of the bucket, hard! They should fly out and all."

I balance each foot on a cone and position myself off frame, near the camera. The birds struggle under my hand, they are suffocating, the director better hurry. The cones are designed to prevent wave erosion of the shore. They are obviously also used as podiums for human ablutions. The sea breeze keeps wafting a mixture of sun-baked pee, shit and washing powder into my nostrils. Sashi keeps hacking up phlegm and shooting it out into the sludgy Arabian Sea. He says it stops the gagging.

Despite a hair-and-makeup artist standing with the stylist next to the model, Pierre insists on doing the final touches himself. He fidgets with her watch, making sure it is centred on her wrists, he adjusts her collar and gently places a perfect strand of curled hair along the side of her face, framing her jawline.

"*Ma petite fleur*, you are beautiful, just beautiful."

He kisses his bunched fingertips, smacks his lips and throws his open hand into the air.

"And now ladies and gentlemen … we must attend to the pure white doves of love!"

He hops towards Sashi and me, noticing me for the first time.

"*Ma chèrie*, you're white like me … But not as beautiful, mate!

"How did this white girl get here? What is she doing on my set, Kush?"

Kush helps out.

"She works for Luna, mate, thanks to her you have your tilt-and-shift lenses."

"Aaa *putain* (whore), another one in training. You better be competent enough to throw a bird into the sky and make it fly. They must spread their wings as they enter my frame, puffing out their proud chests that are full of peace and love. Their beaks must point up into the direction of the sun. The light must catch the glint in their eyes. You understand no?"

He comes up close and whispers in my ear.

"Better not slow things down, white girl, we're already running late, mate. This fucking country has no concept of time."

He taps on the faces of the three watches on his arms.

"Right, let's roll my fine Indian cockroaches."

I whisper into the bucket, I don't think these birds understand English.

"You hear that little birdies? He wants you to spread your wings, puff out your chests and point your beaks to the sun. Don't forget to make sure that the camera catches the glint in your eyes. Okay?"

Pierre checks on the model one last time.

"Ready my darling?"

His smile is disarming, revealing a striking pair of dimples that make him look like a naughty school boy. He knows exactly how he wants things to look and how to get the most out of his cast and crew. He is in full control. I can see why Kush admires him.

"And roll sound!" he shouts.

"Rolling!" Kush responds.

"Roll camera," he shouts.

"Speed!" Kush responds.

"And action!" he shouts.

In the silence, all that can be heard is the frantic fluttering of wings, claws scratching on plastic followed by the hollow drum-beat sound of Sashi and me banging on the bottom of the plastic buckets. Nothing comes out. The smell of terrified fowl rises up mingling with the aroma of human waste heated by the scorching sun.

"Cut *putain*! Cuuuuuuut! Where the fuck are the birds, mate? Again!"

Kush suggests that we should propel the buckets forward without letting go, just to give them a push start.

"And ... roll sound ... roll camera ... and action!"

A few weak flutters, a moment of suspension and the birds fall one by one into the Arabian Sea.

"Kush, your fucking Indian birds are shithouse! If you don't get your ADs to get them to fly I will twist your titties 'til your eyes pop out, mate."

We refill the buckets with more pigeons.

I turn back to see if the Frenchman is ready. He is hopping from cone to cone swearing into the sun. The turn-ups of his white trousers are brown, he is drenched in sweat. His face glows red with frustration and heat. Dhiraj, my favourite spot boy, moves toward him with an umbrella.

"Leave me alone. You stink!"

He misses the cone trying to avoid Dhiraj and scrapes his leg on his way down. Kush breaks his fall just in time. A spot of blood seeps through his trouser. He shouts towards The Producer.

"*Putain*! I'm bleeding to death here, mate, while you sit on your fucking fat arse! I need a medic!"

"Well, you crazy Frenchman, that's why I produce and don't direct. You white people are all the same."

"Look at this shithouse! You owe me a new pair of pants, mate."

The banter between director and producer is lighthearted and familiar. They go back a long way. Other than Cook, no one dares to speak to The Producer like this.

There is of course no medic. This is not a Western set. Pierre makes the best out of some disinfectant and a plaster. We continue to shoot under the beating sun.

We fill the bucket with the last few birds that are left. They are suffering from heat exhaustion. Pierre calls again. Sashi and I propel the birds as high as we can. Our efforts are in vain. The birds are finished. Not one of them attempts to fly. They fall to their death, drowning in the sea.

It's too hot to carry on and Pierre has come to peace with the fact that his background will not have doves displaying peace and love. He settles for a clear blue sky instead.

We break for lunch. Pierre refuses to touch the food. He only eats at the hotel. After lunch, Pierre works quickly and we wrap by 4pm. I am exhausted and find Kush.

"Where are we tomorrow?"

"We don't shoot tomorrow. We are in office."

"Oh why?"

"We need to prep for the next montage."

"What is the product by the way?"

"Deodorant. Tomorrow we prep for a lake scene with a boat and a fisherman, then two days prep to shoot in Delhi."

"How many days all in all?"

"Another five days shoot over a week."

"Wow, that's gonna be interesting with your French mate over there."

"Isn't he great?"

"He's great, but rather you than me. I'm sticking with Kiran Cooper. He's my baby!"

I brush as many feathers off me as I can before I get into Balkran's sacred BMW where The Producer waits. I look like a plucked turkey. The sweat and salty spray from the sea have acted as a feather magnet. I have bird shit on my shoes. I look back into the sea. Over fifty birds float dead on the water. If this were a Western commercial, animal cruelty organisations would be appalled.

Fuckland

Pierre is an excellent storyboard artist. He draws all his own boards for the next leg of the shoot. We sit around him taking instructions. He entertains us with his stringent requests, threatening us with his animated vulgar use of language and strong French accent. He includes every little detail right down to exactly how he wants the fishing rod for the fisherman in the boat to look. Kush and I take it upon ourselves to find the 'authentic wooden' fishing rod. He takes me to Chor Bazaar, which means 'thieves market', to find the rod.

"Bring your camera, we are going to a very interesting part of town."

Chor Bazaar is in the Muslim part of Mumbai. There are a lot of goats wearing jerseys. This is obviously common practice. They are being well fed out of tin buckets. Their bellies bulge over the knitted hems of their attire. We find a fishing shop. Kush bargains for the perfect-looking rod. It looks just like the one Pierre Bordeaux described. There are too many things going on in Chor Bazaar and too many people. We are closely packed on top of each other. I am being swamped with stares. Men take full advantage to touch me. I get groped from all sides. I'm scared my camera will get snatched so I give it to Kush to carry.

"Let's get out of here. I want to show you a road that will blow your mind, mate."

Kush and I walk down a few streets with old crumbling colonial buildings. They are beautiful, but have been left to decay.

"Where you taking me?"

"Bombay's sex street, Falkland Road, where the cage girls live."

"Bombay has a red light district?"

"The oldest and second largest in Asia."

We enter a long street lined with old crumbling moss-laden wooden buildings. Each window and entrance is framed with peeling light blue paint. The ground floor has cage-like structures painted in light blue, a curtain hangs closed in front of the cages when they are 'busy'. The girls are very young. One of them tries to entice Kush by lighting a cigarette and seductively wrapping her brightly painted red lips around it. She toys with her tongue. A little boy of about five laughs at her, grabbing the cigarette and running off. The over-painted girls are dressed in very revealing Western clothes and some wear very bright saris. The makeup smothers their features. Some of them have plastered their faces in white base so if you want 'white', they've got white. Above these cages, the buildings rise three or four storeys and at every window there are more girls, maybe a little older, sitting together on the peeling blue windowsills combing their oiled hair, smoking seductively, beckoning to potential customers. They vary in age from eleven-year-olds to sixty-five-year-old former madams. The street is traffic jammed. Horns honk incessantly. Insistant vendors selling fountain pens, medicines and Western books that have been photocopied scratch at your nerves the more you say no. But there is an unmistakable smell that only exists in this street. The smell of cheap hair oil and perfume, stale alcohol and cigarette breath infused with bodily fluids.

I lift my camera to record it. The reaction is harsh. The women throw insults and whatever they have in their hands at me. I quickly put the camera away. How dare I think I have a right to come in here and judge? This is their only means of survival. A young girl feeds her child in a cage. Her breasts hang out for all to see. They are full and swollen. The dark veins bulge under her skin.

The baby suckles frantically on a flaking nipple. Kush and I stand looking up at the Falkland Road houses. He begins to explain this community of prostitutes. They can be divided into four groups. There are the street girls, who hire rooms from madams by day and sleep among beggars on the pavement by night. There are the transvestites, who have heterosexual as well as homosexual clients. There are the posher girls with rooms on the upper floors and then there are Falkland Road's most famous inhabitants, the cage girls, ridiculed and abused by the rest. No one seems to know where the idea comes from, but the cages are used to protect and display their contents, not imprison them.

It feels wrong of me to let my tourist curiosity get the better of me.

"You're not the first to try. I saw on the net that Alfred Dyer wrote, 'No educated native thinks he has properly "done" Bombay unless he has seen the seething hell of European vice.' The American photographer, Mary Ellen Mark is the only Western photographer to have got inside and recorded what goes on in there. It took her more than ten years to get in. Eventually, she moved in with them for three months."

"How much do they charge?"

"Thirty Rupees for 'short-time' and 150 Rupees 'for the night'."

"What about Aids?"

"It's a very big problem, mate."

"This road is such a contradiction. Bombay's dirty little secret."

"I know. In an article on the net, Richa Kaul Padte wrote, 'Falkland Road is, for many, a symbol of the city's underbelly: full of depravity, loose morals, and the one thing "Indian Culture" well and truly shudders at: sex'."

A curtain from the cage directly in front of us pulls open. A man steps out still doing up the belt of his trousers. The girl behind him has smudged red lips. Her bright pink sari falls seductively to one side exposing part of her left breast. She is barely twelve. The man looks up at us, mortified. I recognise him immediately.

"A fish in the boat is worth two in the bush"

The Producer has gone to Delhi leaving Alisha to oversee the fisherman part of the shoot. She picks me up just after 4am. Her driver is drunk again so she drives. It is dark and the streets, although busy, are manageable. We play loud music and laugh about yesterday's floating fowls. Alisha has the most positive aura I have ever encountered. It is contagious and always puts me in a fantastic mood.

We enter what is meant to be the most established golf course in Bombay. It looks a little brown to me. A panicked Pierre is standing on the bank of a dam with Kush. His long limbs wave continuously as if he is trying to keep his head above water. The dials of his three watches glow fluorescent green in the dim light. Again, he is dressed all in white. The rest of the crew set up. A floodlight illuminates the water where a red boat with peeling paint rocks unsteadily. A male model dressed in fishing gear sits nervously clinging to the sides of it. He is calling for a life jacket. He cannot swim. We are pressed for time. Pierre wants to catch the magic light, the moment when the sun just begins to rise, throwing a sea of sparkling diamonds onto the water's surface. He wants the light to cast a golden glow on everything it touches. This moment does not last long and must be carefully planned for.

The model is incapable of doing anything. He won't let go of the sides and use the oars to position the boat for the cameraman to frame and focus. The cameraman sits on the bank trying to mark the position, but the boat keeps moving.

"Kush, this guy is fucking shithouse. In the audition he said he had boating experience and could swim really well."

Kush suggests that they send the spot boys into the water with rope and rocks to anchor the boat. Kush speaks sternly to the five spots. They are always eager to help. They begin to tie rope around rocks. I watch them struggle to stay afloat. They have not thought this through, but this is their duty and they are determined. I can't watch the pathetic effort. I go in search of Alisha who is looking for the rod and the pink-bellied trout that Pierre Bordeaux requested.

Alisha is shouting on her phone. Her face is red with fury. She holds the authentic wooden fishing rod Kush and I bought yesterday; it is in two pieces now.

She is frantic.

"What are we going to do? The fucking thing broke in the truck. There is no way …"

Her eyes are wide with panic. She looks at me, pleading for a clever answer.

"We can fix it, here let me see. I remember my father fixing my brother's fishing rod when we were little. Like joining a bone, we need a pin and some tape."

She finds me a nail in the toolbox and some brown gaffer tape from the camera department. Luckily, they always have an array of colours.

Sashi's ironing is done. He offers to help.

"Alisha, who were you shouting at on the phone?"

"Dhiraj. He was meant to be here with the fish. Pierre wants them to be in the boat as if the fisherman caught them. And we need to hook one onto the end of this broken rod."

"Fuck, I don't know if I can fix this thing to take weight. Bring me two splints and more tape. How big are the trout in Bombay?"

Alisha is stressed and irritated.

"How long is a piece of string, Gené?"

"Okay, well how far is Dhiraj?"

"He is only going to reach us in twenty minutes."

"Did he find pink-bellied trout?"

"I really hope so or Pierre will kill us all today."

"I hope they're dead. I don't want to watch another animal die in vain."

Kush comes to get the rod and the fish, he finds us trying to solve the problem.

"Oh fuck and now, mate?"

"Stall him, we need twenty minutes."

"I told Dhiraj to get the fish yesterday."

"Well, he has a problem finding freshwater trout in Bombay. Do you blame him?"

"The sun will be up in the next hour, he better be here in twenty or we are all screwed."

Alisha keeps calling Dhiraj. As usual, twenty minutes ends up being forty. He runs toward us with a dripping muddy hessian bag slung over his shoulder. It is full and moving. The fish are still alive. He swings the heavy bag around his body. The fish hit the ground with a hard thud. The fish slide out, sloshing and flapping furiously. They are covered in mud. They are huge black fatheaded catfish with long whiskers. Ugly mother fuckers!

"Fuck, mate."

Alisha starts to scream at Dhiraj in Hindi. His eyes are glazed over, saturated in alcohol. He is drenched in sweat. I can smell him from where I'm standing. The fumes of cheap alcohol are seeping from his pores. He is still drunk from the night before. I feel for him.

I start thinking fast, the artist in me wants to help.

"Why don't we spray paint them? The props *petti* has a whole lot of spray cans. We can cut their whiskers off, paint their tops silver and bellies pink?"

Alisha stops screaming.

"You think it will work?"

"We can only try. Kush, tell him we have a problem, but we're dealing with it."

"Okay, do one and come and show him before you mutilate all of them, mate."

We stand quietly behind the truck waiting for Pierre's reaction to the bad news. It comes. Loud and clear. He is seriously pissed off.

"This fucking place, mate, always a fucking problem, I never get what I ask for, never. You fucking people, I twist all your fucking petite balls until they pop out of your fucking eyes, mate. How can I work like this, how?"

I get a silver and a pink can of spray paint. I ask Sashi to find some old cloths. I make Dhiraj hold a muddy fish. He is reluctant and looks like he wants to gag. The smell of mud and fish makes me want to heave. I don't even have a hangover. The fish flaps vigorously under his shaking grip, I tell him to hold harder, Sashi climbs in to help.

"Madam, we are putting the fish through makeup? Are we giving the fish a costume I must be ironing?" His lighthearted humour is much appreciated. Even Alisha sees the funny side.

I pour a bottle of water over the fish's back and wipe as much of the mud off as I can. I begin to spray silver, the fish is terribly unhappy. Sashi and Dhiraj push down hard to keep the fish still. I feel terrible. They flip him over and I repeat the process using pink spray paint for his belly. He puts up a fight. Alisha walks away. I hold the scissor to his face. His dark bulging eyes flick back and forth with fear. Sashi and Dhiraj look away. I cannot bring myself to cut his whiskers off.

"Let's first see if Pierre is happy with this look before I hurt him."

I go first, carrying the rod, Sashi carries the fish, Dhiraj follows staring at the ground, Alisha stays behind the truck. In his fit of rage, Pierre has slipped into the muddy bank of the dam. His white attire is smothered in mud. He is barefoot. Kush sits beside him, wiping his white moccasins with a rag. He looks beat and the day hasn't even started. He looks up at me and begins to rant again.

"*Bonjour* girl. Where the fuck is your fat Indian boyfriend? The last I heard, he was the fucking producer, no?"

"He's in Delhi, sir, preparing for the next leg of the shoot."

"If his preparations are anything like today, I must run away while I can. I need production, mate, where the fuck is production?"

Alisha comes out from behind the truck.

"Alisha, I squeeze your titties until they pop, you understand? Where is zee art department? While your fucking fat partner sits pretty in Delhi, I have to bear zee consequences of his cutting corners. I will not work on another shoot unless I have a full art department at my side. I suggest you call him and let him know that there better be an art department waiting for me in Delhi, mate. Show me zee fucking fish."

Sashi holds one end and Dhiraj the other, they turn him over exposing his bright pink belly.

"Might work mate, it's a shithouse clown fish, but better than ugly catfish, cut zee pussy hair off its face and paint zee others. I make it fucking work."

Kush calls the spot boys in the water to bring the boat to shore so that we can load the fish and give the model his rod. Pierre has not noticed the break in the rod. Kush holds his hand over the joint.

They have marked the position of the boat with a balloon tied to a rock with string. Being a golf course dam, it is no deeper than eight feet. We will return the boat to that position once the fish are painted and put in the boat with the model. Alisha, Sashi, Dhiraj and I return to the truck. I paint, the boys hold and Alisha cuts the pussy hair off the fish's faces. I can't do it.

Dhiraj carries the hessian bag to the boat, he tips the scared, fighting fish into the boat, the model seems more scared than the thrashing fish around his feet. As the spot boys wade through the water pushing the boat to its mark, the model drops the rod and lifts his feet away from the fish causing him to rock out of control. He begins to squeal like a little girl. The spot boys surround the boat, trying to stabilise it. Pierre gets worked up all over again.

"We need to kill the fucking fish, mate."

"Leave the boat where it is, send this fucking boy with his bag to get them. They must be dead for the shot. That stupid model is a nightmare, mate. He can't swim, he's scared of fish, kill them! I need my shot."

Kush sends Dhiraj in to get the fish. He is a useless swimmer. He clutches the bag in his teeth and begins to doggy-paddle. It takes forever for him to get to the boat, he keeps going under.

"Kush, I think he's drowning?"

"No chance. If he has not drowned himself in the amount of alcohol he consumes, then this morning swim will only but do him good, mate."

He hangs off the side of the boat, limp like a rag doll. The spot boys help him put the thrashing fish into the bag. Dhiraj and the other spots swim back to shore. We all stare, amused, two little drunk Indians doggy-paddling across a dam. The more we stare the longer it takes. They struggle, spluttering and spewing with the hessian bag between them. They push each other under as they struggle. No one says a thing. None of us want to get wet. Pierre has his head in his hands.

"Ah *putain*! I cannot believe what I am seeing. This is real shithouse in a shithouse country. You fucking people stink mate."

Dhiraj stands dripping in front of Pierre, holding the wriggling bag, waiting for instruction.

"Kill the shithouse fish!"

Kush repeats Pierre's request in Hindi. "*Macchi ko maro!*" he shouts to Dhiraj.

Shivering from alcohol poisoning, dripping with fish slime and dirty dam water, Dhiraj is circled by staring eyes. He gingerly takes a painted fish from the bag, holds its squirming body under one arm, holding its gills closed, pinching its nose between his thumb and index finger. Dhiraj scrunches his face, dreading what he has been asked to do, shuts his eyes tightly and looks away. We stare, nothing happens, the fish fights under his arm and Dhiraj stands frozen, waiting for the fish to suffocate.

Dhiraj's pathetic effort pushes Pierre over the edge. He grabs the fish out of Dhiraj's arms and takes it by the tail. He swings the heavy fish above his head. His rage propels the motion. The fish comes crashing down, smashing its head on a sharp rock next to Pierre. He does this again and again, until the fish no longer moves. Its head is mangled, he throws it across the lawn towards me.

"Touch up, mate!"

He grabs another and another. As he kills one by one he purges himself of all his pent-up anger.

"This is shithouse! Where the fuck is production *putain*? Where the fuck is the art department? Where the mother fuck is fucking animal cruelty? Now I kill because I can!"

Sashi and Alisha help me do the touch ups on the slippery bloodied fish. Their makeup has rubbed off with the deadly beatings. Dhiraj puts them back in the bag and doggy-paddles back to the boat. They place the dead fish around the whimpering model's feet and hook the lightest one onto the end of the rod. Pierre gets two takes out of the golden light, we missed the better part of it. During the second take, the rod snaps. Pierre snaps with it. Without a word, he walks to his car, gets in and speaks to the driver, loud enough for us all to hear.

"Hotel, mate!"

He looks back at us.

"I see you tomorrow on the flight to Delhi, mate, be fucking ready. Tomorrow I kill your fat fucking boss."

What to do?

Delhi goes by smoothly. We shoot for two days, the winter is very cold and the fog hangs heavy. The story about me tricking The Politician into believing that The Producer had a white maid has spread to every corner of Delhi. Anyone that is anyone knows about it. Some important people stop by the set to see The Producer and hear him tell the story first hand. They shake my hand and congratulate me on fooling one of India's politicians.

I begin to feel anxious again. I have less than six weeks left in India before my visa expires. I don't want to go home. The Producer and I have not slept together since Hong Kong. Is he distancing himself because my stay is coming to an end? I really want to ask him for an extension. I don't know how. Maybe he's done? Was six months enough for him? Just when I am starting to love him and my life here, it's time to go.

We get back to Bombay late at night, but I don't sleep. I cling to the idea of staying. But The Producer has given me no indication of how he feels about me. I obsess in the darkness about not knowing. I get up and run on the treadmill until my legs are jelly. I go back to my room, shower and dress. I smoke a cigarette on the verandah. It's 4am, the servants are waking up. Maybe I can get some coffee.

I open the kitchen door. Sai and Kutty are not here. Cook

cannot look at me, not after I saw him coming out of the cage in Fuckland. He crawls past me on all fours, motions to the stove.

"Madam, coffee?"

"Please."

I don't want to make this anymore uncomfortable than it is. I go back to my room. When Cook gets drunk and disappears for days, that's where he goes ... His wife and five-year-old daughter live upstairs with Gaya. Do they know?

Goa-way

Summer has arrived. The heat in Bombay is getting unbearable. So is my mood. I worry all the time. Where will I live and what will I do because I have no money? I think about the friends back home that I no longer speak to. I have lost complete contact with everything I left behind. India is where I belong. These are the people I want to be with. I don't want to go back.

I do one of my last commercials with Kiran Cooper and Bly Avibath. I say goodbye. I am so sad. I hug Kiran Cooper, thank him and start to cry. He is taken aback.

"You cannot leave my dear, aa ... we still need to do a film together."

Balkran drives me home. I hug myself, my sleeves smell of Kiran Cooper's perfume. I take it in and hold it for as long as I can. I really love that man.

The Producer has two commercials coming up that need to be shot in Goa. He thinks it will be good for me to work on one of them. That way, I get to see one more place in India before I leave. One commercial is being shot with a sweet Indian director who has a mop of white hair. He reminds me of an Indian Andy Warhol. The other commercial is for an Indian cola, Thumbs Up. Kiran Cooper is the director. Although I'm not assisting Kiran Cooper this time, we will all be staying in the same hotel. One more dose of my favourite director. We can have dinners and drinks together in the evenings. Alisha is the perfect producer for this trip. She loves making sure people have fun while they work.

Samson Night comes to The Producer's house one evening to discuss the beverage commercial. The servants are beside themselves with excitement and dress in their Sunday best. When he arrives, Sai and Kutty serve him like a king. He is kind to them. I see him slip them a few 1 000 Rupee notes each.

Samson Night soon announces he wants to go to a Mediterranean club in Bandra called Olive. I compliment Samson Night on his Hugo Boss shirt. He rips it off and gives it to me. Am I meant to want it? I thank him profusely, go to the kitchen and give it to the servants to fight over. He has another shirt in his car. His dressman helps him dress. He does a few push ups and oils his muscles with mango body butter. We leave with an entourage of bodyguards.

Samson Night orders lobsters, oysters, prawns and champagne in excess. His girlfriend is in Russia visiting her family. The three of us sit at the bar surrounded by his bodyguards and people wanting to touch and talk to him. He is kind and polite to all his fans. They leave him alone once they have got an autograph.

Once The Producer gets up to talk to someone he knows at the other end of the room, Samson Night asks me how I am doing and if I am enjoying India. I tell him too much. I explain that my visa expires and that I really want to come back. He does not see the problem.

"Well, just renew it and come back."

"I can't. I need The Producer to want me back."

"Let me have a talking with The Producer. And stop worrying *yaar*. I will make sure you come back *na*?"

"Please do, I really need your help on this."

"When Samson makes a promise, Samson keeps his promise."

If anyone can twist The Producer's arm, it's him.

The Producer will not be on either of these commercials. He is going to Delhi again. He seems very secretive about Delhi, but I dare not ask him why.

We prep in the Luna office for a week and I go out with Dhiraj to take photos as Kush is too busy to join us. I need to get as many photos as I can before I leave.

We fly to Goa in high spirits. This is my last shoot in India. I'm going to give it all I've got. We settle into the hotel and go on a recce. Our whole shoot is on a beautiful beach with palm trees that bend with the wind. Rich coastal vegetation of rice paddies and coconut plantations surround us. The water is clear and clean with blinding white beaches that stretch on for miles and miles. Only I dare to swim.

We are ready to shoot the next morning. Kush's team will only start shooting after we wrap. Their shoot is bigger and longer. They will use the gear once we have completed. They arrive a day after us, while we are shooting. We wrap and go back to our hotel. It has been my best shoot day ever. I run the floor like clockwork. After we wrap, Alisha books us a table at a restaurant on the beach. We walk past a beautiful Catholic church on the way. Alisha, having gone to a convent school, understands the beauty of lighting candles.

"Baby, do you want to light a candle for your family?"

We go inside. I light four: one for my mother, one for my father, another for my brother and the fourth for my grandmother. Alisha lights one for her children and one for her late husband. We say a prayer and leave. I am not religious, but I ask God to let me come back to India.

Dinner is extremely festive. People come from all over the world to party in Goa. It is known as the Ibiza of Asia. I can see why. Alisha orders a local drink called *feni*, a very strong alcoholic coconut drink. We are drunk. I swim to sober up. We all lie in a row in the sand and watch the stars. I bury Sashi in the sand and give him the biggest pair of breasts with perfect pointed nipples. Alisha gets a call.

It's after midnight. Kush is at the hospital with Kiran Cooper. He is worried as they need to start shooting tomorrow. Alisha and I get our driver to take us to the hospital where they are. We find Kush and Kiran in the emergency room waiting for a doctor. He has curd rice stuck on his moustache and on the front of his shirt. I have watched him eat before. He is a messy eater. His hands drip with curd and rice and he tends to get it everywhere. He has big ears. I can see why the bug chose his ear.

"What happened?"

Kiran slurs slightly.

"I aa ... wazz aa ... drinkinggg my peg and all then I wazz curd rice eatinggg aa ... sssomething of a bugs came into my ear and all aa ... it was astonishing and I sssstuck aa ... my finger to make it come out, but ... but it went further and deeper and it is sitting in my brain. I cannot think aa ... its buzzing is maddening."

Kush speaks. He is drunk, but in control.

"I tried to look inside, but sir used a finger that had curd rice on it. All I can see is rice. It must be buzzing behind the rice and all."

"At least the bug has a decent supply of food in there."

Kiran is rocking himself to stay calm. He holds his head. It must be a horrible feeling.

"Thisss bugging is tickling my brain."

I rub his back trying to comfort him.

"Heavenly my dear, thank you."

The doctor arrives, he's been woken specially. His tired eyes widen when he sees his patient. He becomes animated and alive. He shakes Kiran's hand vigorously. He does not let go.

"Mr Kiran Cooper Sir! What a pleasantry surprise! I am enjoying to watch much of your work, you have one solid grasp on comedy."

Kush interrupts to explain the problem.

The doctor begins to extract rice with a pair of tweezers. He goes in deep until he gets the bug. He does not talk about anything, but film. He wants to know about the stars. He squeezes the bug between the tweezers and kills it, adds it to the curd rice that is sitting in the stainless steel bowl.

"We are done here, sir. All the best for tomorrow."

Kiran is a different man. He seems sober and strong.

The doctor bobs his head from side to side. A pleading grin spreads across his face.

"*Achcha*, just one teeny weeny favours and all?"

He hands Kiran his script pad and a pen.

"Your autograph, please, sir?"

"Most definitely, doc."

Kick ass – kamikaze!

The suicide goat did not die in vain. Kush has been accepted into NYU.

The office decides to throw him a farewell party. We are going clubbing at Eclipse in town. The Producer allows me to go because Nisha will go with me.

His conditions are: no more than two drinks and home by three.

The Producer only gave me enough money for two drinks, so I am grateful for the extra ones that Kush buys me. We start at the top of the shots menu and work our way down. We dance and smoke and laugh and talk. Kush is different towards me when The Producer is not around. His guard is down and he is attentive and kind. He can afford to be nice. He's not going to get fired for being nice to his boss's girlfriend. Sometimes I think The Producer gets intimidated when young good-looking boys pay attention to me. It feels good to be having fun with people my own age rather than the older glitterati of Bombay who are out just to be seen. We are all young and our lives are just beginning. The young Indians in the club stare, not because I'm with a famous producer, but, as always, I'm the only white person here. It does not bother me anymore. I fit in just fine. We end off the night with a flaming Lamborghini. When we get to the car park, the front tyre has been slashed. I suddenly don't feel so good. The flaming Lamborghini is not staying down. I go down onto all fours and projectile vomit every colour of the rainbow with such force that it comes out of my nostrils. Kush sits down next to me. He holds my hair and rubs my back.

"Just be getting it out. You will be feeling much better after."

Kush calls us a cab. Nisha and I get in.

"Juhu, it's almost 4am, we must be dropping me first!"

The taxi driver takes us the wrong way. I would never have known, but Nisha notices immediately. I am smoking a cigarette, trying to replace the taste of vomit in my mouth. Although I'm drunk, I do feel better. I sit slap bang in the middle of the review mirror. The cab driver keeps looking at me as I suck on the smoke. I don't care, not tonight.

Nisha starts shouting at the cab driver in Hindi, but he ignores her and drives faster.

"Put that damn cigarette out, you're encouraging him."

The driver laughs at her through the rearview mirror and pulls into a gas station. He gets all the attendants' attention; they know him. They circle the car, he points to me.

"*Gori hai, gori hai* (she's a white girl)."

Nisha is scared. Very scared.

"He brought us here on purpose."

I'm confused.

"For petrol?"

"No, to show you to these men."

"Not a fucking chance, I'm not scared!"

I am drunk and stupid. Liquid courage flows through my veins. I'm sick and tired of being leered at, touched and seen as a sex symbol. I lean past Nisha and open the door.

"Get out, I'm gonna give these fuckers what they deserve."

Indians are not fighters, in fact they are like little girls when it comes to a good fight. Compared to South Africa I feel safe and unintimidated. Nisha tries to stop me. I climb over her. "You're making it worse. Stupid girl!"

She gets her mobile phone and starts to call the police. She gets out after me. We stand, two girls against five men.

"Come on you fuckers, if it's white skin you want, look here."

I arrogantly point at my chest. I'm wearing a low top. Nisha moves in front of me. The men get greedy, they move forward. I move past Nisha and push one of them as hard as I can in the chest. He is shocked and falls back. I keep walking. Nisha runs after me.

We walk until we find another cab. I took a big chance with those men, but it worked.

It's just past 5am. The servants are up. Sai opens the door.

"*Arrey*, madam, full drinking *yaar*. Boss angry. What time I'm telling you come?"

I don't want him to lie for me.

"Tell him five because it is five."

I fall asleep to the whistle of the rice steamer. The smell of onions comes through the air conditioning. Cook is preparing our lunch for the office.

I sleep through my alarm. The Producer comes in and stands over me. He is angry.

"What is going on here? Why you not up? What time did you reach?"

I try to adjust my thoughts. I'm still wading through my dream. The Producer flicks the light switch.

My head. I say the first stupid thing that comes to me.

"Bad chicken."

This makes The Producer even angrier. He shakes his head.

"I hate it when you lie."

He leaves without another word.

I have never skipped work. The guilt sits on me and I can't go back to sleep.

Sai comes in. He is scared for me.

"Madam, boss going. What you doing *yaar*? This is big tension."

"Coffee, please Sai?"

I catch a cab to the office. Kush has not come to work. Nisha is sitting with her head in her arms. I walk slowly, checking for The Producer. Alisha sees me first. She speaks.

"Hey baby. He's in his cabin. You better pray The Producer never finds out about last night. Standing up to those men. What the hell were you thinking? And what's this bad chicken excuse? Pathetic darling."

"Is he pissed?"

"Extremely pissed, I suggest you stay out of his way."

"Have I blown my chances of staying?"

"Probably."

"Fuck."

"I think knowing you got drunk with Kush makes him even angrier."

The Producer comes out for lunch. He ignores me completely. He tells Alisha to make us clean the studio. It's a nightmare job.

In the evening Alisha comes to check on us. She tells me that I must ride with her. The Producer has gone home early. He is sitting on the couch playing chess when I arrive. I am dreading the fact that I have nowhere else to go. I greet him. He grunts. I head for my room. I am exhausted, dirty and want my bed.

"Where do you think you're going?"

"Bed."

"No you're not. Gaya has invited you to a pre-Holi party she is hosting at the JW Marriott."

"Please can I be excused? I really need to sleep."

"You cannot be rude. Go shower. She will be here in fifteen minutes."

"Are you going?"

"No."

"Why can you ...?"

He cuts in, angry.

"Just do ..."

His jaw begins to clench. I have to obey or there'll be hell to pay.

Do not come back ...

Gaya is waiting for me on the couch. She smiles kindly, too kindly. I don't understand why The Producer's ex-wife would want to spend time with me. She leaves me standing alone and joins her friends. They make it known that they are talking about me. I feel spare. I order a drink at the bar and watch them gossip, snicker and sneer. They are all dripping in money. Gaya keeps looking at me with her Mona Lisa smile. It makes me uncomfortable. I see the woman who lives above us with her husband and two girls. She's alone. Thank god for her. She joins me at the bar. Before I am able to strike up a conversation, Gaya grabs me and drags me onto the dance floor. Her nails dig into the palm of my hand.

"Dance. This is my party. You must dance."

Her friends begin to circle me. They scrunch their eyes, curl their lips and thrust their hips around me. I am forced to move with them. We dance. Gaya makes me do shots with her. The alcohol lifts my hangover. She is getting drunk, fast.

The woman from upstairs whispers in my ear.

"I'm very surprised to see you here. She's up to something. Watch yourself."

Gaya leads us to the swimming pool. There are buckets of champagne and platters of delicious-looking food. I am not hungry. All I want is my bed. The evening gets stranger and stranger. An old short man introduces himself to us. He looks like a bullfrog. Gaya straddles him and begins to get intimate. She proudly tells me that this is her new boyfriend. She obviously wants me to take the news back to The Producer. He runs his hand along her exposed thigh with his creepy hands. I squirm. Things are getting tacky. Gaya gets louder, starts patronising me.

"You must be really happy to be going home where you belong?"

"I'm actually very sad. I have loved being here."

"Well, you're not one of us, you will never be."

Her best friend, whose name rhymes with pimple, spits out her bitter thoughts.

"She's right. Look around you. You don't belong here. I suggest you go home and forget about this little holiday, we will most certainly be forgetting about you."

I am sitting next to Gaya and her man. His hand keeps wandering down my back and into the nape of my neck. No one sees. I pretend to be listening. The mortified look on my face has nothing to do with what she's saying.

Gaya wants to swim.

The man licks his lips.

"You girls should be taking off your clothes."

Gaya grabs my hand.

"Come."

I don't want to, but she insists.

Maybe she really wants to be my friend. I should show that I am fun to be around.

I let her pull me to the edge and we dive in fully clothed.

Gaya surfaces. Her face is bleeding. She has misjudged and hit her lip on the bottom of the pool. Her nasty friend comes to the side of the pool and begins to scream at me.

"You bloody caused this, *firang!* Gaya, how you can be letting this white trash be dragging you down? Ha? Come. Get out before the bloody press see."

All I think about while she ridicules me is that her name rhymes with pimple. This stops me from crying.

She leads Gaya to the bathrooms.

The woman from upstairs helps me out the pool.

She wraps a towel around me.

"Come sweetie, let's get the hell out of here."

We drive home.

"That bloody boyfriend of hers stuck his hand down the back of my skirt while you guys were in the pool. They're the trash, not you."

"He did it to me too, that's why I agreed to swim. To get away."

She hugs me.

"You okay?"

"I will be once I have had a good sleep."

"I hear you're going to Bollywood's biggest Holi party, day after."

"Can't wait."

"Good ending to your stay."

"Definitely."

Picture perfect

The Producer and I function under the same roof for three days without speaking. In the house, the car, the office. He has not said a word about Gaya's party. I don't tell him about her new boyfriend because it's none of my business and I only have one week left here. As far as I can see I won't be coming back. I try not to worry about it too much. Today is Sunday. Today is Holi.

I am surprised to hear The Producer speaking to me.

"Wake up, fatsy, time to party."

I pull myself from sleep and open my eyes. The Producer is standing over me holding a crisp white *salwar kameez.*

"Today you have to wear white so that the colour shows up. Hurry, you can skip your run, just for today."

Why so nice? I go with his good mood. I'm grateful for the change. The Producer is wearing all white too. I dress and meet him on the verandah.

"Gené, today your wish comes true."

"Why?"

"Bly will be at the party and it's Sunday. If you time it right you can sit with him when lunch is served."

"Me and the other thousands of people at the party."

The streets are more alive than ever. Bombay has become a rainbow. As an artist, colour is a priority, but I have never seen colour like this before. People run, dance and parade through the streets drenched in colour. Every colour imaginable is being thrown in the form of powders, liquids and gels. There is a constant sound of *bhangra* drums and music flowing through the streets in time with the people and its saturation of colour, colour, colour.

We decide to walk to the actor's house where the party is being thrown. He does not live far from The Producer. The streets are too crowded and Balkran fears for the gold BMW. People are high on *bhang*, a preparation from the leaves and flowers of the female cannabis plant prepared as a cold beverage with almonds, spices, milk and sugar. Today is all about the party and having a lot of fun.

The press surround the actor's house. There are plenty of people walking in. The security are on high alert to protect.

There is a metal detector and we are asked to show our invitations by the security at the door. A helicopter hovers above us with three cameramen recording what's happening in the actor's back garden from above. We enter and before I know what's hit me I am thrown into a huge trough of yellow colour. I climb out of the trough and am attacked again with purple, red, blue and green powders that stick to the wet yellow of my entire body. They do the same to The Producer. Bly manoeuvres on his crutches towards me, balancing on one crutch to give me a hug. I hardly recognise him under the intensity of colour. He puts a smudge of red paint on my forehead with his thumb, like a *tikka* (red dot), a sign of goodwill. He is such a dignified man. Even though he is outshone by the younger generation of stars, they lack his class and his gracefulness. Money cannot buy these two characteristics. You either have them or you don't.

There are troughs filled with different coloured powders spread across the lawn and people are being attacked with it. It comes from all directions. There are more people than I imagined. Every one of them is famous or important. Samson Night comes at me from behind. I am submerged into the green trough. People are being dunked all over the place. Alisha grabs my hand. I turn to kiss her. She dunks me in pink. I hurl her into the green trough. She is unrecognisable. We laugh and laugh and laugh. There are exotic food stalls in every corner cooking up the most glorious delicacies. There's a champagne and oyster bar, and a dance floor that is packed. The JW Marriot hotel is catering. Waiters, who are less drenched than the guests, walk around with trays packed with little clay pots filled with *bhang*.

Alisha takes three and hands one to The Producer and one to me.

"Drink, you've got some catching up to do."

I'm nervous. I don't like the idea of getting high on such a special day. I want to remember every second.

"What will it do?"

"Just drink."

The Producer and I drink. We drink again and again. I do remember everything, but in a way that can only be explained as the most colourful day of my life.

Bly takes my hand and I push him to the dance floor. He has moved to his wheel chair, as the party and the *bhang* are taking their toll. We dance to my favourite Bollywood song, "It's the time to disco". People circle us and dance with us. Bly manoeuvres his chair like a pro. He swivels and turns on the back tyres flipping the front of his chair up as he moves to the music.

I find The Producer sitting on the grass, laughing uncontrollably. I have never seen The Producer laugh like this before. He cannot stand. He wants to, but he can't. He gets me going, I cannot stop laughing. Our ecstatic mood persists for hours into the night. *Bhang* makes us hungry. We find food. We eat and drink and dance and throw colour. As an artist I am in heaven. Bombay is my canvas. Each and every person who has been a part of my stay here has painted a smudge of colour onto the canvas of my soul forever. My canvas is rich with colour and texture. It is complete. Every person I have met here, rich, poor, old, young, ugly, beautiful and famous, has created a ripple of memories that have changed me forever.

I wake up in The Producer's arms in his bed. I am happy. He is awake, smiling at me. We are naked. The sheets are stained with colour; so are our bodies.

The Producer squeezes me tight against his plump, hairy chest.

"Did you have a good time?"

"The best."

"Do you want to come back? Maybe for a year this time?"

"Madam home going"

I take Alisha with me to South Africa. I show her Cape Town and Johannesburg. We go on a safari. She loves it. Going home has made me realise that in a strange way I am better off without a salary and just the perks. The Producer always flies me business class, I have no living expenses and he overcompensates by allowing me to have more than I could ever afford with just a salary. If I earned money, I would be expected to fend for myself.

The down side? The Producer has all the control.

The Producer gives me a wad of traveller's cheques. I go to town. I replace my CD player with an MP3 player. I get Chanel face products, a new wardrobe and some new camera gear.

I return to India three weeks later with a visa for one full year.

My room is as I left it. The blinds are drawn closed as they always are. It's dark and ice cold inside here. The air conditioner hums me a welcome tune. Sai has put a small oil burner with sandalwood beside my bed. The sweet scent, combined with the wall-to-wall mirrors reflecting dark wood and slippery blue silk sheets, remind me of the exotic richness that India carries within its underbelly. This is my India, my land of spice and rice.

The Producer is in Delhi. My household companions treat me like a queen. Kutty keeps pinching my cheeks. He is thrilled when I give him a wrapped gift with a big green ribbon around it. He has never been given a gift before. He opens it. It is a smart shirt that fits him perfectly. I hug him, he lets me. Sai gets sunglasses. He wears them around the house while he works. While The Producer is out of town we sit in the home theatre and watch Bollywood films all night long. We dance to the item numbers. I make everyone wear my hats, scarves and sunglasses. We are film stars, just for tonight.

Not long after my return, The Producer becomes withdrawn. He seems worried. He retreats into his shell. Being a Cancerian, it's his defence mechanism. He goes to Delhi all the time. When I ask if there's a problem he clams up.

I cannot understand it – we are not fighting and there is plenty of work.

We are shooting a biscuit commercial with the famous cricketer Sachin Tendulkar. The Producer leaves Alisha in charge. Pierre Bordeaux directs. Sachin is humble and kind natured. He gives our dressman Sashi a signed cricket jersey, which he wears with great pride.

On the last day we wrap early and Alisha drops me home just before 5pm. Sai is surprised to see me home so early.

"*Achcha*, Gaya Madam is coming."

"Where?"

"In bedroom coming."

I don't knock.

I push the heavy wooden door open. The naked woman door handle is cold in my palm. My thumb rests between her bronzed breasts. Gaya and another woman stand over my bed. The woman seems to be chanting. Gaya swings burning incense in a jar around the room. They have a candle burning on the side of my bed. They stop. Gaya does not know where to put herself. She begins to talk. Fast.

"Welcome back. Did you have a good trip? I believe Alisha joined you. How nice. How is your family? We are here to wish you well."

She flashes her Mona Lisa smile at me.

"Hello, Gaya."

She looks at the other woman. The woman nods. Gaya walks to the door. The woman follows her. She has dark-set eyes and very long jet-black hair that hangs loose. Her hands are full of rings with different stones in them. She has different materials wrapped around her wrists. Her skirt, made of dark coloured silks, falls loosely around her body.

Is she a witch?

As Gaya makes her way across the room, her disturbing Mona Lisa smile follows me. Before I can answer any of Gaya's questions, they are out the door and gone. I am confused. I blow out the candle and sit on the bed. She has hung a new painting on the wall, it reads:

This castle holds no memories
abandoned by your caravan
the doors stay locked,
behind the rough stone walls
even the light dares not enter
an eternal wait for the sound of footsteps
from the dunes
this castle holds no memories.

It did not take Gaya very long to find out that I was back.

The servants must have told her. They always know what goes on behind closed doors.

Sick

The monsoon begins to wrap its blanket of cloud and persistent rainfall around Bombay. The Producer is unreachable. I am worried, but more distracted by my health. There is something very wrong inside my abdomen and I cannot work out where the pain is coming from. I notice it for the first time when I am in a tuk-tuk with Nisha. I feel heavy inside, like there is a leaking tap in my abdomen. The bumpy ride causes a shooting pain from my coccyx up into the front of my abdomen, where my uterus is. The pain becomes debilitating, it persists and gets worse, it keeps me up at night and makes it hard for me to run and work.

I tell The Producer between his ongoing trips to Delhi and his moods. I am sent to see the only doctor he knows, his house doctor, Dr Bollywood. Dr Bollywood is ever so pleased to see me. He makes me lie on the bed. He sends his assistant outside. We are alone. I am in too much pain to care. He does his usual breast examination. Once he is satisfied, he puts a rubber glove on and inspects me internally. He inspects both cavities with his fingers. I am so embarrassed, but I do not have a choice. I am desperate!

He begins with a strawberry milkshake injection, like the one I had when I was sick with Delhi belly. The pain disappears. I go to bed. I sleep well.

But it keeps coming back. I deal with the pain during the day and then have an injection at night. Dr Bollywood sees me every night after work. Balkran takes me once we have dropped The Producer at the airport. I am grateful for the lift, a tuk-tuk would be too painful. All I need is my precious strawberry injection and I'm gone. Balkran drives me home, the injection works quickly. I drift into numbness as we drive. By the time we get back to the house, five minutes away, I am heavy and dull. I go straight to bed and float, trip, fly. I carry on as best as I can, but I'm only masking the symptoms of something serious. What is wrong with me?

The pain becomes unbearable. I notice a little blood coming from my anus and plenty in my urine. I am so scared.

Dr Bollywood now consults with a gastroenterologist; I am convinced the problem is in my anus. Of all the problems I could have, why does the most embarrassing hole have to have the problem? I want to fix it with the least amount of fuss. I am scared The Producer will send me home if he senses that I am not coping so I try to deal with it on my own. Dr Bollywood admits me into hospital – the gastroenterologist wants to do a colonoscopy to see what is going on inside my plumbing. The Producer is in Delhi. He insists that Sai sleep in the hospital with me because hospitals in Bombay are known to be dangerous for female patients staying over. Many of them get raped in the night. I am given a vile laxative concoction that they mix up in a colddrink bottle. It is soapy and makes me want to vomit. I am forced to drink three bottles. I shit all night long until I am so empty that I begin to vomit bile. Sai stays with me. I don't care, I am beyond feeling embarrassed. The Producer's household staff are the closest people to me. I love and trust them.

Alisha comes to see me before the procedure. She is kind and motherly and I feel safe with her around.

I am wheeled into a sterile operating room with green sheets everywhere. I am placed on a steel bed. The doctor and nurse are male. They cover my naked torso. I am kept awake while a hosepipe is shoved up me to flush. The water pours out and another pipe with a camera at the end of it is shoved in. The doctor fiddles around, pressing my stomach as he moves the equipment around.

He finds nothing. I am so upset by the outcome. What is wrong with me? I have lost more weight, even The Producer notices. The Producer's doctor advises that I see a gynaecologist next. I have to wait a few days as she is fully booked. He advises that I stay home and rest until then. The Producer's doctor continues with the injections. They take the edge off my pain. In my hazy state, I watch my favourite DVD over and over again for comfort. *Love Actually*. I rewind the part where Hugh Grant comes dancing down the stairs in his presidential home. I stand up and dance along in the hope that I will get my spark back. Nothing. I am so devastated by the outcome of the procedure that I lie on the home theatre floor and sob for hours.

As if she could feel my pain, my mother calls, worried. I cannot cope with this alone and so I break down over the phone. She insists I come home and see my brilliant gynaecologist. I agree; something is very wrong. I call The Producer's doctor and thank him for his help. I would prefer to see my gynaecologist back home. I know he will figure out the problem.

I pack a bag and leave, taking *Love Actually* with me. The Producer is in Delhi. I call him to say goodbye and he reassures me that it is better this way and that I can return as soon as I am well.

Stitched

I am anxious all the time. I want to be back in India from the moment I land. I need to find out what is wrong with me, fix it and get back. I can't afford to lose out on this opportunity and if I stay away for too long, The Producer might lose interest in me. That casting couch is empty – anyone could fill it while I'm away.

My brilliant gynaecologist takes one look at me and diagnoses me with endometriosis. He needs to operate and perform a laparoscopy so that he can get inside and fix it. The cells of my womb lining appear to have grown around my bowel and bladder. They bleed in response to my menstrual cycle, explaining the pain and the blood in my urine and anus.

I have two operations in ten days. Once I'm released from hospital and there are no more nightly injections. I begin to feel strange. I am agitated and ratty. I go back to my doctor. He asks if I was taking any painkillers in India. I tell him about the magic strawberry injections. He gives Dr Bollywood a call and confirms that the injections are opium based; he explains that I am suffering from slight withdrawal. My fingers and toes keep curling in like I want to claw at the walls. I am irritable and irrational. I don't care about my recovery. I am given a course of injections that will control the endometriosis. I have to have one every six weeks for eternity. I get a year's supply. Dr Bollywood can administer them when I get back to India. Against my family's and doctor's advice I leave with undissolved stiches inside of me, six external stitches around my belly button and four on either side of my pelvis. Dr Bollywood can remove the external ones. I don't care – I just have to get back before the red velvet casting couch gets filled … by someone else.

Life-saving beauty hamper

I fly via Dubai and land in Mumbai at 4am. I fly economy this time. The flight is full and with all my stitches I cannot lie anywhere and I am forced to sit on them.

I push my retarded trolley through the green zone at customs. I have nothing to declare. A man wearing a khaki uniform and a hat shaped like a paper boat stops me. He opens the suitcase and rummages through a large toiletry bag containing my year's supply of injections and a tub of vaginal cream, which I have been instructed to insert with an applicator at night. The cream contains an antibiotic and will prevent my internal stitches from becoming infected. He is very perturbed by the bag. He tucks it under his stained armpit and escorts me down the passage, his mouth full of *paan*. His cheeks bulge full of saliva mulched with *paan* syrup and tobacco. He holds his lower jaw forward creating a bucket to prevent any spillage. He looks like a pelican.

"Parcel not be clearing."

He points to a doorway leading into a small office lined wall to wall with turbid cream linoleum. Flies buzz around and around having been trapped in this confined space for days. I hope I don't end up like them.

The grease ball places my bag onto a laminated table. Another officer in a khaki uniform with a maroon turban and a long henna-stained beard sits behind the table picking bits of his lunch out from between his teeth with his long-nailed pinky. He looks up, peels what looks like yellow dal out of his fingernail with another nail and wipes it on his pants. He pokes my bag with his swagger stick, folds his arms across his bloated stomach, spreads his legs wide apart, bent at either side of the chair. He begins to rock back and forth on its back legs. The grease ball sits down on the chair next to the maroon-turbaned officer, concentrating on cleaning his ear with a matchstick. He flicks the contents on the floor, explaining in Hindi why I am standing here with my toiletry bag. The overhead ceiling fan circulates fumes of old garlic, ginger, dal and whisky. On one of his swings forward, the turbaned officer pushes the parcel towards me with his swagger stick.

"*Chalo* (all right), open it."

I open the bag, turning the opening towards him. He digs his stick into the content pulling the bag toward him.

"This is drugs taking?"

"I have a letter giving me permission from my doctors to travel with this medication, sir."

"Is this medication life-saving, madam?"

"Yes, sir, this is the letter explaining exactly what it is."

He ignores the injections and the letter favouring the vaginal cream and its applicators. He pulls at the applicator, pumping it so that it blows a soft breeze into his face.

"This is manual fan."

His greasy sidekick laughs, taking another applicator and mimicking his colleague's actions.

Monkey see, monkey do.

The turbaned officer unscrews the lid of the tube, squeezing a dollop of cream onto his yellow dal-stained finger.

"This not be looking life-saving cream to me. Looks like beauty hamper."

His sidekick takes the tube and copies him again. I watch as the two custom officers proudly dab dollops of white vaginal cream across their faces and down their necks.

"I am younger looking *na*? How much this beauty cream is meaning for you?"

I understand the question. I dig into my wallet and cough up 1 000 Rupees. At this stage I will pay any amount to have my precious cream back.

Balkran is patiently waiting for me at the airport. He is alone.

I have bought him a "The Best of Michael Jackson" CD. I am relieved that the custom rats did not confiscate it or my *Love Actually* DVD. Balkran idolises Michael Jackson. He immediately puts it on and hums in an out-of-tune, high-pitched makeshift way. I sing the words. He tries to pronounce them too. Balkran drives us carefully through deeply flooded streets. When we get to the house, The Producer is waking up. He has to leave early for a shoot in Panchgani, a lush hill station southeast of Bombay.

"Good you're back. Feeling better?"

"Pretty much."

"You should come with to the shoot. I have a new director from Germany working on it."

"I wouldn't miss it for the world."

"Good, go freshen up, I will see you in an hour."

He is as closed off as he was before I left. At least the servants make a fuss of me, my ever-faithful house companions.

The Producer decides to drive. I sit in front, next to him. His skin oozes his favourite perfume Terre D'Hermes. He has lost weight and seems very chuffed with himself. He strokes his chin, sucks in his stomach and cheeks, holds a body builder's pose, flexing his biceps as he eyes himself in the rearview mirror. Something is definitely up.

We pass the armless man. I give him what I have, he is always grateful.

I ask The Producer about the commercial and the new German director.

"It's an Avenger bike ad."

"Motorbike?"

"Yes."

"What's the director's name?"

"Darko, young, very talented."

"As talented as Pierre?"

"Seems to be. Very driven."

"Most Germans are. How long's the shoot?"

"We shoot here today and then three days in Kerala."

"Can I go?"

"We'll see."

"It's your birthday in a week's time."

"Unfortunately."

"Fifty is not the end of the world."

"It is to me."

We arrive on set and walk over to a very young-looking white guy. His hair is geometrically spiked with hardened strawberry-scented gel that has begun to flake. His eyes bulge out on stalks behind his small square spectacles. Hands on his hips, all dressed in black, he tries hard to be cool in the humidity of the monsoon. He drips with arrogance and self-importance. A young ambitious-looking Indian guy stands next to him shouting instructions at the crew in Hindi.

Alisha taps the white guy on the shoulder.

"Gené, this is Darko, our talented new director from Germany."

"Talented I am *ja*. And you are from where? What are you doing here, you seem a little pale to be one of them?"

I feel an instant disliking towards this Darko character.

"I am from South Africa, but I work for Luna as an assistant director."

"Shame, poor you, Africa *ja*? I hope you were not intending to assist me? You're three days late. I think I will stick to Indian assistants who speak the language. Can't be easy for people like you."

"Well, if there is anything I can do for you, I'm here so please let me know."

"Coffee, you can get me a coffee *ja*. Try make it better than Santa's little helper over there."

His accent irritates me, he irritates me and now he's being derogatory about my darling spot boy Dhiraj. He's in rural India, what fucking coffee does he expect? A cappuccino in the middle of nowhere?

I vent to Alisha.

"Be prepared darling, we still have the Kerala ad to get through next week."

"Will we be back for The Producer's birthday?"

"We have to be. Gaya's throwing The Producer a huge bash."

"Gaya? Why? I thought they ..."

"She's really trying hard to get close to him again. He's been spending a lot of time with her in Delhi. While you were away her sister got married, it was a huge affair. I think spending all that festive time together with the boys as a family has made Gaya think twice. She wants him back."

I want to vomit.

"But she divorced him?"

"No she didn't, they are separated only, have been for almost three years."

I cannot believe what I am hearing. I feel like a thief and a homewrecker. I am tired and sore. Everything is going wrong. I did not even know that The Producer went to a family wedding while I was away. I walk away and start to cry. I thought they were over and wanted to go their separate ways. Now what? I love The Producer, but he is not mine to love.

Balkran has made his way up to Panchgani and he drives us back to Bombay in the pouring rain. It is dark, but I trust his driving more than I trust The Producer's. I am dozing on the back seat when The Producer's phone rings. His voice is soft and smooth like melted chocolate. He speaks seductively. He obviously thinks I'm asleep.

"Yes, you too ... you drive me crazy. Maybe, we'll see ... Me too ..."

There is want and need in his tone. His phone dies. I offer him mine. He jumps in his seat. And turns around surprised.

"Why, you awake?"

I sit up, wanting to ask who he was talking to, but I'm scared. There is no way that was Gaya.

"I heard you talking ..."

"You should get some sleep."

"Do you want to use my phone?"

"No need, my other one is charged."

He pulls out a second phone from his pocket. Since when does The Producer carry two phones?

"You have another phone? Should I save the number?"

Silence.

"Are we okay?"

"What do you mean?"

"I mean you and me and our relationship. Are we okay?"

"The condition of a relationship is what you make of it in your head. Now sleep."

I lie back down on the back seat. Is that it? I must just pretend that it's okay in my head? Is that not referred to as living a lie or, even worse, in denial? Surely pretending you don't know is so much harder than admitting to yourself what you actually know and coming to terms with the reality of the situation?

Balkran wakes me. The Producer is already upstairs. I get out of the car and drag myself to the front door. Sai answers the door. I tell him not to wake me at five because I am not allowed to run until the stitches have dissolved. There is a card with a flower and some strange pods next to my bed.

"Welcome back. Hope you get well soon. Gaya."

As I fall asleep to the hum of the air conditioner, an idea pops into my head. I am going to paint a self-portrait of myself over the dull brown poem/painting Gaya has put on my wall. This is still my room. "This castle DOES hold memories ... memories of me!"

Venice direct

The Producer throws an air ticket to Kerala onto the back seat on our way home. It has my name on it. The Producer is silent for most of the trip home. When his phone rings, he switches it to silent and does not answer. When we get home I am told to go and pack for my trip. I find a very sexy, slinky G-string in my underwear draw. It's definitely not mine and will certainly not fit Gaya. I ask Kutty – he is in charge of the washing. He holds his hands to his mouth, embarrassed. He is unable to explain in English and all I understand is the word 'Delhi'. I call Sai.

"Sai, is someone staying here when I am South Africa going?"

"One madam from Delhi coming."

Like Venice, life on the Kerala backwaters revolves around the water canals. Our means of transport is on ferries. We are taken from the airport to the ferry by a bus. We load our luggage and our gear onto the ferry and make our way down the brackish lagoon to get to our hotel in the heavy downpour of rain. I soon find out our call time is at 4am. We shoot in an open rice paddy without shelter. The grey light strains behind the heavy blanket of cloud, and the rain pours down hard. Dhiraj hands us each a shower cap. We look ridiculous. An elephant cow and her adolescent calf are placed on a narrow muddy track between two soggy paddies, chained together around their massive round feet. Their eyes are full of fear. Their wrinkly skin blends in beautifully with the sky, but they stick out against the rich chloroform green fields. The motorbike that we are advertising will cross the frame in the background behind the elephants. The most important piece of equipment is the camera. It must stay dry. It is wrapped in plastic and four assistants hold a constructed sail, and all the umbrellas we possess, over it.

Darko bullies and shouts at the *mahout* to position his elephants. The *mahout* does not understand and gets confused and nervous with Darko's uncontrollable shouting. He begins frantically stabbing the elephant cow on the top of the head with an *aṅkuśa,* a sharp metal hook. I get hysterical when the blood flows down the side of the elephant's face and into her eyes, the rain making it look more dramatic. I shout above the rain at the assistant to translate so that the *mahout* can stop hurting the traumatised elephant.

"This is my set, stay out of it."

Darko stands rigid and unemotional. His hands firmly on his hips. I notice his fists are clenched and white. His spectacles are misted up, but he does not move to wipe them clean. He is in combat mode.

The elephant's eyes are overloaded with fear. She blinks repeatedly, her eyelashes strain under the downpour of blood and rain. She can smell her own blood, she moves from one foot to the other, fighting the chains around her feet, trying to protect her calf.

The sky becomes light and we are ready to shoot, but the downpour becomes unmanageable. The camera can only see rain.

Hours later, the rain eventually subsides and Darko has a new adjustment to make before we can turn over and smash the coconut.

He wants the calf to stand under the cow as if sheltered from the rain. He refuses to see the obvious: the calf is too big to fit under the mother's belly. The assistant translates Darko's ludicrous request. The *mahout* begins stabbing the calf on its head trying to force it under the mother. The mother raises her head to the sky, curls her trunk back and gives out a distressed bellow. Her eyes swivel hysterically, showing the whites of her eyeballs. She's had enough. The baby calf squeals under the stabbing, they fight against the chains. The *mahout* beats the calf with a stick until it buckles to the floor, stabbing it repeatedly on the top of its head, making it crawl close to its mother in fear. Can nobody see that the calf is too big to fit under her? I frantically plead with Alisha, I cannot watch this anymore. I walk away in a fit of rage. She finally realises that this has gone too far and she asks Darko to stop. He ignores her.

"Hurry up you stupid man, the rain will come again, *ja*!"

"I'm calling The Producer."

Alisha explains to The Producer and hands the phone to Darko.

The Producer talks him off his high horse. We can put the calf under the mother in postproduction. The Producer has spoken. Darko is forced to listen.

Darko is angry and disappointed. He spends the rest of the day making it very hard for all of us. I don't care – he is a heartless maniac.

India has adapted well to life's cruelty. But this is unnecessary, all in the name of bullshit advertising and an asshole director.

Bust

The Producer is back from Delhi and he comes with Balkran to fetch me from the airport. They have come from the office. The Producer has had a DVD player installed in the car to break the agonising silence of our trips to the office.

He is watching *Intolerable Cruelty*. I sit in the middle of the back seat so that I can watch with him. I can see Balkran's eyes in the rearview mirror. Every time there is a kissing scene he is distracted and glances down to the screen installed where the radio was. The scene gets heated, with George Clooney and Catherine Zeta-Jones on a bed with heart-shaped pillows, The Producer sees Balkran watching this time, whacking Balkran hard on his thigh he skips to the next scene.

When Sai opens the front door there is a huge arched arrangement of red roses behind him against the wall. Deep down my heart is begging for them to be from The Producer to me, but he seems to stumble and plays dumb.

"No idea."

There is a note. I take it.

"To the love of my life ..."

Before I can turn it over The Producer takes it from me and marches into the kitchen.

He comes back without the card. "You want them? Put them in your room, they will look good there."

There are over two thousand red roses, the arch will not fit through the door.

"They won't fit."

The Producer tries to distract me from my disappointment, obviously covering something up. He patronises me.

"Come, let me take a photo of you next to them, get your camera."

"I don't want a photo with them; I want to know who they are from."

"If you don't know, how should I know?"

He narrows his eyes teasingly and says, "Are you having an affair behind my back?"

Before I can reply he has turned his back on me, pushing the door to his bedroom closed.

I walk in the opposite direction to my door. My thumb pushes between the cold breasts of the naked woman door handle slide between my fingers. I whisper down at her.

"No, you are."

Raindrops won't stop falling on my head ...

Gaya is going all out for The Producer's party arrangements. I will wait until after the party to start painting my portrait over her poetic message on the wall.

The next morning when I open my eyes she is standing over me. It's just past 6am. "Please get up, this room is needed for tonight's party."

She rings the bell and her servant, Cook's wife, comes running in. Gaya throws instructions at her and she becomes very busy around me. She is on her hands and knees in my bathroom. I step over her to get my toiletry bag. She touches my feet out of respect, holds her palms together in a 'Namaste' and greets me. I cannot look at her. All I see is her husband in 'Fuckland' coming out of a cage doing up his zipper. I will have to get showered in The Producer's bathroom.

When I get out of the shower The Producer is on his bed counting out a wad of money. He wraps an elastic band around it and hands it to me.

"Get Balkran to take you to the Vikram Phadnis boutique and pick up something nice to wear for tonight. I need you to look good. There will be a lot of people attending my party. Go to Nail Bar and do something with that hair of yours. No curls – they make you look like a granny."

The persistent rain does not put a damper on The Producer's party. All of Bombay's who's who and the press arrive. A crowd from Delhi, including some of Gaya's family, has also flown in. If I play my cards right I might be able to figure out who the woman from Delhi is that stayed in my room, The Delhi Robber. Maybe she's here and I can return her panties? Gaya is praised for her décor; she has gone to so much effort. The outside bar and dance floor on the verandah are a hit. She has built a beautiful pergola to protect us from the rain. Enormous flower arrangements, pink spotlights and gauze transform the entire apartment into a glitzy intimate venue.

I order another drink and scan the room for the potential Delhi Robber. A short petite girl catches my eye; she is staring at me. She smiles and approaches me. She has a baby face and looks younger than me. She moves in to hug me. She speaks gently, but excitedly.

"You must be Gené?"

"How do you know who I am?"

She giggles, her enthusiasm bubbles over.

"Easy, you are the only white girl here and I have heard so much about you. My son and I came to stay with The Producer while you were in South Africa. Are you feeling better?"

"You have a son?"

"Yes, he's six years old."

A fresh-looking man joins us; his face is round and soft like hers. He introduces himself as her husband. I am confused.

"How do you know The Producer?"

"He's a very good family friend of ours."

The mojitos are kicking in. I join Samson Night on the dance floor. I don't understand what's going on. Why is The Producer behaving so strangely? I know he has someone else, but who? The harder I dance, the better I feel. Someone is taking pictures of me, but I don't care.

Samson Night, The Producer and I leave the party and go to the nightclub at the JW Marriott, we each down a flaming Lamborghini. It finishes me. Samson carries me out the club over his shoulder. The press and Samson's fans are everywhere. His crew manage to keep my passed-out body away from the cameras. The last thing I remember is Samson Night carrying me to my room. He washes my face and feeds me water. I have vomited all over myself and all over The Producer's shoes. The Producer is annoyed and goes back to entertaining his guests.

The Producer shakes me awake just after 6am.

"Get up. Balkran will take you to set."

"What set?"

"Darko has some pick up shots to do. You're late."

"But you didn't say I had to work today? I feel so sick."

"And whose fault is that?"

The Producer climbs into my bed, he has not slept yet.

"My room is taken, I need your bed."

I have a monumental hangover. I shower and leave quietly. There are passed-out bodies all over the house, on the couches, under the table and in The Producer's bed. Lucky for him he can sleep all day. Dealing with Darko, the rain and my sore head is not going to be easy.

Over the following weeks, The Producer climbs deeper into himself. We don't talk anymore. He guards his two mobile phones like the giant in *Jack and the Beanstalk* guarding the goose that lays the golden eggs. The screens are always facing down and on silent. Sometimes he takes calls, sometimes he blocks them.

I begin my painting. It gives me something to do at night. I find an old copper fan at the market and decide to incorporate it into my self-portrait. The blades signify my freedom; the cage surrounding the blades resembles The Producer's control over me. I go to the beach and get some sand to mix into the paint. I want a piece of Bombay to be part of my painting. I take the poem off the wall, dip a large roller into a bucket of green paint and drown every word. In less than five minutes my canvas is primed and I am ready to paint my self-portrait. I begin with my eyes.

My phone rings. It is Nisha. She is crying and wants to meet me. She comes over and sits with me while I paint. She has a bottle of rum in her bag. We sip from it and smoke cigarettes under the extractor fan in my bathroom. She tells me that things are getting very hard at home and that she is desperate to get married and move out. She shows me bruises on her legs. She's been kicked again by Spy. She falls asleep while I paint. I wake her and Sai and I escort her home. Sai carries me on his shoulders when the water level on the street gets too high. I don't want anything above my thighs to get wet. My stitches are only just dissolving.

We all fall down

The Producer and I drive home from the office. We are bathed in silence while he plays chess. The rain and traffic are insufferable, I feel like my life jacket is coming undone and I am drowning in the presence of The Producer's dampening mood. Will he ever come out of it? My phone rings. The Producer stops his game to listen to my conversation. It is Samson Night. He has booked the club Vie for my birthday, which I had told him about the night when he carried me home. He wants me to invite whoever I want – he is footing the entire bill. I thank him over and over again. We say goodbye.

The Producer does not waste time asking me what is going on. I tell him. He is annoyed.

"Why did you not ask me first? How do you not know I wasn't planning a party for you?"

"I'm sorry, but he just offered, and I didn't think too much of it until now that he's actually gone and done it."

"You should think before ..."

"Sorry, were you really planning something?"

"It's too late now, do what you want. I don't care."

I cannot believe The Producer was planning something, not in the mood that he's been in. The Producer throws a newspaper onto the back seat next to me.

"I hope you are more discreet at your own party. Gaya does not want you splashed across the *Bombay Times*. We need to protect the boys. Can you understand? Can you imagine if there was a picture of you puking all over the place in that club? You must think before you do."

"They spelt my name wrong."

"What do you care?"

"Do you think the press are having a silent dig?"

"At who?"

"At Gaya. They have not written about me, but they have made me the biggest item on the page and it's not even my party."

"The press are friends of Gaya, they would not do that to her."

"Oh. Looks like they are showing and not telling."

"Just do as I say and behave yourself, okay?"

I feel like a reprimanded teenager.

I wake up on my birthday feeling very excited. I have invited all the people I know. Trainer has bought me a silver bracelet. Sai helps him wrap it while I am on the treadmill. He writes a beautiful card and says it's from him and all the servants in the house.

At the office Alisha gives me a beautiful silver watch and an artisanal triple-layered chocolate cake with honeycomb crunch sprinkled between the mousse. According to tradition, the entire Luna crew feed me a piece with their hands. The Producer lightens up and smears chocolate mousse across my face. We drive home early. The Producer wants us to get to the club before my guests do.

The Producer comes to find me while I dress. He makes me close my eyes and hold out my arm, a frosty Swarovski watch is wrapped around my wrist, gently he turns my hand over, his oversized bronze fingers stumble along my soft transparent white skin as he presses the swan-shaped clasp between his thumb and index finger. Click. Its crystal face winks at me as it catches the light. The Producer is soft again, maybe just for tonight.

Vie is on the beach. The rain is softer than this morning. The Producer and I sit at the bar overlooking the tormented ocean.

We order a few cocktails while we wait for our guests. We tumble into conversation, snowballing into laughter and forgiveness. The Producer admits that he has been absent and brash. He opens up about Gaya and the family and explains that he is having a very hard time with her father. He also tells me that he is very disappointed with his film that is due to release and that he fears the outcome. There is a lot of money to be lost. I feel sorry for him.

The venue is packed. Nisha points out that The Producer's ex from Nail Bar is here. Many people I do not know also arrive. French champagne, oyster shots and canapés circulate the room on large trays held high by waiters wearing sequined waistcoats. They serve to please like disco balls. Kush is talking to Dhiraj from the office. Alisha asks me why I invited him. I told him about it, but did not think he would come. He is out of place, but Kush is looking after him.

Everyone is getting very drunk very quickly. The music is turned up and the lights are dimmed. The Producer pulls me onto the dance floor. We have attended so many parties together, but he has never danced with me before. We move together. He kisses me in front of everyone. We do our own version of the tango. Everyone joins in and the floor heaves under us. Together we rise and fall, an unstoppable ball of energy that the press squashes into their lens, portraying us as the envy of Bombay's party scene. I am ripped away from The Producer and find myself spinning in the arms of Dhiraj. Holding me tight around the waist his pelvis grinds into me. He has a red rose in his mouth, taken off one of the tables, he tries to out do The Producer's tango and dips me. He is too drunk to keep control. Falling backward, he drops me. Before I register that I am on the floor, The Producer has grabbed Dhiraj and is dragging him out by his shirt collar. Probably the best shirt he has ever owned is tearing under the armpits, the buttons shooting off in different directions. Alisha helps me off the floor. Once out of view, The Producer will hit Dhiraj. Kush has the same thought and chases after them. He convinces The Producer to come inside. Balkran has come to help. Together Kush and Balkran frogmarch Dhiraj away from the party.

When Samson Night, who is paying for all this, arrives the party takes on a whole new shape. His girlfriend is with him, but not for long. They have a fight, so she leaves. Samson catches up with us by chasing shots and downing his rum on ice.

I find Nisha buckled over a toilet in the bathroom. Kush is with her. He is holding back her hair. Kush seems to be taking care of all the problem cases tonight.

"Can you call her fiancé? He needs to take her home."

I find Arin in a corner away from the party. He is talking to a stylist who often works with us at Luna. He looks annoyed by my interruption.

"Duty calls, bud, you need to get your wife home, had too much to drink."

"Can't Balkran take her?"

"No, he can't. Get your ass out there and do what's right."

"*Arrey yaar* Gené, you killing my fun."

Kush carries Nisha to the car for Arin. They go out the back so that The Producer does not see how trashed she is.

Arin joins us again.

"Where's Nisha?"

"Called her a cab, I don't want to leave."

"That's not safe when she's so drunk."

"She's fine."

I notice that Arin has developed spaghetti arms. They keep flailing towards the stylist. I go outside and call Nisha. She answers in a very sleepy voice. She's home and safe.

It's 5am; the party is over. The lights are turned on and reality is delivered back to us in bags beneath our eyes. The sky is a heavy grey, a dull light persuades its way through thick cloud on the horizon. It's raining again.

Arin, Alisha and the stylist walk out of the club with us. We go our separate ways. The Producer is in very high spirits. I do not care if it's the alcohol speaking; he is being such good company. When we get home he asks me to join him in his bedroom. Sai brings us chai and chilli fried eggs. We eat and what we do after that feels like making love. I want him to because I want to. The

Producer asks me to stay in his arms and sleep with him. We have not fallen asleep yet when my phone rings. It's the stylist. She is sobbing and sounds terrified. She tells me that Arin followed her home, pushed her off the road and when she got out of her car he held her down and tried to rape her. She got away. The Producer can hear what she is saying. Before he can react, his phone rings, its Samson Night's girlfriend.

She is also crying. Samson is not home yet. She cannot get hold of him. The Producer talks to her calmly and says he will phone her back. He calls Samson. Samson answers in a fast-asleep voice.

"Where are you brother? Your girlfriend is freaking out. You need to get home."

I can hear his reply. He has fallen asleep at the house of the actress that he was chatting to when we left the club.

"I suggest you get your ass out of there and go home. I'm sending Balkran to you now."

The Producer calls Samson's girlfriend back. In his sweetest voice he tells her that Samson fell asleep at the club and that he is sending Balkran to get him home.

He unravels himself from me and goes to the kitchen to wake Balkran, who has slept on the kitchen floor with the other servants because we got home so 'early'. Balkran looks very annoyed, but he obeys and leaves immediately. The Producer goes and sits on the couch. He starts playing chess on his phone.

"Are you okay?"

"No, I'm not. I need to figure out what I am going to do with this dick Arin."

There goes The Producer's good mood.

I go to my room and climb into my silk bed. The sheets are cold and slippery. I can hear the crows outside. A palm leaf casts a shadow against the maroon blinds. It's a beautiful shape; just like my beautiful party, it took fantastic shape until we all fell down.

"I don't"

Nisha does not know yet, but her wedding plans and her perfectly planned future are about to come crashing down on her. The Producer plays chess until 8am and then calls her. All he says is, "You need to come over now."

I am woken by Sai and told to go and sit with The Producer. I have only had an hour's sleep. I sit opposite him. He concentrates on his chess game, not looking up to answer any of my questions.

"When Nisha gets here I want you to tell her exactly what happened. I want her to hear it from you."

"Okay."

Nisha walks through the door, her head bent forward. She looks at the ground.

"I'm so sorry, I did not mean to get so …"

"Sit. This is not about that."

She looks surprised and relieved. When she catches my eye I can see she starts to worry again. I am dreading what I am about to tell her.

"Tell her."

I tell her what happened after she was sent home in the cab. She drops to the floor and starts to sob. Her face pushes into the cold marble, her nose squashes under her. She rolls to the side, becoming hysterical. She curls into fetal position and covers her face with both hands.

"Get up, you're not a baby." The Producer bends over her and helps her onto the couch.

Nisha looks at me, her nose swollen red, her mascara runs.

"You are lying. You are jealous and you want to get me back for stealing your perfume, I know it's not true."

She covers her face again and sobs. The Producer motions for me to leave. I go back to my room. My heart is breaking for her. I cannot go back to sleep. I continue painting my portrait over Gaya's poem. I plug into my MP3 player. I don't want to hear her pain.

Lead balloon

When I walk into the office on Monday morning, Dhiraj is standing at Alisha's desk with his head hanging heavy like a lead balloon, staring at the floor, his hands folded respectfully behind his back. I catch the tail end of Alisha hissing. He turns and walks away. His head stays down. Alisha turns to me, she is seriously pissed off.

"It's your fault I had to fire him."

I'm shocked.

"Why did you have to fire him?"

"Because of what he did at your party. What the hell were you thinking, inviting a bloody *peon*?"

"You can't fire him, he's been part of Luna from the beginning, he's Dhiraj."

"I have to."

"Why?"

"The Producer wants him gone."

"Then why doesn't The Producer fire him?"

"He won't, he makes me do it every time."

"Why?"

"He can't. Same goes with his girlfriends, he is unable to dump them when he is done so he makes it so unbearable for them that they end up leaving him."

"Really? That's insane."

"That's The Producer for you."

"I'm so sorry."

"You should be, that man just lost his job."

I feel infected with the horrible disease called guilt. I cannot look at anyone. Everyone loves Dhiraj and now he's gone because of me and my stupid 'show off' party. I'm a homewrecker, an engagement 'vandaliser' and a job destroyer. Kush comes to cheer me up. He holds the *Bombay Times* in front of me, wriggles his hips and in a girl's voice sings, "*Achcha*, you do it again … you show off your face, you're such a disgrace."

I am in the papers again. They get my name right, but not my profession. They say I am a top South African model, which could not be further from the truth. Lucky for me The Producer is in Delhi so I'm in the clear.

The music launch day for The Producer's film has finally arrived. When the party begins, everyone seems to be enjoying it, except for The Producer. It throws him into a deeper depression. Samson Night and his girlfriend arrive. The press can't get enough of him; their flashes work overtime, a blinding frenzy on the red carpet. They turn their cameras on me, I don't think too much of it. I am the girlfriend of the producer that's releasing his film and I am behaving, there's no drama tonight. We leave very soon after we have arrived. The Producer is utterly ashamed of his film.

'Miss' understanding

The Producer sends me to the office with Balkran. On the days that we shoot, Alisha picks me up before sunrise and brings me back after wrap. The Producer stays in his room watching TV, chain smoking, eating and playing chess on his phone. He is unreachable. I leave him be, disappearing into my room to paint while my *Love Actually* DVD plays, keeping me company. My self-portrait is almost complete. I am so alone I make friends with the shadows on the wall, pretending we are shooting an item number with Bly in his wheelchair doing crazy moves on his wheels. I dance with my tripod in front of the wall-to-wall mirrors along my cupboards. I have become obsessed with Michael Jackson's "Man in the Mirror" song. I imagine that Bly and I have choreographed all the street children that I have photographed to dance with us at an exhibition opening of my paintings and photography based on their lives on the streets. The words are perfect. I sing into my hairbrush about how they follow the pattern of the wind because they've got no place to be. I imagine us raising money for them and giving it back to their families. It is just a thought, but it keeps me going forward.

On my day off I wake up to The Producer arguing on the phone. He has left his room for the first time in days and is sitting on the sofa outside my bedroom door in his boxer shorts. His stomach has grown bigger. The Producer's weapon for self-destruction is not drugs or booze, but food. He is talking to Samson Night's girlfriend and they are in a very heated discussion. He is trying hard to get his point across in a calm manner. His fists absorb the frustration. He is holding a *Mid Day* paper with a picture of me on it. The last words he says are, "So sue me". He cuts the call.

"What going on?"

"Samson's girlfiend is trying to get funny. The papers have obviously got their facts screwed up."

Lighting a cigarette, he throws the paper at me. I wish I could have one, but with his mood I don't dare smoke in front of him. I read the article attached to my picture. It's all about me and that I am Samson Night's girlfriend's sister, the prettier sister who will land a film faster that her.

"Did you give the press that bullshit story that you are Samson's girlfriend's sister aspiring to be an actress?"

"I've never spoken to the press. I never left your side at the launch, don't you remember? They took this picture when we were walking down the red carpet. I swear, I've never ... Why would I ...?"

"Okay."

"Now what?"

"Nothing. The sulky bitch is pissed off because they think you're her sister. She wants to sue you if you said it or the press if they said it. Don't worry, I've sorted it out. She must take it up with the papers. We've got fuck all to do with it."

It's Sunday and we are not shooting. I'm trying to figure out how I am going to keep myself occupied. I am always alone. The voices in my head are starting to sound like a thousand people sitting at my dining room table so that I cannot hear what they are saying anymore, too loud, too many.

The Producer calls me to his room. Samson's girlfriend has

made the press write a new article correcting the mistake. She has made sure that it is clear to anyone who cares that I am NOT her sister and will not be landing a Bollywood film anytime soon. Is she worried that I'm trying to ride on her 'fame' or is it because the press thinks I'm as pretty as she is?

She can't even spell my name right.

I get up to go back to my room.

"Where you going?"

"To watch *Love Actually* and finish my painting."

"How many times can a person watch the same film over and over?"

"Many times, it makes me feel good."

"Really? I need to feel good. Okay, bring it here, we watch together."

Is The Producer reaching out to me? Are we actually going to spend the day together?

The Producer calls Sai to order in pizza and ice cream; he enjoys the film.

"I want to make the Bollywood version of this film."

I laugh at him.

"No, really, thank you, it's a beautiful film Gené-baba. I will make this film."

I have managed to touch the inside of the place where he can still feel, even if it's just for today.

Bombay begins to dry out; the monsoon season is over. The Producer is more secretive than ever. He takes all the calls on his old mobile phone, but rejects or ignores every call that comes through on the new one. He keeps it face down and on silent, but it vibrates all the time. He sporadically checks my phone, scrolling through it, often querying numbers I have dialed or numbers that have called me. He never responds to my reasons, it makes me feel guilty even though I have done nothing wrong. It's the fucking Spanish Inquisition around here.

Roti has developed severe epilepsy. His seizures have become part of our daily life. The servants protect his large limbs and body from getting hurt when he has the fits. He is never alone – there is always someone by his side with a cold cloth and a sock for his mouth. I can see the toll the seizures are having on his body; apparently it's his heart that is taking the strain. Although he is still walked every day he is quieter than before and he is greying around his eyes and nose. His big brown eyes reflect a deep-seated sadness that cannot be cured. I know The Producer sees it too.

To date I have worked on eighty-seven commercials. I am ready to move on. Kush and I have one last commercial to work on before I go on to Kiran Cooper's film and he goes to NYU. New male blood has joined Luna; they will be taking over from us.

After working flat out on our last commercial, I get home having only had very little sleep in four days. I want my bed. Nisha calls and wants to take me to a party. I cannot turn her down, I have not seen her since the disastrous break up. After her break up she became terribly depressed and would not speak to me. I sent Trainer to see her. He put her on a healthy eating and exercise plan. Now that she is looking and feeling better we speak almost every day. She accepts what has happened and is in search of a new man to marry. I would like to believe that she does not hold any of what happened against me. I want her to believe that her ship will come in one day and she will find happiness. I must accept her invite.

The Producer, as usual, is in Delhi. I decide not to tell him. He won't be checking on me, he never does when he is in Delhi. Something is keeping him way too occupied over there. I give Sai and Kutty some bribe money and tell them not to say anything when he returns. It's just an innocent party so I don't feel deceptive although I know The Producer will see it differently. The Producer will only land at 8am tomorrow. There is plenty of time to party.

Nisha and I have a fabulous evening. I meet a friend of a friend from London. He has played a lot of polo with my friends and we have a lot to talk about. It is nice to interact with a guy my age. It's 5am and the sun is rising when we drop Nisha. When we get to The Producer's building we decide to take a walk on the beach, it's going to be a beautiful day. I see Balkran arriving on his motorbike. I wave, thinking nothing of it.

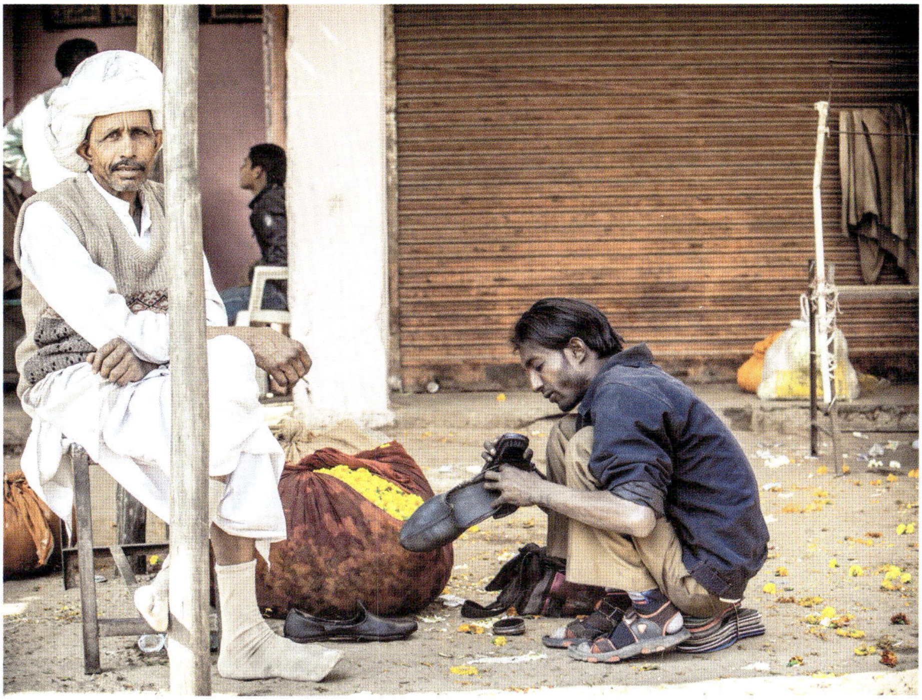

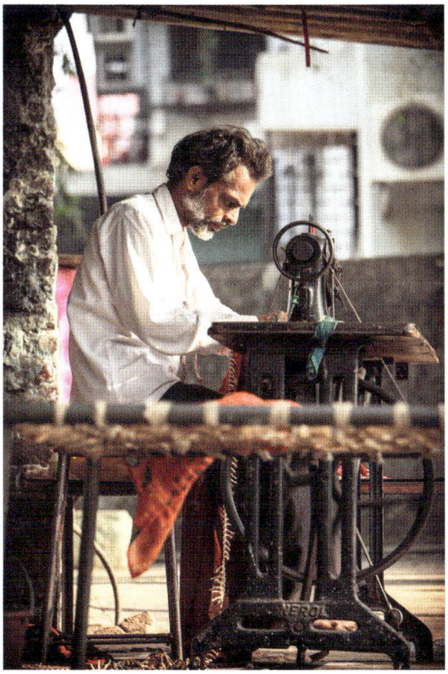

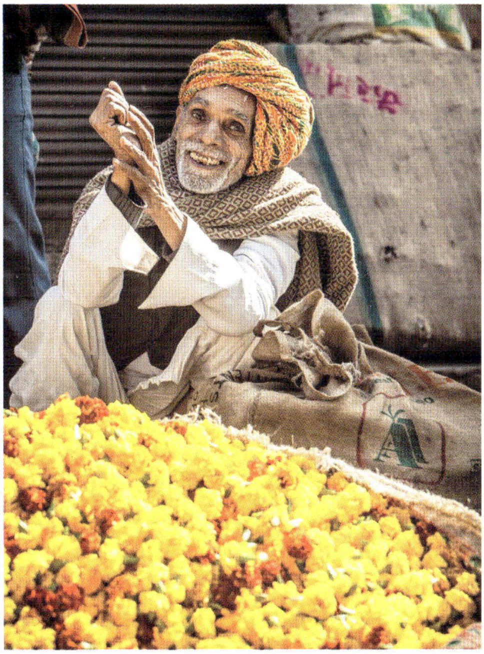

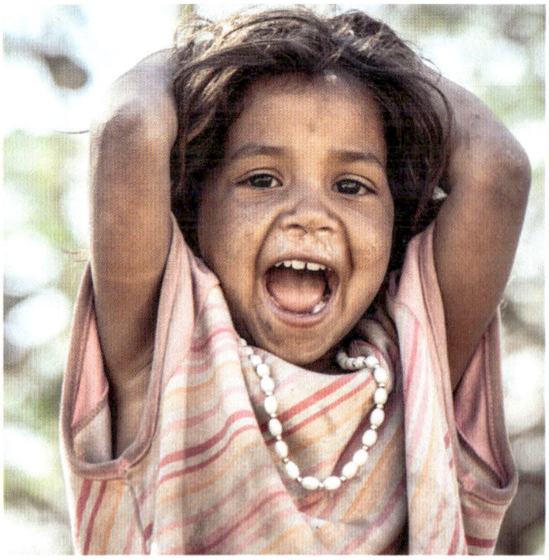

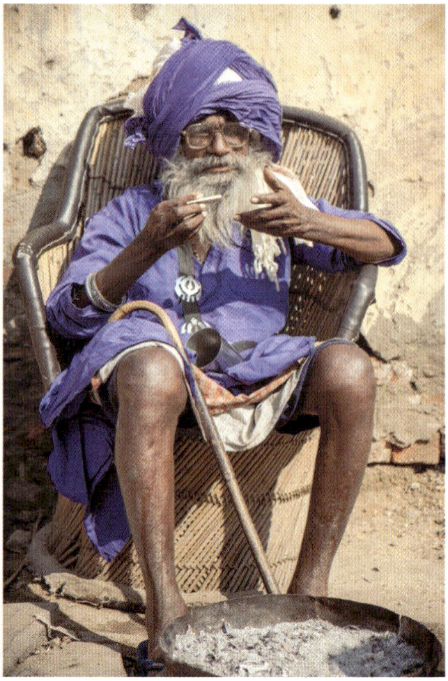

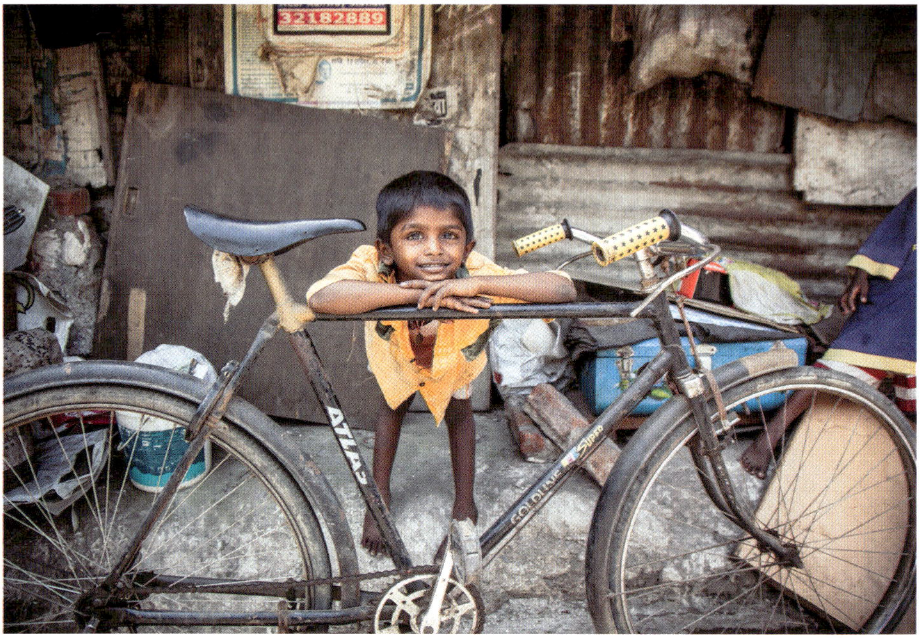
32182889
ATLAS

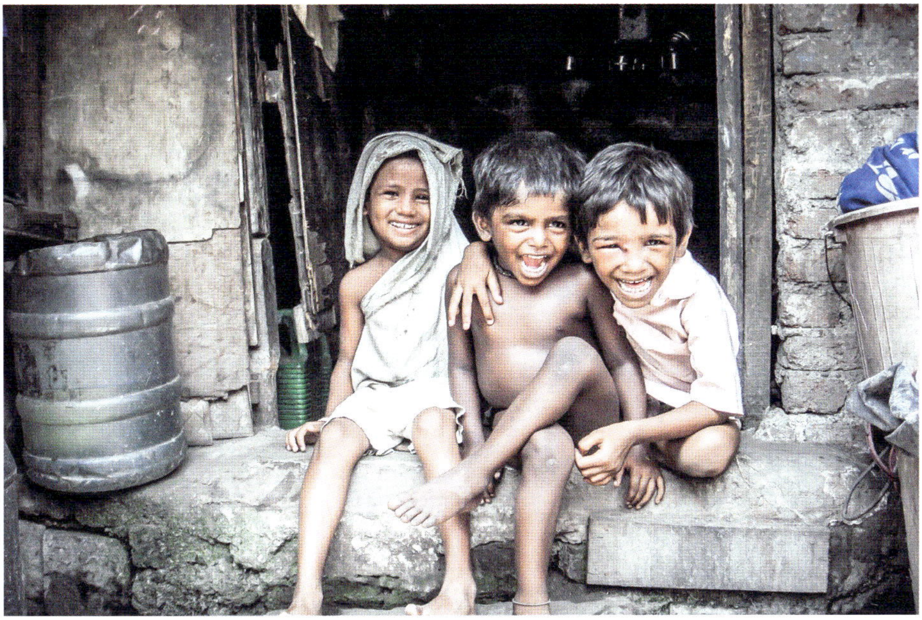

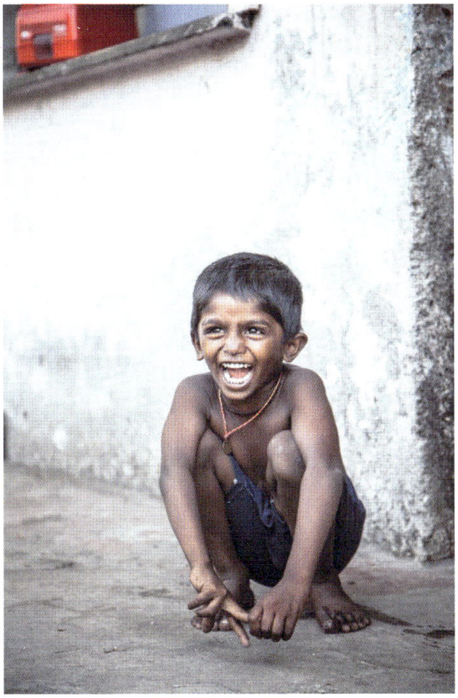

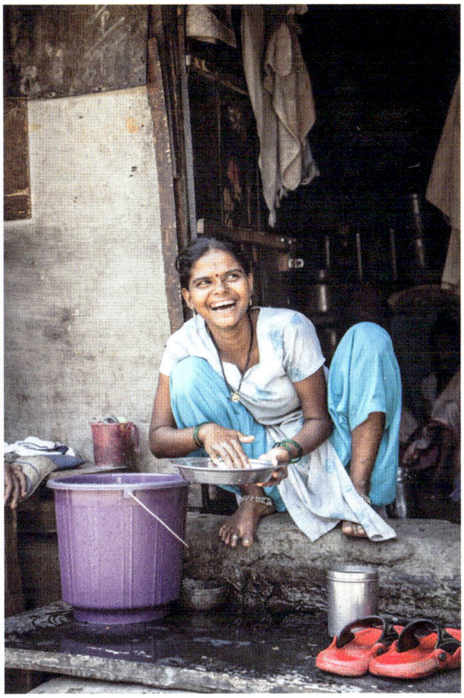

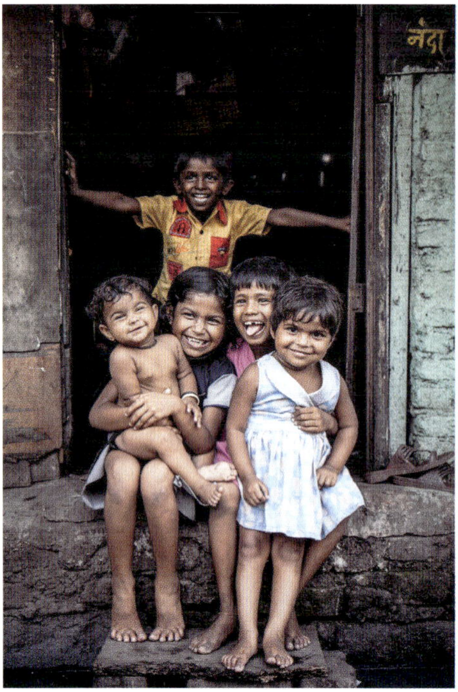
नंदा

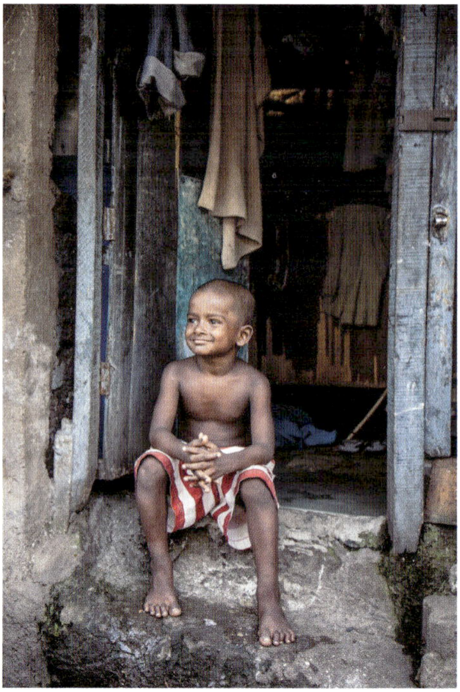

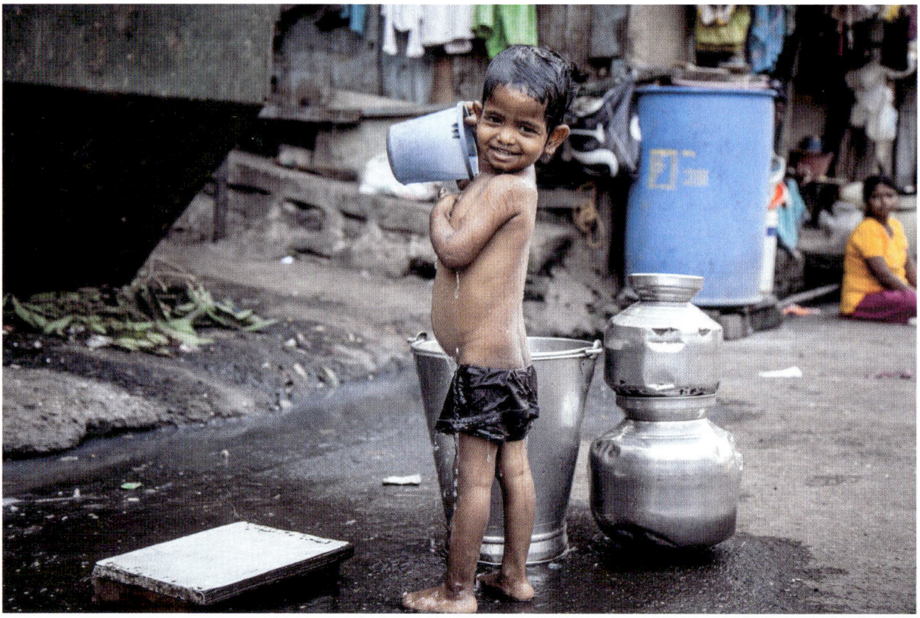

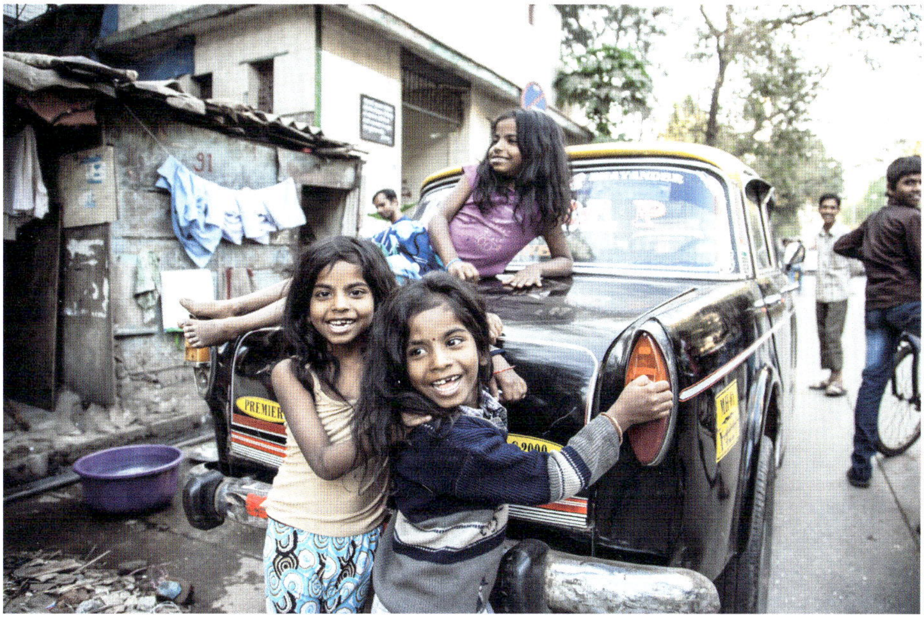
PREMIER

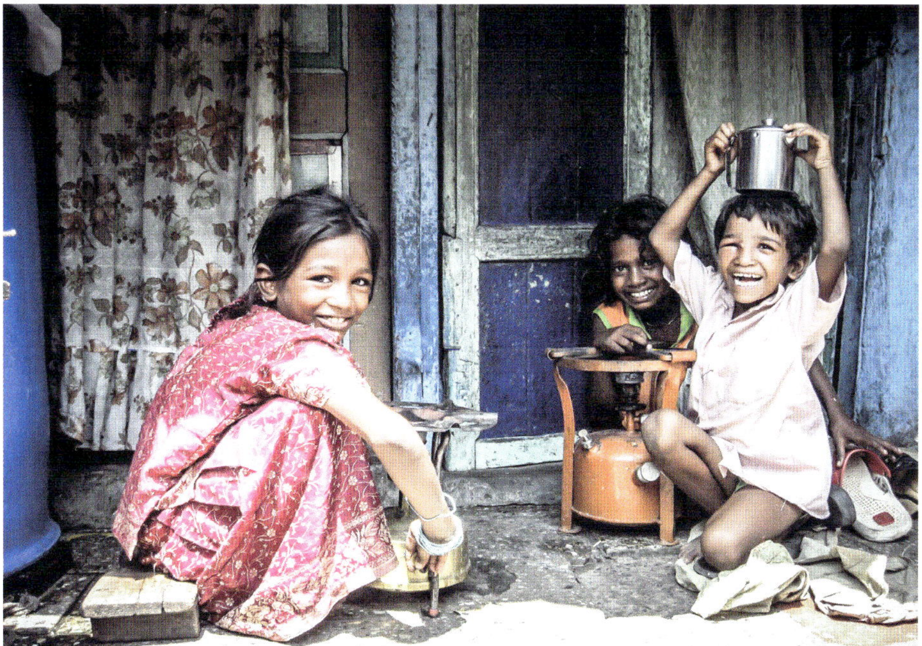

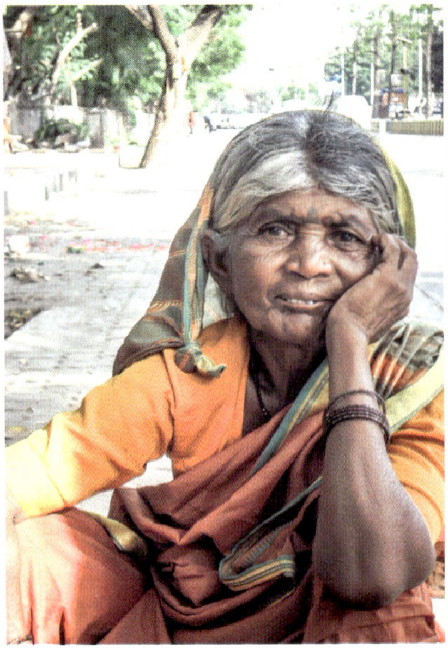
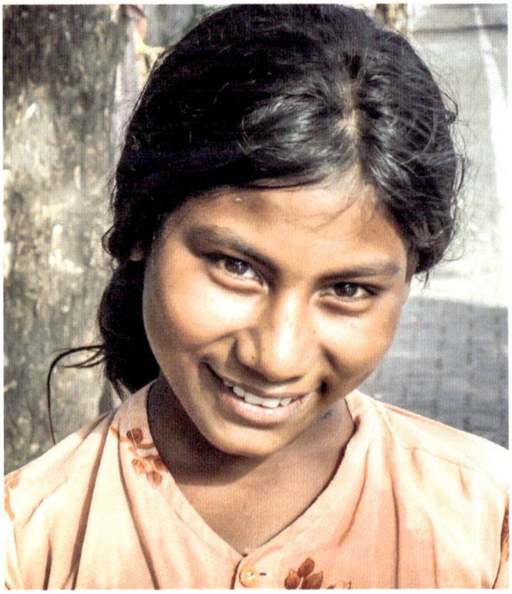
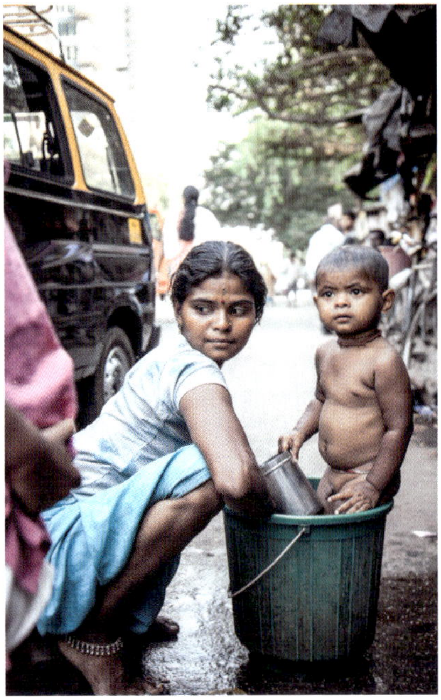
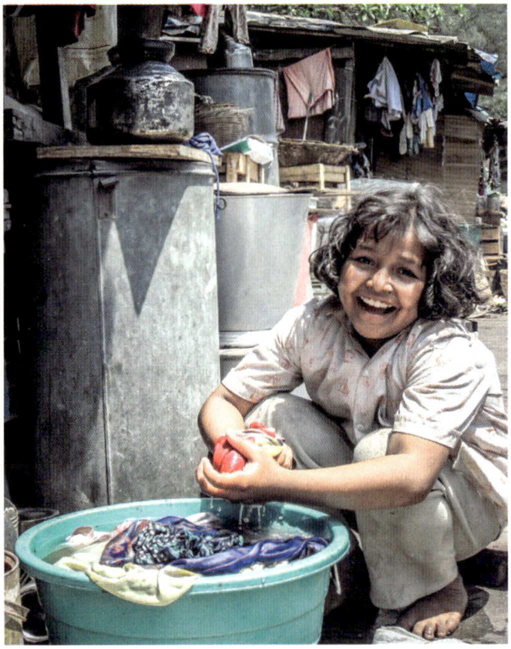

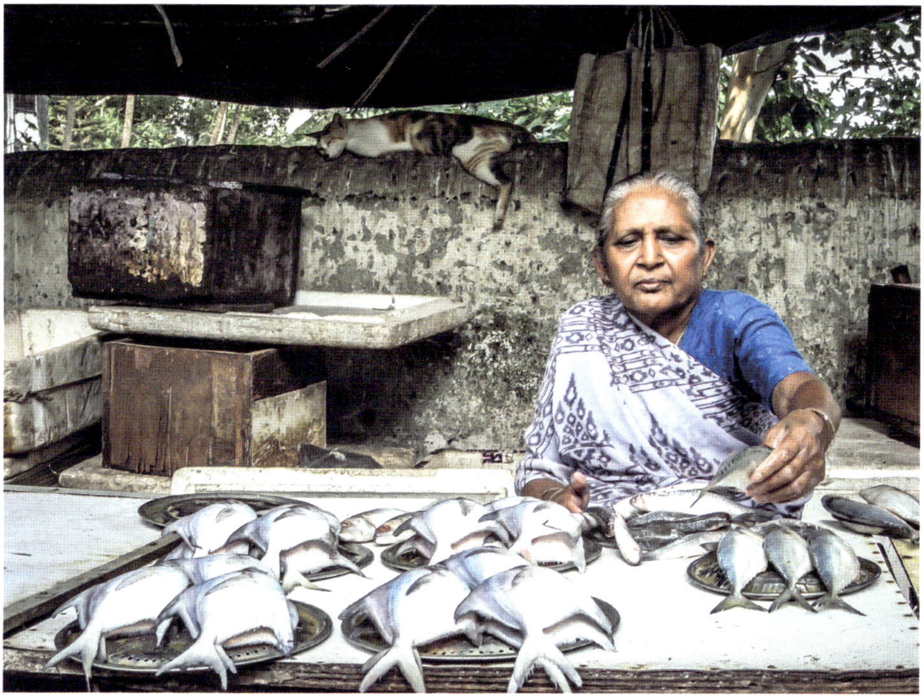

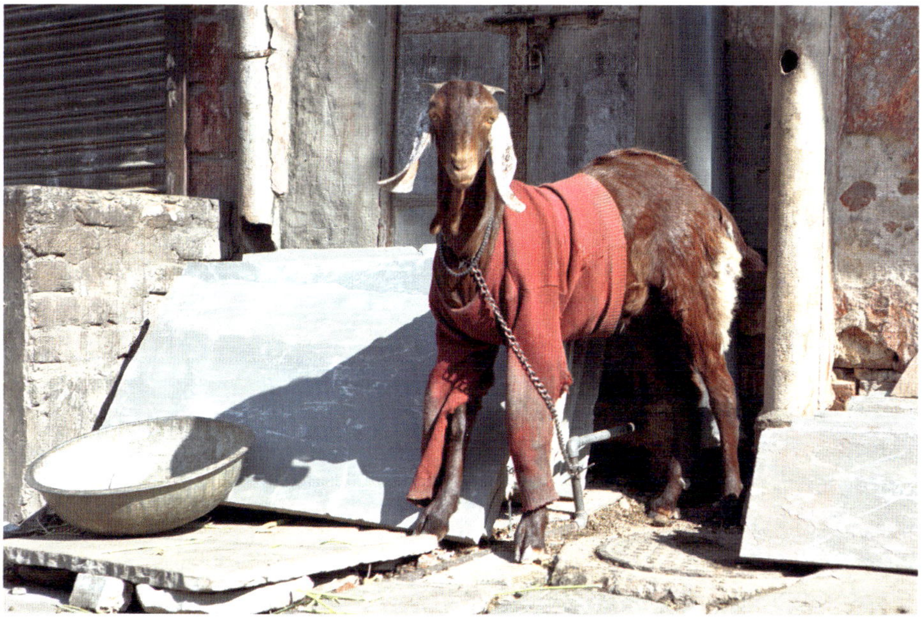

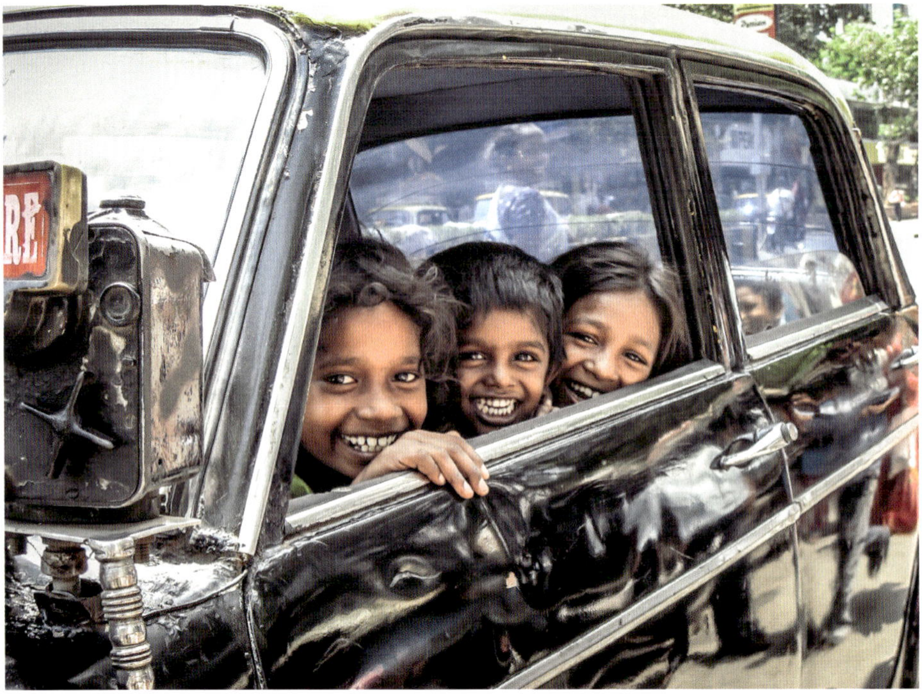

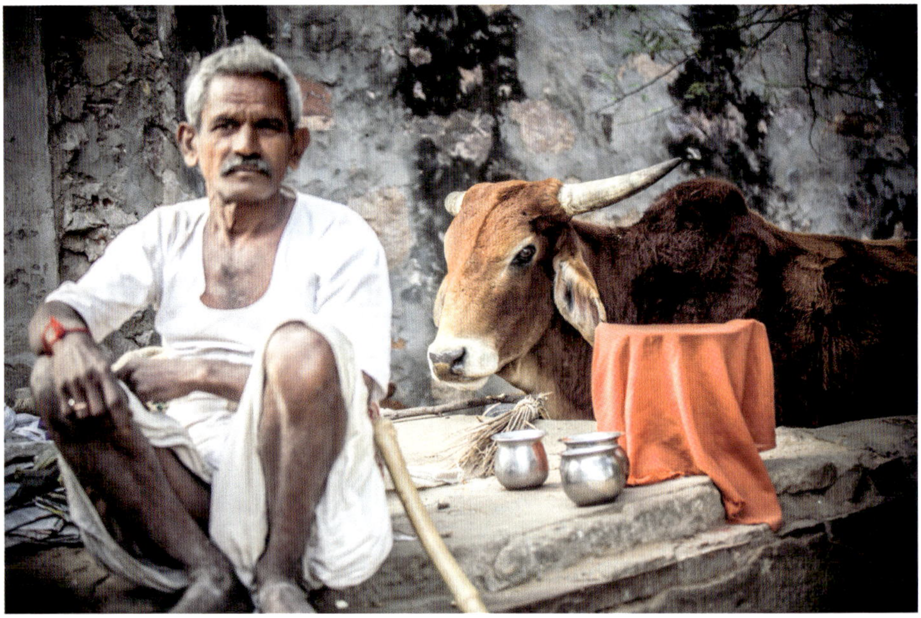

The Producer comes to the office. He leaves early. I get a lift home with Alisha. He's asleep when I get in. I wake up to him standing over me, he is holding another paper in his hand, he is angry. Now what? I'm done with the press.

"You went out while I was away."

"I did, I went with Nisha."

"Obviously."

He thrashes the paper across the silk bedding.

"I told you I hate it when you lie."

"I'm not lying. I just said I went with Nisha."

"What are you hiding?"

"Nothing."

"Did Nisha have a sex change?"

"No."

"Stop fucking lying, you were on the beach all night with Kush, I'm not fucking stupid."

"Kush? No I wasn't, I went for a walk with a friend of a friend of mine from London that I met at the party ..."

"Are you sick in the head?"

"No."

"You know what? I don't care anymore! Just stay out of my fucking way. You're embarrassing me. People will think you're having an affair behind my back. I suggest you sort your head out."

"What about you having an affair behind my back?"

"You will never know if I'm having an affair."

His phone vibrates. He doesn't take the call until he has exploded out of the room.

Balkran, why? It was just a walk.

Love? Not actually

The only conversations I have with The Producer for the next two weeks are the ones in my head. They are fuelled with confusion, frustration and anger. He makes me feel horrible about myself. I become as miserable as he is, but I cling to the idea of working on a real Bollywood film with one of India's greatest directors. At mealtimes, we eat in silence, the food sticking in my throat. I want to scream across the table for a reaction. I don't, instead I pile my plate with chillies and eat them all. He says nothing. I chew on them quickly, my eyes water, I hold back the tears. I bite a hole into my tongue; it bleeds. The chillies sting the open wound. I taste how pathetically needy and desperately weak I have become. I get sick alone in my room, it feels like I am breathing flames, the masticated chillies repeat on me; I'm on fire. I am desperate to love him but he won't let me. Please … Please let me love you?

Alisha sends Dr Bollywood to the house to see The Producer for high blood pressure. He is put onto strong tablets to keep it under control. At this stage he is the perfect heart attack candidate. I take the opportunity and ask Dr Bollywood to administer my injection so that I don't have to be alone with him in his consulting rooms.

My spirits lift when Kiran Cooper comes to visit The Producer to discuss the film. He is finalising the script and music. Music always has to be created first in a Bollywood film so that the dance sequences can be shot and the actors know which words they are miming to. The script is based on *One Flew over the Cuckoo's Nest*. Samson Night will play the part of Jack Nicholson.

The film will be shot in two countries, Romania and India. There are two heroines in the film. We have confirmed one of them for the Indian part of the film, but we have still not found the heroine for the Romanian part. The dates are confirmed – we will shoot in Romania first. Samson presses The Producer to give his girlfriend a break and let her play the Romanian part; The Producer refuses.

In the evenings groups of musicians have begun visiting The Producer's apartment to pitch for the music. There are usually three men in a group. One will tap or clap out a rhythm with his hands, a second will take up the beat making a variety of clicking, raspberry and other sounds with his mouth and tongue, the third man sings. They are so talented that they can harmonise beautifully, creating a perfectly balanced song. Kiran Cooper and The Producer listen to their suggestions and call one or two groups back, listening to them again and again before making their final choice. I never get tired of the harmonious sounds permeating the previously empty silence of this cold marble house. I am in awe of this prehistoric method of making music.

Kiran Cooper wants me to be more that just his assistant. He has always encouraged my photography. He suggests that I handle the stills on set as well as the continuity over and above being his assistant. The Producer agrees. He likes the idea, he will save some money not having to employ, fly and accommodate a photographer in Romania. I will simultaneously take care of continuity. This suggestion is beneficial to all of us. One person, three jobs and I will ride on The Producer's accommodation and share with him.

The Producer flies to Delhi. The heaviness lifts.

My phone rings. It's Kiran Cooper.

"My dear aa ... Harvey, my art director, is coming to town tonight. We would love you to join us for dinner aa ... we are staying next door to you at the Holiday Inn."

I know I should not, but I would be creating a reason for another episode with The Producer. I cannot explain The Producer's hold on me nor his jealousy – not to the man who is about to make a huge film with The Producer. Besides, he would find it absolutely ludicrous and it would sound stupid if I were to say "no sorry, The Producer will get angry."

"I would love to join you, Kiran Cooper Sir, what time?"

"Eight-thirty."

I find Harvey and Kiran Cooper seated in the hotel restaurant. Harvey has just returned from an overseas trip. He gives me a full carton of cigarettes as a gift.

"Try these, they are really good; you can't get them in India and all."

A crowd gathers around our table. They want Kiran Cooper's autograph. Kiran Cooper speaks kindly to his fans and poses with them as they stretch out, pushing their mobile phones at him. Something catches his unpatched eye from behind a pot plant that isn't a camera flash.

"My dear aa ... isn't your boyfriend out of town?"

"He was when I left home."

"Then aa ... I think he has sent someone to spy on us."

I push the chair from under me; my body moves without thinking. I storm towards the large pot-plant in the middle of the restaurant. Between the foliage, two human eyes stare at me, blinking like Christmas lights. My blood boils. "SAI!!!"

When I get home I put my full carton of cigarettes next to my bed in clear view.

The next day, Alisha drops me home after work; I sit in my bedroom painting. I know The Producer will want to check my phone tonight; if he wants it he will have to come and fetch it.

I wait. Fifteen minutes go by. I wait. Eventually The Producer comes in.

"I'm back."

"Hi."

True to my predictions ...

"I need your phone."

I do not get off the bed, I hold it out for him to come and get it. As he nears the bed I see him look down at the long metallic red carton, the light bouncing off its shine has caught his eye.

"What is this?"

I carry on painting as I answer him.

"A gift from Harvey Sydnam."

"A what?"

He has developed an angry growl in his voice. It pushes out from his gut, making his words rumble.

"I had dinner with Kiran Cooper and Harvey at the hotel next door. Harvey gave them to me as a gift; he's just come back from New York."

"You think you fucking clever, don't you? You and Kiran Cooper can go ahead and do what the fuck you want!"

His growl has turned into a shout, a shout that is a million times better than his silence. He storms out, taking my carton with him. I skip dinner.

He comes back after he's eaten. Now I'm scared. He does not come in. He stands at the door and hisses at me, his tongue slipping with rage as he spits the words out.

"I suggest you fucking start eating, you getting too fucking thin, it doesn't suit you."

I cannot believe what he is actually saying. I smile without smiling.

He leaves. I watch *Love Actually* ... again.

Last Minute.com

After another two weeks of silent treatment I find myself sitting on the large mustard sofa in the apartment with The Producer and Kiran Cooper the night before we are due to fly to Romania. We still do not have an actress to take with us. The biggest problem is that if we find someone tonight she will need a visa and that takes time. Samson Night's girlfriend sees an opportunity to try again for the part. She knows The Producer is desperate and because she has a Russian passport, she does not need a visa for Romania. She calls The Producer, but he refuses her again. The Producer desperately tracks down an actress who has recently shot a film in Romania – she is called in for an interview. Kiran Cooper is not convinced, he pleads with The Producer to postpone the shoot and not rush into something, but The Producer is adamant he needs to get away from India to avoid his *Stolen Hearts* film release.

The first day of a movie release in India is like waiting for election results. As the attendance numbers start coming in they show how many cinemas have released the film and how many people have gone to the release. This gives the producer a clear indication of how well the film will do. The Producer's mobile phone rings off the hook.

I have finished my painting. I proudly hang it off the nail that Gaya had knocked in. Perfect. I look fabulous up there, give a dog a bone!

The Producer and I fly with Kiran Cooper, Harvey and the director of photography. The rest of the crew will join us later once we are ready to start filming.

We have arrived in Bucharest at the tail end of summer; the weather is warm, the conditions are comfortable. We stay at the JW Marriot. I like it inside, it helps me forget about the miserable outsides. I share a double suite with The Producer. We each have our own three-quarter bed. Because we are in a suite, we get access to a VIP lounge that has Wi-Fi and a free twenty-four-hour buffet, The Producer encourages me to only eat from there, he makes it sound ideal, but I know he wants to save money. There is a casino in the hotel and The Producer gets sucked in straight away. He leaves me in charge and disappears during the day. Sometimes he does not come back until the early hours of the morning. This suits me as I can watch what I want to watch on television and visit Kiran Cooper and Harvey in their rooms.

We need to prep for two weeks in Romania before we can start shooting. The Producer has hired a facilitating production house in Romania called Random Films. The owner of the company is a young Romanian called Bronko. Like The Producer, Bronko is obsessed with the brand Hugo Boss. They have a little competition going on between them. Bronko drives a slick gold convertible and drowns himself in Pacco Robanne Ultraviolet perfume. He smells like the inside of his car, the leather seats have absorbed him. There's not much to absorb – he's a shallow man.

We do not have a finished script. Kiran Cooper is still working on it in his head and adds to it as we go along. We have no schedule and no idea where we want to shoot because Kiran Cooper has never been to Romania. The Producer has – it was his idea to shoot here. Because Romania had not joined the European Union, their currency, Lei, is cheaper than the Euro, making it ideal for The Producer's pocket. The Romanian crew is horrified at how disorganised we are. This is how Bollywood gets things done, fuelled by chaos, bringing fear and confusion to the order of the Western world. We sit around the boardroom table shifting their way of doing things to suit us. If they want to survive these forty days, they are going to do it the Bollywood way.

Italy is Romania's main trading partner which means that many of the Romanians speak or at least understand Italian, so I can communicate with them easily. I use this to my advantage and become the go-to girl for everything. This is exactly where I want to be. I thrive on the chaos and excitement of it all and together we find solutions to move forward for the sake of the bigger picture. Magically, everything comes together at the last minute and we are ready to shoot.

Harvey has one last errand to run. He asks me if he can get me anything while he's out – I have been stuck in the office for over a week.

It is safe for me to spend the evening with 'my boys' – The Producer has met up with a friend from school who owns hotels, cellular networks and restaurants all over Romania. They are going to a casino on the other side of town and they will be there all night.

Samson Night flies in with Spy, The Producer's right-hand man on feature films and the cousin that Nisha lives with.

There is a knock on the door. When I open it Spy is standing with a coconut under his arm, the one we are going to smash on the floor after the first take tomorrow. His sweaty assistant, wearing the same thick glasses as Spy, with the same shaped moustache as everyone at Luna, stands behind him with a hotel trolley overloaded with cheap bottled water and instant packet food from India.

"What you are doing in director's room?"

"Hello Spy."

He ignores my enthusiastic manners. His bottle-bottomed spectacles are misted up. He's been busy.

"You must stop drinking water of hotel. Jimmy, you must be coming to my room and your box collecting. I am not running after you. I am noting Kiran Cooper and Harvey, this is room service ordering, but I will be supplying Indian packet food from now on, because we are not wanting you people to be ordering hotel foods because it is expensive, I am chief executive for saving money."

We are initially dumbstruck and then Harvey explodes.

"I haven't worked this hard to be told that I can't eat in the hotel I am staying in, the hotel is in my contract, and now we are being told to eat packaged food and all. Who the hell does he think he is?"

"The Producer's cousin, 'chief executive for saving money', so that The Producer has more to gamble with."

Breaking the silence

Samson Night is a loose cannon. He needs to be looked after when he is not on set, especially at night. He loves to party. He has a huge following in Romania. Bollywood films are very popular in the Eastern Bloc. Everyone at Random Films is excited to meet him, especially Sophia, Bronko's assistant.

"So what's he like?"

"He has the biggest heart."

I interrupt her thought by reminding her that we will need a bee on the set, the day we shoot in the church.

"If we have a bee we have to have an animal wrangler."

I'm amused and think about Pierre Bordeaux.

"The Producer will never agree to pay for a wrangler."

"What if the actress gets stung?"

"Then she get's stung and we carry on shooting. There are many worse things that have happened on Indian film sets."

"Is he as beautiful as on screen? Is his body and long hair really that beautiful?"

I had met Sophia's boyfriend, who was very tall and overweight with glasses. Like many Romanian men he was 'unlovely'.

"I guess so."

When Samson walks onto set, Sophia sheds a tear; she is completely in awe of him.

Together The Producer, Samson and Bronko hit the streets at night. The Producer never gets in before three or four in the morning. I can smell him in my sleep. When the strong mixture of mercury perfume and cigarette smoke assaults me I know he's back. My call time is always hours before Samson's. The Producer gets him to set by dragging him out of bed and making sure he's in the car with the body guards before he goes back to bed, hitting the casinos once he's had enough sleep. He comes to set when we wrap to keep Samson entertained again at night. Playing the neighbourhood watchdog is taking its toll. He looks exhausted. We are like passing ships. I am never asked to join them at night. In the mornings I always hear Bronko talking about the fantastic night and all the girls they've had fun with. I ask Sophia about their recreational adventures, she only has one answer for me.

"My boss is a very naughty boy."

Many Indian men find it essential to behave inappropriately when in a foreign country. It's as if they cannot control themselves, behaving like dogs drooling over a bone. They try their luck with the 'white girls' and will go to great lengths to get themselves into strip clubs and brothels, even though they are married or involved. Romania is the ideal location to satisfy some of our crew's hunger, the drool lies in puddles as we work. The streets are like a candy store with the continuous flow of passing women. It's summer, the dress code is minimal and I am yet to see an ugly girl in this place. Was this the ideal place for Kiran Cooper's film or is it the ideal playground for The Producer's gambling and lust for women? I am relieved that The Producer and I are not on very good terms. The fear of having to sleep with him when there is so much available pussy going around scares the shit out of me. I know his take on condoms and I am too weak to insist; this will open up a whole new can of ghee. I latch on to Kiran Cooper and Harvey who are only interested in the film and sitting in their room drinking whisky over room service and interesting conversation. I find solace when I am with them until The Producer puts a stop to it.

"You are starting your nonsense again."

"What have I done now?"

"Don't act dumb with me. You have been drinking in Kiran Cooper's room every night since we got here. I told you before, you are not to go drinking with them at night. Understand? You have a perfectly decent buffet upstairs. I suggest you stop messing around and concentrate on your work."

How does he know what I do at night when he is never around? Spy!

I explain the situation to Kiran Cooper and Harvey – they are upset.

Harvey calmly comforts my embarrassment. "He is just a very insecure man. For your best interests we must be aware because that goldfish-faced cousin of his will make trouble for you. We have nothing to lose and he cannot harm us, but he can make your life very miserable. Let us stop meeting for a few days. Spy will get tired of checking and then we can take it from there again."

He gives me *The BFG* to read. "This giant might be keeping you good company at night."

In the evenings I occupy my time by swimming in the hotel pool where I meet Donald Sutherland. On my first evening at the pool I choose the lane running along the edge. I am face down in the water when somebody taps me on the shoulder. I stop and look up in surprise. It's Donald, smiling down at me, his silver hair escaping his swimming cap, his penetrating eyes piercing sharply into my bubble of surprise.

"Would you mind if I took this lane? It's twenty centimetres shorter and three degrees warmer than the others."

He laughs at my confusion and nods toward a stereotypical Russian-looking man standing with his bulging arms folded in front of him, wearing a black suit with a wire in his ear.

"Security reasons, just in case."

I happily oblige.

In the early mornings before call time, I catch him in the

VIP lounge at breakfast. He often sits with Sissy Spacek, who is shooting a film in Bucharest. I ask him to autograph a napkin for me, which he graciously obliges. Starting and ending my days with this star reminds me why I'm here; I still want to believe in the magic of film.

I get back from set exhausted. I decide to skip my swim, have a shower and go straight to bed. I start drifting when a mobile phone that's not mine tears me away from my land of nod. It's The Producer's mobile phone and it's not on silent. Is he here? I scramble for the light, suddenly in shock. Has he been here all along?

"Hello?"

Nothing.

I give myself the creeps. I find the light and adjust my bleary eyes.

No one.

The phone starts ringing again. I keep thinking it's impossible that The Producer would leave his phone, but he has. He has because he has hardly slept in days. The mobile phone is in the pocket of a pair of jeans. I cannot resist. Before it cuts again I answer.

"Hello."

An annoyed women's voice snaps back at me.

"Who is dis?"

"Gené. The Producer left his phone here, can I take a message?"

It's not Gaya. I don't recognise the voice.

"Where did he leave it?" She becomes angry.

"In our hotel room, can I give him a mess …?"

She hangs up without another word.

I turn off the lights and go back to sleep.

The phone beeps, a message has just come through. I have to read it, I cannot resist. For so long The Producer has made his phone out to be the biggest sacred secret. Now here it is available for me to scrutinise like he does mine. I read the message. It's sharp and nasty.

"You bastard. You will not get away with this. I will make sure the truth comes out. Do you not have blood running through your veins? Do you even know the meaning of love?"

I read it again and again. I cannot believe what I am looking at. I forward the message to my phone. I have to keep it, one day I'm going to need to use it, but now is not the right time. I have to finish this film. I cannot have come to Bollywood without doing a Bollywood film. Ninety-seven commercials don't count. I put the phone back where I found it. I cannot sleep so I go down to the pool. It's almost midnight. I slip under the dark still water and start doing laps.

I sit under the hair dryer in the cloakroom. The noise does not block out the raging thoughts and accusations that are flying across my mind. I sit in the VIP lounge alone playing with the snacks on my plate that I have taken off the buffet. No one comes in while I am there. At 4am I go back to my room to change for work. The Producer is still not back from his night trip with Samson and 'the boys'.

I drive with Kiran Cooper to the Orthodox Church where we are shooting. Harvey has dressed the church for the funeral scene with plenty of candles and flowers, a beautiful silk-lined coffin balances on a pedestal. The grips are helping our actress climb in with her wedding dress. She lies as still as possible, looking dead while Samson puts glycerin in his eyes, pretending to weep.

The bee arrives on set in a jar. It is lifeless and cannot fly. Kiran Cooper decides to artificially replicate the bee in post-production. Problem solved. We move on.

There is absolute silence on set as a choir sings mournfully. Samson cries hysterically over the actress in the coffin, trying to swat an imaginary bee. The Producer charges into the church like a bull, shouting. He is spitting; his finger points at me.

"What the fuck do you think you're doing you fucking bitch?"

He grabs me by my shoulders and pushes me up against the wall. His purpling face pushes up against mine. His breath smells like a bad lifestyle.

His words tumble down on me like an avalanche.

"Who the fuck do you think you are? You think you clever, huh? Sneaking around on my phone, forwarding my messages to other people, how dare you? Don't just fucking stand there acting dumb."

Nobody moves except the actress in the coffin who sits bolt upright. He has woken the dead. My mouth goes dry; the blood drains from my face. Out of the corner of my eye I see a cameraman, high up on a crane, signal to the grip to lower him down onto solid ground. The front of my T-shirt is twisted and balled up in his fist; his knuckles dig into my sternum. He shakes me back and forth; I feel like a limp ragdoll.

"I'm sorry, I only sent the message to my ..."

"Don't you dare, dare fucking lie to me now, you hear me?"

The local priest comes running down the aisle. He asks us to leave, this is the house of God.

Samson leads us down the aisle, out the double stain-glassed doors. The Romanian crew stands with their mouths open, their eyes wide. The Indian crew look to the floor. They know what it's like to be at the receiving end of The Producer's wrath.

The Producer comes for me again; this time Samson holds him back, pushing us apart.

"I said I am sorry, I only wanted ..."

I had failed to realise the obvious – when forwarding the message he would see it had been forwarded. The woman had obviously got hold of him again. He would also have seen that I took her call. My voice begins to crack. I cannot get another word out. I start to cry; I'm in shock.

Bronko stands at the door, watching in horror. Samson's arm leans against me like a boom keeping me at arms length from The Producer, I push it away and start walking. I am done. I'm tired of pretending. I walk and I don't look back. I need to get to the hotel, get my bags and catch a cab to the airport. There is nothing left here for me; without The Producer I cannot stay. I want to say sorry to Kiran Cooper and Harvey, but there's no chance I'm going back, not now. I keep walking.

Someone is following me. It's Samson Night.

"Gené, please stop. Hey come on, we can work it out. It's just a small misunderstanding and all. Come back so I can help you. Hey Gené please, stop. Kiran Cooper needs you, we all need you, especially The Producer."

He catches up to me, grabbing hold of my arm that's been swinging at my side with purpose. I stop and turn to him pulling my arm away from his grip. His two bodyguards stand at his side. Behind him are over a hundred fans who have followed us, all trying to get a piece of him. Great, my personal issues have just been shared with half of Bucharest.

He takes my hand.

"Please? You can't go like this, not after all ..."

I want to be true to Kiran Cooper and say goodbye properly.

Samson takes me back to the church. He buys me a soda along the way.

"Your body needs the sugar."

The Producer is standing against the wall smoking a cigarette. Bronko is calmly talking him off his rearing horse. Everyone is standing around; they cannot shoot without Samson. We walk past The Producer, back into the church. The more the crew tries not to look at me, the more obvious it is that they are looking at me. I stand next to Kiran Cooper not saying a word. He calls for order.

"Okay, let's start from the top."

The Producer does not enter the church again.

When we break for lunch, I sit with Kiran Cooper and Harvey; I don't want to be anywhere near The Producer. I hope he gambles all night again so that I don't have to see him in the room.

I can see Samson talking to The Producer and I know it's about the fight. I don't want to know what his version of the story is. After lunch, Samson calls me over. Pulling my hand towards The Producer's he cradles them together.

"Say sorry to each other."

I've never seen The Producer listen to anyone like this before.

"Sorry."

"You can do better than that, brother. Give her a hug."

It all feels so fake, I don't want a sorry or a hug. I know The Producer is appeasing Samson. The Producer is trying to run a business, not a sorority club. He hugs me in front of everyone. Then we move on to the next scene and The Producer goes back to the hotel to do some 'work'.

Kiran Cooper sits me down after wrap. He becomes solemn, takes a deep breath, holding my hand securely in his, and speaks gently, but assertively.

"My dear aa ... Why aa ... you let him abuse you like that? I never want to see you cry like that again, instead aa ... you fight back."

Job offer

We have a week to go before we move to Brasov. I get back to the hotel after wrap and find The Producer and Bronko waiting for me in the foyer. They want to take me out for dinner. They have something they want to discuss with me. Strange. They seem in good spirits. I can't imagine what I have done wrong this time.

We sit in a Lebanese restaurant.

"What's going on?"

The Producer smiles at me.

"We have a job proposal for you. Bronko and I want to bring more work to Romania, he wants to attract more Bollywood business. You understand Romanian, but you also understand Bollywood and how we work. You will be the ideal mediator between the two countries."

Bronko interrupts.

"I have seen how you work and you are very good at what you do. I can give you a place to stay, a car and a much better salary than The Producer."

He laughs at The Producer.

"Watch what you promise, you may be surprised at what we pay her."

"What does he pay you?"

The Producer answers for me.

"Let's keep the monies for later."

"So what you think, Gené?"

I look at The Producer.

"What about this film and my work in India?"

"I have told Bronko that you can join him in January after we complete this film. It's time to move on, besides, you've learnt everything you can in India. There is no other level for you to move up to, for a white girl that does not speak and read fluent Hindi you have reached your peak."

I don't know what to say, but they both look so convincingly chuffed.

"Okay, as long as I can finish my film with Kiran Cooper."

"Of course, and don't worry, I will see lots of you. Bronko and I plan to do a lot of work together."

After dinner The Producer comes back to the room.

"Don't discuss any monies and what your deal was with me; I will handle your contract for you."

His mood flutters lightly, a butterfly that has just discovered its wings. A weight has lifted off his shoulders. Is it because he's just found a way to get rid of me without having to say the words, "it's over"? Alisha's not here to do it for him.

We shoot in Bucharest continuously for forty days. On the last day, Kiran Cooper needs a European nun that can speak Hindi and act beside Samson Night. There aren't any so Kiran Cooper chooses me. Samson and I have a lot of fun doing the scene, my bad accent makes everyone laugh. I will leave Bollywood having not only worked on a film, but acted in one too.

When I get back to the room there is a bag full of gifts spread out on my bed. They are all beautifully wrapped in red paper with big gold ribbons. The Producer is in the shower.

"Hi sweets."

He comes out wrapped in a towel; he gestures to the bed.

"For you. I had a good win today. I thought I would pick up some things for when you come and live here."

I unwrap them slowly, my feelings unravelling with them. I'm confused and unsure about this Romanian idea, but The Producer is right that India is over. I can only have a piece of India if I am with him. I become overwhelmed and concentrate on the gifts to stop the tears. An orange-and-cream snow jacket with faux fur trimmings, a pair of snow boots and a beautiful handbag from Guess. A few new pairs of jeans and some warm tops all with some bling on them.

"It's not going to be warm like this when you get back here in January."

"How cold will it be?"

"At least twenty to thirty degrees below zero."

I get up to hug him. He holds me gently and starts kissing me; his moustache is a little damp. He wants this to go somewhere.

The Producer orders room service while I shower. When I come out he has a massive spread waiting. We are a couple again, sharing each other over the one thing that keeps us connected – food.

I leave Romania convincing myself that The Producer will come and visit me as often as he can. I make the relationship what I want it to be in my head, just like The Producer said I should do. My future holds promise, promise for a life that is mine to control, promise that The Producer will come and see me as often as he can, promise that he will miss me. It is not perfect, but maybe this way we could become permanent. I love him more than I have ever loved anyone before. It's going to be perfect.

Game of dice

I walk into The Producer's house to find that Cook has gone on another drinking and fucking binge. This time The Producer does not want him back. He has employed a very experienced cook who has trained in Germany.

The cook lasts all of four days. It is Diwali and The Producer wants to have a huge party in his house. He hires rolette and black jack tables that come with croupiers wearing cream suits with pink bow ties. The Producer makes the cook cater for a hundred guests. My room is turned into a card room where the men will roll dice all night long. Sai, Balkran and Kutty do the rest of the planning for the party. Gaya has not been asked to decorate. Pierre Bordeaux is in town shooting a commercial for The Producer. He does not gamble, so we sit together at the bar for a catch up.

"Forty days of shoot! *Putain*! Three shithouse days is enough."

After midnight Nisha and I watch the magnificent fireworks from the rooftop. The cook is lying on the stretcher that he brought complaining about how hard he has to work. The next morning I see Balkran standing with the new cook – he has a bag and his stretcher under his arm. We watch him leave.

"And now, Sai?"

"Now I am cook making."

Cheeking on me

I fly to Chennai alone. The Producer stays in Bombay – he has been away from Luna for a very long time.

Chennai is colourful and glossy. It feels like it's been dipped in coconut oil and painted with enamels. The people are darker in skin tone, when they stand in the shadows they disappear, leaving eyes and wide bright smiles like Cheshire cats. Brightly painted Hindu temples adorned with godly figurines cut through the sometimes-modern sometimes-colonial skyline. The streets are highlighted with brilliant white Ambassador taxis cramming to get through the congested traffic.

Spy comes straight from Romania to Chennai. He brings his narrow-minded law down on everyone. He has turned Harvey's job into a nightmare, making him beg for everything. It is Harvey's job to make the sets look beautiful, but Spy does not see it that way. I am booked into the presidential suite at the Park Hotel in Chennai. It's a boutique hotel with plenty of character, old Bollywood film posters decorate the walls, vintage cameras and film gear adorn the halls. My room even has a television in the bathroom.

The only reason I am in such a luxurious suite is because I am sharing it with The Producer. Spy does not let me forget it.

"Because of The Producer you are too spoiling. If it were up to me ..."

I interrupt.

"If it were up to you I would be sleeping in the slum next door after kicking my legs in."

"Don't you be cheeking on me. You think you are very clever in Romania. I am big boss now. This is my ruling and you are to be listening. My job is being very difficult, very hard. I must be on set one hour before you. You being removed off production, you now just be pictures taking. Not so difficult. This is small job of insignificance. I am big money saving for The Producer."

As well as being India's topmost director, Kiran Cooper owns a percentage of South India's cinemas, sound studios and rental houses, all of which have the best American camera equipment. The south of India has its own film industry that turns out Tamil Malayalam, Kannada and Telegu films. The set that Harvey has built at AVM studios is that of a mental asylum.

He has used Salvador Dali's melting clocks as a decorative theme.

"For you Miss Gené 'G'."

Samson Night gets dragged onto set with a huge coffee mug and sunglasses most days. He is either still drunk or very hungover. It doesn't matter – he is playing a mad man and gets to lie in a hospital bed a lot of the time. Stumbling around and walking around looking retarded comes naturally when one has a monumental hangover. The main set is a hospital ward with two rows of beds, off to the side are smaller sets making up a bathroom area, reception and consulting rooms.

The Producer comes and goes depending on the commercial workload back in Bombay. When The Producer is with me we share quality time together in the mornings before going to set. We are both at our best and conversation is easy. The Producer's worry has not begun yet and he is able to give a little more of himself without distraction. We take up walking eight kilometres on the beach before sunrise, after which the heat makes walking impossible.

Chennai's Marina Beach is the widest beach in the world and

colonies of people, alive with fishermen, their wives, children and dogs, live on it in makeshift tents made of cloth and sticks. The wave of inhabitants expands and contracts depending on the tides, a mobile nomadic slum on the beach.

From the first day, without fail, a little scruffy white dog with long thin legs and a big curly tail meets us on the beach at the start of our walk. He keeps us company for the full eight kilometres, disappearing back to somewhere in the colony of people when we're done. I name him Ashok. Every morning I reward Ashok's loyalty with food from the hotel breakfast buffet. He develops a taste for the chocolate croissants.

The walk becomes our bonding ritual and my heart is light and fluffy with happy thoughts for our future. Before returning to Bombay, The Producer gives me the usual grand lecture about not getting familiar or socialising with the actors and crew after work.

"This is an Indian shoot and people talk. If I hear you've had a drink, even if it is with the director ..."

I stop listening. I know the rules. Read the manual and follow the instructions. His continual bleating constipates me.

We have a week of shooting to go before we move to Ooty (a hill station tucked away in the mountains), when there is a huge accident. The Producer is in Bombay.

A set light falls from the bamboo scaffolding, destroying the set with the hospital beds. Normally each bed has an actor playing a patient lying on it, but we have broken for lunch. Thank god. Some technical crew were up on the scaffold and fall with the light, one of them loses his hand, the other is knocked unconscious. We have to stop shooting. Spy does not care about the wounded, he only cares about his precious pennies. Harvey consults with him, there is no way they can rebuild in a day – they will need a week at least. The Producer calls and tells us to move to Ooty as soon as possible while the set gets fixed. This way time and money are not completely wasted. Spy runs around booking flights and arranging everything; he is a very busy man. His fish-eye spectacles are permanently fogged up, sweat creates puddles under his armpits. We go back to our hotel. There is nothing else we can do. Samson

Night takes this as a very big party opportunity. For the first day in weeks we will be able to sleep in tomorrow. By the time Spy gets his shit together it will be the day after tomorrow before we can travel to Ooty.

Just before I fall asleep, Spy knocks on my door. His moustache twitches with satisfaction, the whiskers of a rat resonating at different frequencies. He hands me a ticket.

"You will be travelling by train. You must be down in reception at 4am tomorrow morning, driver taking you to station. You will be travelling with spot boys and technical crew."

"How long is the trip?"

"Thirteen hours it is taking. You will be finding me at station; I am to be making sure no crew is forgetting behind."

"Are you coming with us on the train?"

"This is positively not, I am to be flying in evening."

Blue train

The station is chaos at 4:30am. Lepers and beggars grab at me; their desperate hearts dripping off their sleeves. Hacked up phlegm splattered in patches, piss, human shit and spice copulated together for today's special, 'bodily fluid served on a bed of concrete, madam?' Crows and pigeons pick at the menu on the floor. Coolies packed like mules move up and down collecting money for their efforts. It's a small price to pay, saving one the trouble of putting your back out. Let them do it, it's the duty they were born into, their crooked spines leaning to the side – a wider surface area along the torso for extra packing space. Buckled and bent they shout for their supper.

Spy stands at the carriage of a waiting train, an executioner's smile bends like a banana beneath his moustache.

The inside of the carriage is an enormous chipped-blue-paint iron box. The sides, floor and seats are all metal with a layer of grime and the sour smell of old sweat and rusting iron. The engine shudders and very slowly pulls itself and the carriages out of the station. Spy walks away. I throw a zap sign at him which he does not see. We rattle and rock through Chennai and its outskirts before sluggishly creeping through the countryside. The seats are hard and slippery, making it difficult to stay in one place. I give up trying and join

Sashi who is sitting in the open doorway with his legs dangling out. A bottle of Old Monk Rum is being passed around, I take a few swigs. We throw the drink back without letting our lips touch the bottleneck. The toilets are unusable. When we start climbing into the mountains, our toilet overflows on the uphill. It pours down towards us, snaking through the seating until we are forced to change carriages. The smell assaults us; we move to the front of the train. A man selling samosas calls his friends to leer at me. Sashi gets rid of them in a disorderly fashion. A fight breaks out, fuelled by the Old Monk.

When nature calls, I resort to hanging my ass out of the train door and pissing into the wind while Sashi turns his back and keeps watch for incoming passengers.

We pull into Ooty station thirteen hours later. I am gutted. A driver takes me to the Taj Hotel where The Producer, Spy, Samson Night and his entourage are having drinks. I want to know where my room is.

The Producer's smile is laced with sarcasm.

"Did you enjoy the trip? I thought it would be good for you to see more of India before you leave. The train is the best way of seeing it, wouldn't you agree? 'The ultimate Indian experience.' We've just ordered food; you want something?"

"No thanks, I want a shower and my bed."

He pulls a key attached to a wooden disk out of his pocket and throws it at me. I'm staying with him again. How convenient. The entire crew, including Spy, Kiran Cooper and Harvey, are booked into another hotel. Samson Night, his entourage and I are booked in the Taj with The Producer. I know he has done this on purpose. The other hotel is on the other side of the forest, a half hour drive from here. There is no way I can see them after hours. I am so tired of the same old shit.

The spying elephant

Once we are up and running The Producer leaves for Bombay. We are shooting a dance scene in the forest and I need to wee. Being the only female crew member, this always poses a problem when we shoot on secluded locations. The trees surrounding us have trunks as thin as telephone poles.

I eventually find a place where the land drops away and much bigger, stronger trees grow up from below so that their top halves reach the level of the ground I am standing on. I climb into the topmost branches. The foliage is dense and perfect for what I intend to do. I hold onto a branch with one hand and undo the buttons of my jeans with the other. The tree begins to shake. I look down, meeting the beady eyes of an irate elephant pushing his head against the tree trunk with increasing violence.

I try to retain my balance, my jeans around my ankles, but the impulse to stop pissing is overridden by fear. My pee splashes off his snaking trunk, spitting him in the eye. This really pisses him off. He begins to rock the tree backwards and forwards, cancelling out the intended advantage of not getting my shoes wet. As the momentum of the tree's swing increases, I realise I cannot afford to let go of the branch to pull up my jeans and clamber back onto stable ground. I have to scream for help. I am so scared I am going to fall and get stomped to death.

Sashi hears me first.

He helps me out of the tree, looking away. I roll onto the ground face down and wiggle my way back into my pants.

Everyone claps. The entire crew are watching us. I cover my eyes and walk back to them in shame.

Kiran Cooper puts his arm around me.

"One day my dear aa ... we will be making a fantastic film about this."

The Producer flies in for the last two days of the shoot. He comes to set and ignores me; I can see he's stewing. When we get to the room I shower and climb straight into bed. He is lying on the bed in his boxers playing chess.

"Are you okay?"

He does not answer. I lie along the very edge of my side of the bed, my back to him, my eyes wide, and I stare at the ochre-stained cupboard. Now what? I'm so tired of this shit. A chill goes up my spine, the shit's about to hit the fan.

"Whose room did you sleep in the other night?"

"Whose room? I've not slept in anyone's room but my own."

"You did, you fucking did! I want you to fucking tell me."

His fist hits the sheet, denting the mattress and leaving an awkward shape that I want to crawl into. I get off the bed and start taking my belongings out of the cupboard.

He gets louder.

"Spy saw you at breakfast the morning after the party Kiran and the crew had at their hotel, who's bed did you share?"

"Ask Samson or Kiran Cooper, ask whoever you want to ask, but get your facts right before you accuse me. I was invited to join them for breakfast one morning because we had a late start. I've never slept in their hotel. The driver took me there in the morning."

I have never spoken back to him, but I cannot do this anymore.

I start to cry, wheeling my bag out the door.

"I'm done, I'm fucking done!"

I become frantic with anger and frustration. I want to scoop Spy's throat out with a spoon!

"Shut up, people are sleeping."

I slam the door behind me, rolling my bag as fast as I can down the path and into the forest. I want to go home … Now!

The Producer comes after me.

"Stop it, come here, there are dangerous elephants in this place."

"Oh don't I know about that! I want to go. Let me go."

I sit down and I cry and cry and cry. Resting my head on my knees I sit frozen, desperate to be proven innocent. I am a child again. The Producer pulls at my arm. He uncurls my fingers off the handle of the suitcase and pulls me along with it. I follow him without a word and we walk back to the room. I fold a blanket on the floor in the corner of the room. I go to sleep. Nothing more is said. We wrap and move back to Chennai. The Producer lets me fly back with the others.

Unforgettable (tsunami, 2004)

It's Christmas but we cannot stop shooting. We pick up where we left off before the accident. The set looks as good as new. The Producer wants to walk on the beach again in the mornings; maybe we can use this time to patch things up before I leave.

There is no magic to my Christmas morning. It's just another day in India. We walk our eight kilometres, go to set and shoot until 11pm. We only have the studio for five days – it was already hired out to another production before the accident. We are forced to work extreme hours to get our film done. We shoot a stunt scene where a man is thrown through a sheet of glass. The sugar glass is of low quality and the stunt man ends up looking like he has been pulled through a cheese grater. Everyone seems to think that it's okay. He gets put into a car and sent to the hospital to get stitches. It is his duty to sacrifice himself for the film. Safety on set in India is not first priority. Apparently he knew he would end up badly cut, and the crew consider him a hero.

When we get back to the room, The Producer gives me a folded piece of paper.

"Your Christmas present Gené-baba."

It's an e-ticket with our names on it.

Mumbai – New York, New York – Orlando, Florida

Orlando, Florida – New York, New York – Mumbai

"Oh my word, you're taking me to New York at the end of the week?"

"For New Year's Eve. I thought it would be a good farewell gift."

"Wow, that really ..."

"And I'm taking you to Florida, we gonna go to Disney World. I want to check out the Epcot Center there – I believe it's fantastic."

"Really? Okay. I always wanted to see it as a kid."

The Producer wakes me at 5:30am for our walk. I am too tired.

"Please? We got home so late last night, please can we skip today?"

"Come on, lazy bones, get up!"

He rips the duvet off my warm cocooned body.

"Please? It's Boxing Day, in my country that's considered a holiday, please?"

"Well, we are not in your country now are we?"

"It's so dark I'm sure it's raining."

The Producer goes to the window.

"A little."

"Please, I need to finish my dream, it was a good one, I need to know how it ends, please, just one more hour?"

"Okay, fatsy, just for today ... I'll wake you in an hour to get ready for set."

The Producer gets the newspaper, goes into the bathroom and shuts the door. I hear him turn the television on. We are back in the presidential suite at the Park Hotel with a television even in the bathroom.

I slowly fall asleep again.

The Producer shakes me roughly. He is distressed.

"Did you feel that?"

"What?"

"That shake. How could you not feel it?"

"What? What shake? Where?"

"All over, it was all over. Like an earthquake."

"There's nothing now."

"I know, dumbo, but there was."

"Okay."

"Come, go shower it's time to get up."

I reluctantly sit up. I'm so heavy with fatigue. Thinking of our New York trip gets me moving with a little more enthusiasm.

I let the water spill over me; I don't move, I just stand with my forehead pushed against the tiles holding me up. I am so tired, but four more days and then New York baby! I wish I never had to leave just as things ...

The Producer pushes the shower door open. It hits my backside.

"Ouch!"

I turn, wiping the water out of my eyes.

He's frantic. I have never seen him consumed by fear. His hands flap in front of him, his eyes cannot get any bigger or his eyeballs will fall out. He can't get his words lined up properly.

"Get out! Come! See! Hurry! We must go! We must ... We must get out of ... Something terrible is..."

He pulls my arm with him towards the window, my brain gets left behind.

"What?"

I look out. In the distance the level of the ground is much higher than it was yesterday. It's risen and it's moving, it ... it's water.

The Producer scrambles to the television mounted on the wall beside the window I am looking out from. He turns it on. Every news channel is broadcasting in detail what is happening outside my hotel window. I cannot believe the horror of what I am looking at. There are human beings and animals in this water. Some of them are not moving, drowned, face down, their bodies bob with the movement of this water monster that is destroying everything in its way. The live bait (humans and animals) are fighting for their lives. I can see their faces, each and every one of them, panic stricken beyond functionality. I can see the fear of death pulling them down. They desperately grab and cling to anything that comes their way.

They have been sucked into a natural disaster that has no exit. Disfigured, mangled, twisted objects plough through the water at a rapid rate hooking, cutting, piercing, drowning, sinking, dragging, pushing, coming towards my window for a close-up view.

The Producer leaves me standing at the window. I can't move. I think the hotel phone is ringing. Is it? Or is it my head? Must be, The Producer is holding the receiver. His lips are moving. Are they? Is this? Is this really ...?

A voice booms through the room over a loudspeaker. The Producer throws the phone pointing to the ceiling.

"Shhhhhhh ... Listen!"

I have not said a word.

"Attention, attention ... pause ... dis is your hotel manager speaking ... pause ... A very big natural disaster is bin taking us by surprise. At five-thirty ... pause... dis morning an earthquake is causing a very big wave to hit our shores ... pause ... a Tsunami is its good name. We are requesting that all guests ... pause ... remaining calm be coming to the turd floor to gather in the banquet hall. We are ... pause ... to be counting heads. Nobody is to be going out of hotel ... pause ... Please ... pause ... be making your way at lightning speed only ... pause ... using the stair only ... pause... Thank you."

He repeats the exact same speech in Malayalam and Hindi. The Producer and I look at each other. Silence.

"Say something Baloo."

"Thank god our room is on the tenth floor?"

He throws a towel at me.

"Get dressed, we need to go."

"Have you spoken to Kiran Cooper?"

"There's no mobile reception. Only the internal hotel line is working."

We make our way down the crowded stairs. Nobody says a single word. Everyone seems to be staring at their feet, hoping that the better they follow the rules the better chance they have of surviving.

Whatever any of us were worrying about before seems trivial. My little world and all its little worries has been taken away with the terrifying wave of water outside. I feel like I'm in a movie about the world coming to an end.

People wear the strangest things when caught in the middle of a disaster. We all stand huddled together in the dark. A generator comes on, a few spotlights flicker, taking on a low glow as the generator picks up speed. If it runs out of fuel we will be in the dark again. Samson Night is just another face in the crowd. We wait for our names to be called out. They call Samson's name first; people turn to look at him, but not for long. They go back to staring at their feet, wallowing in their fear.

While I wait I start to think about all the people living on the beach. They would have been taken first. The force would have been too much to survive. I don't think many of them could swim.

I squeeze The Producer's hand and whisper in his ear.

"Ashok is gone."

We sit in the hotel for two days, waiting. Waiting to be told that we can fly back to Bombay. Waiting for the roads to be cleared so that we can get to the airport. Samson Night is first on the list, we will go with him.

India is crying, the world is crying, I am crying. The Producer cries with me, as the papers start printing and the world begins to cover the disaster, rubbing salt deeper into the wound.

We get back to Bombay on 28 December. I call Kiran Cooper to say goodbye. I will never see him again. I ask after everyone, he starts to cry. Some of Harvey's crew were building a piece of set for the next day on the beach when the wave hit, they were found dead, buried in the sand, yesterday. We cry together. I say goodbye. I love you Kiran Cooper you have a very good heart. It's Samson Night's birthday. He tries to lift spirits by throwing a party at Vie, the lounge where he threw my party. The Producer and I are flying to New York in the early hours of the 29th. We drop in to the party before we leave. I have not even been back twenty-four hours and the press are starting their nonsense.

They are thrashing the dress that I'm wearing. "Same dress again, Gené?"

My dress is brand new. After what's just happened in the world, is there nothing better to write about?

Make believe

New York is no different to how I imagined it. It's just like the movies. It's brutal but beautiful, colourful and yet so grey. When it's hot it can be so cold. New York can be safe but make you feel so insecure, clean but so dirty, happy and yet so sad. A balloon filled with contradictions leaking out from inside of you.

We spend three days shopping, eating and enjoying each other. I cannot let go. I don't want it to end. The Producer does not deny me anything. We watch the ball fall at midnight in Times Square as a reflection off a building. It's too crowded to actually get anywhere near Times Square on New Year's Eve.

On our last day, in Disney World, The Producer plans to meet me in the park for lunch. I have had a lot of time to think. I want to stay in India.

I sit on a baby-blue bench waiting for him, thinking about how I am going to convince The Producer to keep me. The sweet smell of candyfloss and fresh popcorn wafts past me and I start to cry. The Producer sits down next to me, putting his arm around me. We are in a foreign country – here he can show me affection.

"And now?"

"I don't want to go."

"Of course you do, we just bought you a whole new wardrobe

for a whole new life."

"But I love you."

"I will come visit."

"When?"

"When the time is right."

"I love you."

"This is a fantastic opportunity for you, you know there's nothing left for you in India."

"What about Kush's film when he gets back from New York?"

"When Bombay freezes over, I will call you, okay?"

People stare at us as they walk past and realise we are touching; we are such an unsuited pair. The Producer becomes solemn. Something is bothering him and it's not the staring crowd; he is never fazed by the way people look at us when we are outside of India.

"I just heard the most shocking news."

"What?"

"Alisha is getting married to a man half her age."

"What? To who? She wasn't even seeing anyone."

"Apparently she has been, for almost a year. He's about your age. An aspiring actor, how convenient for him, marrying the producer so that he can get the job."

"Maybe they really love each other?"

"Please, he will use her and spit her out. She's older than him, she won't look like this for much longer, and then what? What's she going to do to keep him?"

Romain here …

I spend my last week in India saying goodbye to all the people who have been the building blocks in my life for the past three years. Nisha stays at The Producer's with me. We sit under the extractor fan smoking cigarettes and sipping on neat rum like naughty children. I sit on the kitchen counter for hours helping Sai peel garlic. We talk about 'the inside story', gossip. I love my housemates so much.

I know Romania is the wrong decision from the moment I put foot on that plane. I fly via Frankfurt, but get stuck there for two days sitting on an airport chair waiting. President Bush has come to Frankfurt and the whole country has come to a standstill. There is a blizzard, the coldest European winter in thirty years. All flights are cancelled, but the American President gets priority.

When I finally get to Bucharest my luggage has been lost. They promise to bring it to me when it's located; I have no clothes until then. It is minus thirty-three degrees. Sophia, Bronko's assistant, picks me up, full of smiles. She wants to know about Samson Night and if he will be coming to do another film soon. I tell her not to hold her breath.

My apartment does not even have a bed. I must sleep on a battered couch. There is a small toilet and a two-plate stove. A broom without bristles stands in the corner of the one-room apartment.

Living in Bucharest at the JW Marriott was like living behind glass. Without The Producer and his money involved I cannot survive. I love the idea of how glamorous my life had become. The more I obsess and want it back, the harder it is for me to stay here. I can't make the most of this. I won't make the most of it. This is not what I want for myself.

There is no car. I must walk on the frozen snow to work every day. It takes me forever. I fall a lot. I have never felt cold like this before. When my bag finally arrives the locks are gone and most of my warm clothes that The Producer bought for me have been stolen. After the first month, I have not been paid, I am broke. I ask my father to wire me money via Western Union. When I try to confront Bronko, he gets slippery. I call The Producer from a call box. He tells me to be patient. He gives me the number of his friend, the one who owns half of Romania. I call him. He is in London with his wife settling his children into Eaton. He says he will take me for dinner when he gets back. I crave a fancy meal. There is no work and Bronko cannot pay me again after the second month. I get a mobile phone with my father's money. I get phone calls from strange men. They breathe heavily and play "I'm horny, horny, horny, horny". I have visions of being kidnapped and trafficked. Romania is where it happens most. I call The Producer.

The Producer's friend comes to see me. The Producer has obviously sent him to check things out. He is horrified, the heating has been turned off and I wear every piece of clothing I own. He takes me back to his mansion on a golf estate. His maid cooks me a decent meal and I have a hot bath. He sits me down.

"This is obviously not working, but on principal The Producer and I have decided that you should wait for Bronko to pay for your ticket back. He got you into this mess."

Bronko does not budge. I wait, desperate to leave. The Producer's friend and his wife let me stay with them. After another month has passed, The Producer's friend goes to see Bronko in person. He comes back with a ticket.

The waiting room

My ticket is to South Africa, not to India.

I find it hard to fit back into South Africa. I become depressed, I join a gym, and this is all I do at first. I have no friends left back in South Africa; I abandoned everything and everyone in my life when I went to India. I don't fit in here any more and I will not allow myself the chance to try. I don't want to relate to people my age and my race. I am in a transitional phase of finding out who and what I am. I am no longer like any of the people I have left behind. I am different. I am stuck and I cannot move forward. I want to go back to where I came from, India. I can't make any decisions for myself. I have been controlled for far too long. I don't know what is right or wrong; everything feels unmanageable. HE tells me HE's working on it. HE tells me to wait. I wait. I wait for six months. I go to Hindi lessons to hear the familiar sounds coming from the people that make me feel I'm where I should be. I take up a job at an airport shuttle company so that I can see the departure lounge and the aeroplane that I am supposed to be on every day.

The endometriosis comes back with a vengeance and I have to have another operation. Then one day the blessed phone call comes. The Producer is starting another film – I have no idea under what conditions I am going back on, but I am going back.

In transit

I land in Mumbai at midday. I find Balkran waiting for me at Arrivals. He takes my trolley and I follow him to the car. It is September, the monsoons are coming to an end, it is hot and muggy. The air is thick and creamy with the smell of rot. If the world was a kitchen, Mumbai would be the garbage can.

The Producer sits in the front seat of the BMW playing chess on his mobile phone. I reach through the window to hug him.

"Get in," he grunts.

I slide onto the backseat, excited to see him.

"I missed you so much."

He does not look up.

"Hmm."

I sit back into the cold porous leather; the car coughs its way through the jammed streets. My eyes burn dry trying to focus through a cloud of The Producer's cigarette smoke and the blasting air conditioner. So much for my romanticised expectations, the joyful reunion of two people in love longing to be in each other's arms, me dressed up as 'The Bride' in Chagall's painting, the goat in the background gently playing the violin. I pull my arm through my denim jacket sleeve, it's so cold in here. My lucky bead bracelet catches on the button, it breaks. Beads roll off my arm one by one onto the floor and under the seat. I bend down, frantic to find them. It's impossible. Is this an omen? Is the universe trying to tell me something?

Why is it that I only miss The Producer when he is not next to me? The moment I'm around him he makes me feel down.

I try to lift my spirits by killing the silence.

"Whose film are we shooting?"

"A new up-and-coming director. You don't know him."

"What's the film about?"

"It's based on *Love Actually*.

"My *Love Actually*?"

"Yes, you gave me the idea. I got this director to write a Bollywood version. It will have all of India's best actors, including, of course, Samson Night. Huge cast, the biggest any Bollywood film has ever seen."

The only person left at Luna that I can relate to is Alisha. Everyone else has moved on. Alisha looks different; she is glowing. It seems a younger man can make all the difference. I congratulate her on her marriage, and she tells me all about her new life. I ask her about The Producer's servants and what has happened in the last six months. It's easier to get answers out of Alisha than out of The Producer; he is like an onion, too many layers to get through.

"The film you did with Kiran Cooper did not do well. The Producer went into a very deep depression. He got really ill too, he has developed severe diabetes type two and has to inject insulin."

"Really? He didn't tell me any of this."

"A lot has changed Gené."

"Like what?"

"Things are really bad with Gaya and her family. Her father is screwing The Producer in the divorce settlement. You won't be staying with The Producer, he has moved you to an apartment across town."

"Really?"

"It's been a very ugly divorce and if there is any proof of you being around ..."

"I get it."

"Is anything like it was?"

"I'm still here and happy to see you."

"At least that."

I hug her for some time; she's the only support left.

"Come, let me walk you through the British Airways commercial that we are shooting next week in New York. You are the only one going because you have an Italian passport and don't need a visa."

"Who's the director?"

"Same guy that's making the *Love Actually* film."

Alisha introduces me to two young male assistants. Both of them look unimpressed. They are as westernised as Kush, very eager, but lack in experience. I spend the rest of the day dragging all the information I can out of them for a British Airways commercial. The director comes to introduce himself in the evening; he is the Indian clone of Darko with a serious case of halitosis. He is arrogant and rude. He likes to get in your face when he talks to you. I gag; he stinks. He speaks to his assistants in Hindi. They laugh at his jokes and praise him for the things he says. What have I come back to?

When they leave, I go and find Alisha.

"They hate me."

"Of course they do, you took away their chance to go to New York. They've been prepping for over a week, then you come in, the white girl with the right passport, and get to do the fun part of the job, travelling to London and New York."

"It doesn't seem like I'm The Producer's girlfriend anymore."

"No, it doesn't."

"Are things over between The Producer and me? Has he told you it's over?"

"Only you would know. Ask him. But if I were you I would let the dust settle first."

"Am I really staying somewhere else?"

"You are, flats in Lokhandwala, the suburb after The Producer's suburb."

"Oh."

"I took some things from the prop department for you. There's a bed and a dining table. I got you some bedding, very nice, yellow. It's a happy place; you will like it there I'm sure."

The Producer interrupts us.

"Is Alisha telling you about your new apartment? Come, let's go and see it."

I fall asleep on the back seat of the car. I'm exhausted. The Producer wakes me when we get to his apartment.

"Sai and Balkran will settle you into your new place. There is a houseboy staying there with you, for now I will send food with Sai until you are more settled. Enjoy."

The Producer walks up the stairs to his apartment, Sai comes down and sits next to Balkran, and we drive to my new home.

Lokhandwala is fifteen minutes away from The Producer's house in Juhu. It is an aggressive version of suburbia consisting of raw concrete high-rise apartment blocks that shoot up through the ground exposing gutted out and incomplete pigeonholes decorated with dripping air conditioners along their walls. Rows and rows of these domino buildings populate the area, building rubble pushed into pyramid-shaped piles get rummaged through by crows and the ever-hopeful homeless. There is very little vegetation left until we turn into a dirt road leading to a cluster of buildings built in a semi circle around a swamp. Green foam lies stagnant, the water beneath it is unreflecting, a thick bubbling stew of sewage, grass, rubbish bags and mosquitoes. Black hogs with spikey tufts running along their spines rummage through the thick stew, swallowing great gulps of it as they wade forward. The smell stops me, I cover my mouth, my salivary glands work overtime to keep me from gagging. Sai blows through his nostrils; Balkran clears his throat and shoots it out through his mouth, just missing his shoe. I am led to the entrance of an ugly marked concrete building called Sweet Home.

A watchman sits tilted back on a red plastic chair, snoring. Balkran flicks his ear as we walk past him to the rusting elevator gate.

"*Arrey*, bloody black Indian! This is watchman."

The three of us squash into the linoleum-lined elevator. Sai presses number eight slamming the beeping rusty trellis door shut, it stops beeping at us and the box begins to move up slowly. We pass sweating cream walls that blister and peel in front of our faces, squashed toward the gate gasping for air. Nothing seems sweet about this home so far.

Sai knocks on the door. A small man, no older than eighteen, opens it. He does not smile. He nods, gesturing for us to come in. His eyes follow me slyly, his mouth curls upward as I brush past him. Troll.

Sai bombards him with questions in Hindi. He hands the troll dishes sealed with foil.

"This, madam, is your dinner eating. I am making."

The troll takes it to a narrow brown kitchen, opens the rattling dirty cream fridge, its light illuminating the floor as a cockroach runs past, waving at me in spite. Sai stamps on it and shouts at the troll to clean it up. He leads me to a dining and lounge area. This room looks onto the swamp.

"Madam, windows closed keeping, this is air conditioner only."

There is an ornate white dining table with a glass top, eight curly white ornate chairs are pushed in around it. A telephone sits in the middle of the table. Balkran holds the handset to his ear to check that it's working.

"Boss putting 'dring-dring'."

"Why?"

"This is checking, madam staying in house."

He laughs; he thinks it's funny. I don't.

The Producer has had the treadmill moved to this room. It stands next to the table facing a small television on the floor on the opposite side of the room.

Balkran points to a cable running across the ceiling.

"This is my cable TV giving, English." He takes the remote and flicks to the HBO channel.

Sai leads me to my room. It has a padlock on the door; he tells me to lock it when I sleep.

My room has a bed and a row of cupboards, the bedding is bright yellow, and so are the curtains. They are yellow voile, transparent and useless at keeping light out. I look out of the window; it also looks onto the swamp. There are two bathrooms, a maroon one and a blue one. The blue one has been claimed by my house troll. He has put his toiletries on a shelf at the mirror above the basin. Both have showers only. I wish I had a bath. My bathroom is very dark and small. The toilet freaks me out. It has wings with ridges on either side of the seat, obviously to stand on the seat and squat over the hole. The shower spout is shared with the tap next to the toilet that is used to wash one's bits when you are finished shitting, I hate the whole set up. My towels are yellow.

We go back to the dining area. The house troll has rolled out his mattress in front of the television. He has changed channels and is transfixed. Sai snaps his fingers in front of the troll's eyes, saying something stern in Hindi. The house troll stands, putting his hands on his hips.

Sai speaks to me. "Madam, this is houseboy, making food and cleaning. He not speaking English. If you need translation you me calling, I am telling."

Balkran and Sai leave. The house troll lies back in front of the television. He has claimed his sleeping area, in front of the television, with remote control in hand. I won't be getting a chance. I walk to my bedroom, I need to repack my suitcase for New York. I am happy to be leaving again tomorrow night – I can face this place later.

I look down, watching Sai and Balkran get into the BMW. They are both covering their mouths and noses. So this is where The Producer puts his girls when they've reached their expiry date.

I heat my own food that Sai has made for me and eat it in my room. I don't want to sit alone at the eight-seater. The telephone rings. I let the house troll pick it up.

He knocks on my door.

"Come in."

He does not say a word; he is mute. He uses his hands to signal for me to come to the phone.

"Hello?"

"Hello, Gené-baba, do you like your new house?"

I lie. "Yes, it's great, thank you."

"You always wanted your own place."

"Yes, my very own basket."

"Good. What were you doing?"

"I was eating."

"Good, I better not hear from that guy that you're smoking, and no going out, understand?"

"No, I won't. Please can this guy not live here with me, I will be fine on my own."

"Definitely not, you cannot stay on your own."

"But I always ..."

"It's dangerous, don't make me ..."

"Please?"

"Go finish your dinner. Balkran will pick you up at eight. Don't forget to carry your bag for New York. We are going to go straight from the office to the airport tomorrow night."

"Why can't I have Kutty then?"

"My mother would never allow that."

Wet dog mixed with poo

The Producer and I fly with the director and his halitosis to New York via London, where we stop off for three days for a drawn-out meeting where the agency flagellates and masturbates over every little detail pertaining to the shoot. Then we fly to New York.

The facilitating producer in New York is Indian. He is slippery and disorganised. The Producer takes an instant disliking to him. He pushes the guy up against the wall and sticks his obese finger into his face.

"Get your shit together, you're embarrassing me."

The British Airways client and the creative agency watch with wide eyes.

I am given my own room; The Producer does not make me share this time. We use my room as an office during the day. After a day with the director in my room, I air it and spray as much deodorant as I can. The Producer comes to see me.

"Did you spray something in here?"

"Yes, my deodorant."

"Why so much?"

"Because the director stinks; his breath makes my whole room stink."

"Is that what the awful smell was in here earlier? I kept checking my armpits to make sure it was not me."

On our last day in New York, we shoot in Central Park. The slippery facilitating producer proudly hands The Producer the signed permit giving us permission to shoot in the Park.

It's a Sunday and I feel like I'm living the American dream. Families with strollers and dogs walk up and down; ducks eat bread that's being thrown at them by little girls with blonde ringlets; big red, blue and white helium balloons are being sold to children; some let them go and cry. Lovers lie under trees on checked blankets with picnic baskets, reading, loving and napping while joggers come past plugged into their driven need to stay healthy. It's a perfect day until we arrive.

We start to unload our aggressive-looking equipment. The grips start to carry tracks and a dolly across the park. I get the models changed and into position. The camera gets placed; the director makes me move a family having a picnic. They are annoyed. The Producer pulls the permit from his pocket to show them we have permission; they move away. We are about to begin filming when a sudden police siren nearby draws all the attention to us.

The policeman begins to speak. "Please put your hands above your heads where I can see them. You have the right to remain silent."

He gets out and comes toward us. Two more cars arrive as back up. The Producer steps forward, his best smile in place.

"Can I help you, officer?"

"You sure can, mister. Who the hell gave you permission to shoot in Central Park on a Sunday? Never in the history of New York has any crew been given permission to shoot in Central Park on a Sunday."

"I have a signed permit, officer."

The Producer reaches into his pocket and pulls the permit out. The officer looks at it and laughs.

"What a coincidence, my name, my signature, but I definitely did not sign this piece of paper, someone has forged my signature!"

"Sorry?"

"I said someone has forged my signature. Who gave this permit to you, sir?"

"My facilitating producer here in New York. I am sure there is a misunderstanding officer, I'm sure we can work this out."

The Producer has his pleading smile in place. He hunches slightly, trying to make himself look small and vulnerable.

"We sure can work this out. I'm afraid I am going to have to take you and your crew in for questioning. Cuff 'em all."

We are all handcuffed and loaded into the back of the cars. The American crew are left to go free. They are innocent.

The officer pulls me aside.

"Ma'am, are you with them?"

"Yes, I am."

"We would like to take you in for questioning too."

The Producer looks at me, begging me to comply. I do.

"Sure."

We are lined up on a bench and told not to talk. The Producer is taken to a room and I am taken into another.

The director and the agency from India are left sitting on the bench. The director thinks it's a joke, but the agency looks very worried.

A woman officer comes to search me. She removes all my clothes, just leaving my panties. She checks inside my mouth and probes with her rubberised fingers around my naughty bits. I have nothing to hide. Once she is satisfied, she asks me to dress and takes me into another room. A male officer joins us.

"Ma'am, where do you live?"

"India."

"Where are you from?"

"South Africa."

"Ma'am, what exactly are you doing in India?"

"I work for The Producer's production house as an assistant director and a photographer."

"Ma'am, is that all you do?"

"Yes."

"Ma'am, why are you the only Caucasian travelling with them?"

"I have always been the only Caucasian in the company."

"Does that seem strange to you?"

"Not to me. It's where my job took me and not many people venture out to work in India, I guess."

"Ma'am, have you ever been asked to do anything illegal for these people?"

"Like what?"

"Like carry anything across borders?"

"No."

"Were you aware that shooting in Central Park on a Sunday is illegal?"

"No, I was not."

"How did you come to shooting there?"

"I was told that our location would be there and I reported to work in Central Park because that's where I was told to be."

"Are you okay, ma'am? Have you been hurt by these people in any way?"

I want to tell him that my heart's been broken by The Producer, but I refrain from getting stupid.

The Producer has managed to convince the cops that we had no idea and that he trusted the production facilitator. It was truly an innocent mistake from our side. We are set free and return to our hotel to figure out when we can shoot in Central Park again, but we are denied access.

I am woken up at 3am by The Producer and the director. They have managed to bribe a park supervisor in Brooklyn who will give us between four and five-thirty to get the shot we need. The park has the Brooklyn Bridge in the background; it's perfect. We get the model to the location and get our shot before New York comes to life. We go straight to the airport and catch a plane back to India. The Producer is totally chuffed with himself. All charges were dropped and we have clean records. The facilitating producer has been banned from working in America. I fly over the oceans back to my basket where my house troll awaits me.

Rose-coloured spectacles ... gone

Reality is my worst enemy. I open my apartment door and it hits me. When I lived with The Producer everything was taken care of, The Producer's staff are 'only the best', his house is designed with 'only the best', his life comprises of owning 'only the best'. To survive in a place as harsh as India, I need to live in 'only the best'. This is going to be so much harder than I thought.

The phone rings. It's The Producer.

"Just checking you okay."

"I'm fine."

"You are not to go out anywhere; it's dangerous."

"Okay."

"Did you have your dinner?"

"No."

"Why not?"

"He only knows how to make rice and dal."

"Okay, I will ask Sai to come and teach him to make veg and *paneer* tomorrow. For now eat the rice and dal."

"Why don't you call me on my mobile?"

"Because, you have the landline now."

"Are you checking on me?"

"Ya."

I stand at the fridge. Dal and rice, nothing else. I need some fruit in here. I give the troll some money and call Sai.

"Sai, please ask him to get me some watermelon and a few apples. Also please come show him how to make something other than dal and rice."

"What you want?"

"Maybe some boiled vegetables and *palak paneer*."

"Okay, madam no problem *yaar*."

I lie awake for a long time. Without the busy servants and the tinny doorbell, the silence keeps me awake. The transparent curtains don't help.

I am given a car. Balkran sits next to me. It's my first time driving in India. The old Ford is damp and smelly inside, too many monsoons flooding through its doors. It drives well and gets me where I want to be. Bombay is a maze and there are no road signs and names, I have to set landmarks in my mind and use them to show me the way. It's a confusing ride, but I get used to it. The congestion and the hooting get me into hysteria, but Balkran tells me to hoot constantly and just go. I follow his instructions and it works.

By Friday I am driving on my own to work. I am exhausted by the time I get there.

As I predicted, there is very little for me to do in the office. The director and his halitosis now have six assistant directors.

Spy comes to see me regarding a salary. I am finally going to be paid for my work. With this money I must pay the house troll that I do not want and give him money for groceries. The rest is mine. The Producer pays for my fuel, he has an account running at the gas station near his house. Spy gives me some papers and tells me to open a bank account. They will be paying Rs30 000.00 ($483.32) into it every month. Spy becomes awfully sweet, cocking his head to the side, his goldfish lips part, exposing a smile. He sidles up to me, his eyes squashed behind the double glass in his large tortoise shell square frames, and whispers into my ear, bobbing his head.

"These people are not knowing what they are doing. Full money wasting. I am already pushing over my budgeting and we are still only in the prepping. These people are being rude, the young ones are having no respect. They are making my job even harder, and you know from working with me how hard my job is being."

"I'm sorry to hear that you are having such an awful time. Maybe working with Kiran Cooper was not such a bad thing after all."

Spy ignores my comment and continues to talk.

"The difference between working with experienced directors and amateur ones is that one can be prepared, I must be constantly concerned in this situation, where the monkey is not knowing how to be peeling the banana!"

House trolls

I am so lonely. The Producer does not see me anymore. He leaves no shit beneath his shoe for me to scrape off. I have no idea where I stand with him. Does he have someone else? Are we over? Just let me know so that I can get on with this life I have come back to. I want to make some friends and have a life of my own since he seems to be getting on just fine with his. I am invited out once since being back, a dinner at Samson Night's house. I feel spare and awkward in the crowd. I think the people ignore me because they know something I just don't want to admit. I ask The Producer, but he is as vague as ever. He will not give the go ahead of setting me free, he cannot afford to lose the control, instead his answers are loaded with innuendos.

"You know where we stand. Don't ask stupid questions. You know how it is. Don't act dumb. I need you to hang low while this divorce is going through, that's all."

And of course, my all-time favourite.

"Our relationship is what you make of it in your head."

But of course don't I dare make of it that I'm free to do as I please, heaven forbid!

Nisha will be joining some friends in Goa for December. I am so happy for her – she has her life back. She comes to see me before she leaves with a bottle of rum and a carton of cigarettes, just like old times. I tell her all about the house troll. He has become fat and round; all he does is lie in front of the TV stuffing his face with dal and rice and it's showing.

"He looks pregnant," she jokes.

My days go by way too slowly. When we get the day off on the occasional Sunday, I would rather have somewhere to be. I try to read *Shantaram*, the photocopied version that the book vendors in the streets sell. I eventually leave the book. It's too long and because it's a fake photocopied version there are pages missing. I avoid driving when I don't have to – the cops always stop me. They lean in intimidatingly, pushing their crotches against the widow. I watch their package go as flat as a pancake and then even flatter, squeezing between their sheriff's badge as I roll down the window. They hide their discomfort under their caterpillar moustaches and fake Ray-Ban Aviators. Chasing the American *Top Gun* dream, they are all Tom Cruise wannabes in uniform. They want a bribe and they will not let me go without one. They see me coming a mile away; I stand out in a traffic jam. All my paper work is in place, but they will stand and endure the discomfort until I surrender and pull out my wallet. The Producer does not want me going out anyway. I find some street scenes to photograph and make friends with the children. In the mornings when I go to work they run with the car, pressing their cheeks against the cold air-conditioned glass. I keep biscuits in the car so that I can hand them out. At night they wait for me two streets down, their singsong voices full of hope and belief cheer me up.

On one of my days off I get a surprising phone call. It is late and The Producer has already made his mandatory call to the landline checking that I am where I am supposed to be: nowhere.

It's Harvey. He is in town and is staying in the apartment that he owns in Lokhandwala, literally three blocks from my apartment. While I was away he became so busy in Bombay that it was more feasible to buy an apartment.

"Kiran is also in town. He will be coming over for some Chinese. Can I pick you up and you join us?"

I am totally taken by surprise.

"How did you know I live here?"

"I saw Alisha on a commercial today at Film City and she told me when I asked after you."

We spend the evening together. The three of us sit outside on his balcony, sinking into plush colourful beanbags drinking whisky and smoking cigarettes until the sun rises. Harvey makes us a quick breakfast before taking me back to my place. I tell him about the house troll. When I get out of the car he slips a Rs500.00 note into my hand.

"This will keep him quiet."

I become a regular at Harvey's house, although unfortunately not for long as they both wrap and have to return to Chennai.

Coming and going

I am surprised when I arrive at the office and the director and his brown-nosing assistants are waiting for me at my desk. The director sucks on one of my pens as he swivels around on my chair; one of his slaves massages his shoulders adoringly.

"We need your help."

They never need my help.

"We want you to go to South Africa and find a girl that can play the part of the *firang*."

"South African?"

"Yes, an American gets too complicated with SAG rules; we will never get away with our shooting hours and the way we work, it's also very expensive. Make sure that whoever you find in South Africa can speak in an American accent and she must be blonde or be willing to become a bottle blonde."

I get a free trip home – I cannot believe my luck.

"When shall I go?"

"As soon as possible. Get Spy to book your ticket."

There's a flight out tonight. I will be on it.

I spend a week at home. This time I make an effort to hook up with old friends. A little seed has been planted; maybe it's time to come home? My parents are back together and things are back to normal. I realise how much I've missed them and my old life; to survive India I never allowed myself the option before.

I find the perfect actress. She is with a top acting agency in Johannesburg. Her hair is dark, but she is willing to dye it blonde. I send a copy of her audition to the director. He's happy.

I receive a phone call from The Producer. It's two days before Christmas. I desperately want to ask him if I can stay home for Christmas and fly with the actress in January when we start shooting. I am not needed until then and I cannot bear the thought of sitting alone in India with my house troll.

The Producer is in a surprisingly good mood. He starts telling me about the holiday he has booked for us. He wants me to fly from South Africa to Las Vegas. From there he wants to take me to Los Angeles and then on to Japan and back to India. A round-the-world trip in twelve days.

"When have you booked this for?"

"Tomorrow."

"So soon?"

"What's wrong? You want to turn me down?"

It feels like the wind has been knocked out of me. I don't know what to say. He's had no time for me for the past year and now he suddenly wants to take me on a round-the-world trip on business class.

What the hell is going on? He follows a pattern: every Christmas he takes me somewhere as if he is trying to forget about his boys because they don't want to be with him. If he's had other women, why has he not asked them? They are either tied up with better arrangements or he has not had anyone else, which I find very hard to believe given his behaviour.

Maybe he is trying to rekindle our relationship. I have to say yes; this trip might change things for the better. If I don't go, I will regret that I did not try and make things right. I have to give it one more chance.

The departure lounge

I meet The Producer in a casino in Las Vegas. It's after ten at night. The only element I am able to absorb in the chaos of addiction, greed and money are the lights. Vegas is one big Christmas tree, I have never seen a city as grotesque, vulgar and in your face, yet utterly captivating; its charm sucks me in immediately.

The Producer is on a winning streak, he hands me the room key. I go upstairs and unpack. I come back down after midnight, he is still doing well and does not want to leave; I go to bed alone. When I wake up, The Producer is in the bathroom. He has just come in. Typically, he put back into the casino everything he had won. He needs to sleep. He gives me a couple of dollars and tells me to wake him at lunchtime. I find myself being entertained by sitting on a bench in the street observing the people; a carousel of people that makes my head turn. I wake The Producer at lunchtime. We soon find ourselves talking again like we used to over a Wendy's burger. We share a large slice of cheesecake and again as always food brings us together. The Producer takes me to see a David Copperfield show; the moment it's over he returns to the casino. I find a fun-looking bar and order a margherita.

The Producer comes home in the morning with a ticket for me to go and see Celine Dion alone. He wants sex. We do it and I think to myself that this will be the last time we do. I don't really want to anymore; I don't want him anymore. I know he does not want me anymore either; I can feel it. I am just a possession that looks good at his side, thin, blonde, attractive: his own personal Barbie doll. He does not want me, but he wants no one else to have me either. I hate him for this. I hate him for how lonely I feel. I hate him for not letting me have more from India. I can only have what he allows; I cannot be in India if I am not under his control – he will make it impossible for me. This is my understanding and I am ready to accept it for what it is. He brought me to India and he owns me. I want to finish this dreaded film and leave, I have a long year ahead before I can walk away; another film on my CV will serve me well.

I go to Celine Dion alone. I fade away in the crowd; I am somewhere else digesting the past four years as Celine Dion pours out her movingly powerful legendary love songs. I fall out of love by the end of the concert; there is no love left in me for The Producer. I feel nothing, just gratitude for the time we had together and the experiences he has so generously given me. But we are over. I want nothing more.

As we fly over the Grand Canyon leaving Vegas behind us, I promise myself that I will return here to get married one day, with my cowboy boots, dressed as Pocahontas, to someone who truly loves me. Los Angeles is uneventful. After throwing mounds of money away in Vegas, The Producer complains about the expense. We share a room again and I now manipulate our time with avoiding the bedroom. I am lucky The Producer did not sleep much in Vegas. He falls asleep at 6pm on New Year's Eve. Such a bore, we are in L.A. He's clearly too old for me, I see that now. We get ready to fly to Japan. The Producer is irritated with me. I do things in my own time; I don't run after him and his bags, I move slowly only worrying about myself. I can see it gets to him. He tells me that I'm walking too slowly and that I look lazy. I ignore him, I'm not the one with the weight problem – I can see that now.

Just before we board the plane for Japan, The Producer loses his boarding pass. He becomes hysterical.

"This is America. They will never let me on the plane without my pass; they love to give me shit. Don't just stand there, help me!"

"They give you shit because you look like Saddam Hussein."

He does not hear me; he has run into a duty-free shop to see if he left it there. I calmly walk to the men's toilets. I bet he left it next to the urinal. I ask a man going in, he returns with The Producer's boarding pass. I sit and wait for The Producer. He comes past, irate with me.

"Don't just sit there you lazy ..."

"I really hope you weren't going to say bitch?"

I look at him smugly, holding up the boarding card.

"Oh my god, where did ..."

"In the men's room."

He snatches it from me, wheeling his suitcase behind him.

In Japan, I am in a city ahead of its time that blends in beautifully with its ancient history. Palaces from long ago are surrounded by parks with magical-looking old trees surrounded by skyscrapers, fast trains with tracks built in the sky and technological advancement that makes smoke come out of your ears. We stay in Ginza, the most expensive city in the world. The Producer and I make conversation over sushi. It's cold and snowing. We drink copious amounts of hot sake, numbing us from the cold. It loosens The Producer up.

The Producer takes me to a camera shop that has eight floors. I am in heaven.

"The poster designer has asked me to get you this lens for the film."

He pulls out his phone and reads off an email.

"It's a Canon lens, the 70mm–200mm, F2.8."

I'm not going to complain. Never in a million years could I afford to own a lens like that. I return to India with a beautiful zoom lens. It cost $3000.00, six months of my salary.

Chillies and Champagne

When we land in Mumbai, I go straight to domestic flights and fly to Jaipur with The Producer. The director, his halitosis and the entire film crew are there, ready to start filming. We are scheduled to shoot in Rajasthan for the next four weeks. The desert and the Taj Mahal are first up. When we get to the hotel in Jaipur, I am bombarded by a panicked director and six assistants who smell like they've been up his arse the entire time I was away. The South African actress is here, but she is in a complete state and won't stop crying; they need me again. The Producer tells me to take care of it. He goes off to discuss overshot budgets with Spy.

I find the actress sitting on her hotel bed in tears. She's been here for all of two days and already she wants to go home. She is expected to know the words of a song and the choreographed dance sequence by tomorrow. She will be mounted on a moving truck with camels in the middle of the desert and is expected to dance in sequence with the taxi driver – a very famous Bollywood actor. She feels she has not been given enough time and no matter how many times she listens to the song she cannot grasp the complex pronunciation of the Hindi words whining back at her.

The director comes in. The actress is distraught.

"Please get him out of my room. He does not know how to speak to me properly."

His assistants look at me pleadingly. "Please help her."

The actress looks at me sobbing. "Look what they've done to my hair." She pulls at a tuft of grassy blonde hair. It's burnt. It breaks off in her hand.

"They've ruined it. I told them to use the wig and not dabble in something they know nothing about. These hairdressers have never worked with peroxide. Have you ever seen a blonde Indian?"

She puts her head back into her hands and jerks up and down taking big breaths between desperate sobs.

I send everyone out of the room. I tell her that the Indians do use bleach, but not on their heads. I tell her about my bleached asshole and it makes her laugh. I try to explain to her how it's going to be and that she only needs to do this for four weeks. It makes her cry even more. I tell her I have been here for over four years and although it never gets easier, learning to cope becomes easier. We spend the evening going through the song and the dance moves together. I know the words and write them down phonetically for her.

The actress gets through the first day, but not without tears. There is no safety on the moving truck and the director will not speak to her normally. He stands next to her with a loud hailer and shouts instructions rudely into her ear; it drives her mad. She calls her agent, the agent tells her to stick it out. However, The Producer receives a call from her agent regarding her safety. Annoyed, The Producer comes to talk to the actress. He thinks he can treat her like me, but she is not as obliging and she gives him a piece of her mind, standing her ground. They instantly dislike each other. At night I sit with her – she will not eat the food and survives on chocolate bars. After two weeks, her outfits need adjusting; she loses a lot of weight.

The actress confronts me about The Producer. I am petrified that she will find out that I was, am or no longer am The Producer's girlfriend. I am suddenly terribly embarrassed. Now that a girl my age and my race is with me, I can see how bizarre The Producer and I look together. She finds him repulsive. Her repulsion casts a true light on what I have allowed myself to become: a controlled puppet with no future if I stay.

"He is the sleaziest producer I have ever come across. Is it him that you have worked for, for four years? It's time you come home. You deserve to be with your own kind. As for the fucking director, he's a pig. He stinks. I want to ram that loud hailer up his arse. He has no communication skills.

"Look how he screams and shouts abusively at his crew, it's disgusting."

"I know. Two more weeks; hang in there."

I am relieved that nothing has been mentioned about The Producer's and my relationship; the secret's not out yet. I need to keep it that way. The actress speaks about South Africa every day; she begs me to be brave and come home; she says she will help me get into the South African industry. She is totally spun out by everything happening around her. I begin to see her point; her horror starts to reflect onto me, to see things for what they are. She removes my rose-coloured spectacles.

We move to Rishikesh, a spiritual village on the Ganga River up in the Himalayan Mountains. The Beatles spent a lot of time in Rishikesh, making it famous today. The deep flowing rivers dominate the scenery and the ambience, while the saffron-coloured robes of the priests dominate the colour of the streets. Rishikesh is cold.

It is said that Rishikesh has the power to transform and cure those who have lost their way by showing them a new spiritual path. I am not sure if it's the place or the actress, but I am convinced that my time is done in India; it is time to go home for good. I will cut my losses and leave quietly, I just need to find the right moment to tell The Producer, who has left for Bombay. I will wait until I see him.

Spy comes to see me on a daily basis; he hates the job and the people. But we've only just begun – we have another nine months ahead of us. Luckily for the South African actress, she is only needed for these first four weeks and then she's done. She will never have to see these people or India ever again.

The actress has a crying scene to do on a bridge. She is offered glycerine, but declines. She is so worked up and angry with the director and the way he treats the crew that the tears come easily. Everyone is in awe; they cannot believe how well she plays out the scene. The crew talk about it for days. They have never seen an actress cry for real. They regard her as a true talent.

On our last day in Rishikesh, the Indian actor playing the taxi driver and the South African actress have to complete their song on a rock in the middle of the gushing Ganga River. Crowds line up along the quay and across the steep stepped hillside to see the actor. He is immensely popular and takes the time to talk to people and sign autographs. The director decides out of nowhere that he wants an aerial shot of the scene.

The cameraman does not agree.

"You are not needing aerial shot. I can see through viewfinder. The shot is most definitely good just as it is. You are wasting money, Sir."

Spy calls The Producer, horrified. He has obviously been keeping The Producer up to speed right through and has definitely not been singing their praises. He comes back to the director saying that The Producer rejects the request. The director screams at Spy over the loud hailer in front of everyone.

"Go fuck yourself."

We are forced to wait around until they sort out their differences, with extra days in the hotel adding costs to the production. The South African actress is distraught that her stay has been extended for three days; it feels like the end of her world. The Producer refuses to come to Rishikesh, he stays in Bombay to fight this fight over the phone. He finally gives in to the director.

Getting a helicopter into Rishikesh is not simple. It is an extremely mountainous area making it dangerous and very expensive. The director and his assistants ride in the helicopter with the cameraman and pilot. I watch Spy on the phone, obviously to The Producer. When they land, the director and his assistants strut about so plump chicken-breasted that I expect they might cluck and lay eggs.

We move into the final week of the schedule doing night shoots in Ramoji, a big South Indian film studio, incorporated with hotels and an amusement park.

By this stage, the South African actress has stopped eating completely. She is weak, miserable and completely self-absorbed. She does not come out of her room unless she has to. She talks to no one, only me. She draws in her sketchbook, trying to make sense of her nightmares. We have one night left – I just have to help her get through it. I bump into Harvey and Kiran Cooper. They offer to have the actress and myself over for a whisky in their room before we have to be on set. The actress refuses. She wants to see and speak to no one. I decline Kiran Cooper's offer, although I know Spy has no time to spy on me. I don't want The Producer to have anything on me when I tell him that I'm leaving tomorrow.

I arrive on set at 9pm. It's chaos. We are shooting a typical Indian wedding scene with over one thousand extras. I quietly take my place next to the cameraman. This is my last night on this disastrous film. I can't stop smiling. I have rehearsed my going-away speech to The Producer in front of the bathroom mirror. When we wrap tomorrow morning we are flying straight out of here, by lunch time I will be free. I just have to find a shipping agent, pack my trunks and then I am off. I fantasise about the supermarkets, the clean air, my friends, Cape Town and the beautiful sea. I will be able to do my own shopping, choose my own detergents. I can open all of them, smell all of them and choose any of them – ocean breeze, lemon fresh and potpourri. I will have tampons. I will have Woolworths and their beautifully packaged foods, fresh sushi and beef steaks. I will not feel 'unable' anymore; I will make my own choices; my decisions will be mine. I will have myself back. Best of all I will blend like turpentine, no one will leer at me ever again. I will never have to wake up to my house troll's hawking.

The director's voice bellows over the loud hailer, bringing me back to the disorganised set. He is hugely agitated tonight; his assistants are not managing to control the crowds very well.

The music screams and crackles through the blown speakers; the choreographer leads the crowd into a coordinated dance sequence. The South African actress runs down a flight of stairs in her sari into the arms of her chocolate lover. Saris really don't suit us white girls, we always look too white in them.

As the film camera moves slowly along the tracks I follow, keeping as closely attached to the camera team as I can. We cut to do another take. The cameraman changes his lens; I follow suit. The cameraman is ready, the director's assistants shout for silence and they begin to roll again. I am still changing my lens. As I am about to screw the lens into the shoe, the director screams "CUT", storming towards me, pushing me hard with two hands as he walks on shouting.

"Get out of my fucking way."

He then spins around and walks back to his 'special chair', with his name embroidered on it in gold thread. He sits down and says with a smile on his face, "Okay, ready ..."

I am on the floor scrambling around. My eyes fill with tears – the new Canon lens is next to me in pieces, shards of glass everywhere, under my hands, there are too many, I cannot pick up all the pieces. The set has gone silent, nobody moves.

The director screams.

"I said ready!"

Nobody moves. I get up with what is left of the lens and walk off to the side. I can hear the director and the noise build up again. Everything starts moving. Everyone goes back to what they were doing without a word. Not a single bloody word! He did that on purpose.

I now have no doubts, I have to leave this place. Now.

I find a car to take me back to the hotel. It's almost midnight. Kiran Cooper and Harvey are still up, they pour me a whisky and

I cry. I cry for what feels like forever. After all these years, I can finally let it go. After my cry, we drink whisky, smoke cigarettes and laugh about the stupid things in life. They sit with me until morning. When it's time to leave for the airport, I say goodbye to Kiran Cooper and Harvey. There's a bowl of chillies left on the food tray, which Harvey throws into the melted ice bucket that had a bottle of champagne in it, ordered by Kiran Cooper from room service to celebrate my freedom.

"They need cooling down."

We promise each other that we will do a film together, I point to the ice bucket.

"I think we should call it *Chillies and Champagne*."

I make a promise to myself: I will write my book and return to India to shoot the film with Kiran Cooper and Harvey at my side.

Trapped

I walk through my front door. I feel relief – soon I will be leaving this smelly place. I don't care that I have to step over the house troll, who is lying on his mat in front of the television pushing squashed rice and dal into his face. I phone my best friend in South Africa and tell him that I am coming home. I unpack my bag and repack it. I call the travel agent and make a preliminary booking for next week. I will need at least a week to organise. I wait until 8pm when I know The Producer will be home. I listen to Johnny Clegg's song "Asimbonanga" all the way to his house, shouting out the song as I drive.

I pull into The Producer's courtyard and meet Sai coming down the stairs.

"*Arrey*, Madam Jimmy what you doing?"

It suddenly hits me that I have arrived at The Producer's without being invited.

"Is Boss alone?"

"Yes, Boss television watching. Why coming this hour?"

"I'm going home."

I run into the apartment block, past the rows of the servants' *chappals* (sandals) lined up against the wall, up the stairs, through the front door and burst into The Producer's room.

"What on earth are you doing?"

I throw what's left of the lens onto the bed beside him. The Producer turns his soccer match down on the television; the fans' shouting spurs me on. It is the same support team I had cheering me on when I first had to sleep with The Producer in Kuala Lumpur; now here I am almost four years later.

"I have to talk to you. I hate everything about this film. There is no future for me here. I am wasting my time. I am already 28. I need to go home and sort my life out. I'm sorry. You have been so good to me, and I realise I have been a strain on you. I know you really want me to go, and you haven't wanted to hurt my feelings. I have done nearly a hundred commercials, I need to go back and try to get into the South African film industry. It isn't that I don't like working for you ... but ..."

Months of pent-up anger, frustration and despair burst out as I crouch, crying on The Producer's floor. The Producer looks shocked.

"What are you talking about?"

I tell him about how the director publicly slated him and I show him my lens.

"Calm down."

I hold up some of the pieces of my precious lens.

"Spy already told me."

He shouts for Sai. "Make the madam proper dinner – butter chicken."

"Sit down, everything is going to be fine. Leave the lens with me, I will get you a new one and I will have words with the director."

"No, you don't understand. It is time for me to leave. I need to go home. I cannot work here anymore."

The more frantic I become, the nicer he gets. The Producer turns everything around. He has been so distant and secretive for so long and now he is being sweeter than he has ever been. I don't want to hurt his feelings, but I know it is time to leave India. I feel cornered.

"I really must go home ..."

"You must stay for Kush's film. You can't turn him down."

He hugs me.

"You will be working with your boyfriend Bly Avibath; Kush has written this fabulous script. The two of you have always made a good team. It's what you have always wanted. Do the film and then you can go."

"But how long will the film take?"

"If we start prepping next month we should be done filming by October, November."

"The end of the year?"

"Don't sound so disappointed. Hey, isn't this what you always wanted?"

"It's too long, I need to go now."

"Your season is ending soon in South Africa, so you won't find a job. Go back when the season starts. You can be the first assistant and the photographer."

"Can I go home before prep starts?"

"No, you have just been home. Stay here and do whatever you like. You can paint. Anyway you owe me a painting."

"What would you like me to paint?"

Here I go again, I can't stop myself. I'm agreeing to stay after convincing myself otherwise.

"Why don't you paint me? But make sure you don't put any fat rolls in or double chin!" he says as he pulls in his stomach and stretches out his neck as I have seen him do a hundred times before.

"Why don't you use those black-and-white photos that you took of me in Romania, but without the double chin? Why don't you go and wash up before dinner. You can stay here in your old room for a few days until you feel ready to go back to your basket. I will ask Nisha to come and stay with you."

The Producer goes back to his soccer match. I go to my old bedroom; I lean against the heavy wooden door, the metal woman doorhandle pushes her breasts against my thumb. The Producer has breakfast with me on the verandah in the morning. I have not been to this house or sat with The Producer since December. I notice that a colossal white building going up right in front of his verandah has obstructed his sea view.

"Who the hell got permission to build right in front of you? I thought you said no one could build here, it's holy land."

"It was until Gaya and her new husband-to-be decided to screw me over and steal my view."

"What? Gaya's getting married? To who?"

"To the owner of a huge soap company. And just to rub it in my face they have taken my view and will be living with my sons right in front of my face."

"I am so sorry."

"I don't care, they must get on with it."

Home … sweet home

I go back to my house troll and a blank canvas. Painting The Producer's face is not my idea of therapeutic release; why the hell did I agree to do this? I am so disappointed with myself, but when it comes to Bly Avibath and Kush I cannot say no. I try to persuade myself that doing this film justifies why I insisted on coming back after Romania, it justifies the fact that I have stuck it out for so long, it justifies the sacrifice, the heartache and the pain. I push away the doubt and occupy myself with The Producer's face. This film will look good on my CV; it will give me the experience that I need to go back and find work in South Africa. I rearrange the house and move the television into my bedroom. I create a painting area in the living room near the window between the dining table and the treadmill. I tell the house troll to watch TV during the day in my room, but when I'm done painting at night I want to lie in bed and have the TV to myself. This arrangement does not work. When I watch television at night I find the house troll sitting staring at a blank wall in the living room. He has nothing to do. Even if he had friends he is not allowed to leave the flat. The Producer calls every night on the landline to make sure we are both there. We are prisoners of Sweet Home Towers. I call him to watch with me, but he stares at the English channel I watch and he does not understand a word. He sits on the floor next to me with his dinner plate piled high with rice and dal. He has doubled in size; his face looks like a party balloon. He shoves the food in, sucking his lips together. His tongue slaps his palette. Tswap ... tswap ... tswap ...

I move the television back to the living room.

Nisha comes to visit. She is in high spirits. She has met a man on the Internet who lives in London. He works for the Mittal family and wants to meet her. His family would like him to marry soon. Nisha would like The Producer to represent her and put her forward as a possible bride. The Producer has the financial recourses to offer the family a decent dowry. She has spoken to The Producer and he is willing to put in an offer and get her married off. Things have got very bad for her at home. Spy's abuse has become unbearable.

The house troll comes to ask for bribe money, pointing at the rum bottle and the pack of cigarettes.

I finish the painting in three weeks and deliver it to The Producer. He does not like it.

"You did not make me thinner."

"But then it would not look like you."

"I want to look thinner, my double chin is still there."

In the company of hogs

I have become depressed. I don't get out of bed. I have nowhere to go, and even if I did, I'm not allowed to. I hate my house troll. He hates me. My best friend from South Africa calls me every day and we speak for over an hour. He is a musician. He makes me get out of bed. I put him on speakerphone and he sings his famous song to me, "Can you hear my call." A hog comes to our door with its babies. I take one and let it sleep in my bed with me. I return it to its mother the next day. I feed them; they come and visit every day at noon. I am seriously starting to lose it.

My phone rings. It's Kush.

"Hello mate, I'm back! Let's make this film, are you ready?"

Thank god, I've just been saved.

Through the lens

The last time I saw Kush was when we did our last commercial together, more than a year-and-a-half ago. His hair has become speckled with grey, New York has matured him. Something is different. When I ask him, he gets shy.

"I found true love in New York."

I am so happy for him.

"Is she here?"

He stumbles on his words, looking down at the floor.

"It's a he."

I'm surprised, but not shocked.

"That's wonderful Kush, I am really happy for you. Where is he?"

"New York. It would be too risky for us to be together in India, you know how it is, they will never accept me and I really need to do this film."

"So now what?"

"I will see him in New York when I am done shooting. Please, I beg you not to say anything. Ever."

"Of course."

His vibrant energy and positive outlook put me at ease immediately. It feels good to work with him again. I find myself regaining my sanity as he reads his script to me. The story is unique and for the first time someone is making a film in Bollywood that has not been stolen from Hollywood, how refreshing. He has written the script in English, which means I have something to work off. He has written the character to specifically suit Bly Avibath. There are no typical dance sequences and actors breaking out into song, which is very unconventional for Bollywood.

"I had a meeting with your boyfriend Bly last night. He is excited that you are on the film," Kush tells me. "I have set up a photo shoot with him for next week. He will have a ponytail in this film and we want to see how it registers on camera."

"Where are we doing the shoot?"

"At his house."

"I get to go to his house?"

"You sure do."

Kush's adoration for Bly is as big as mine. The only difference is that he grew up with Bly as his childhood hero. To me, he is my newfound hero and no Western icon comes close. I do not understand what draws me to this man, but the attraction is indescribably immense.

The Producer comes over to join us for lunch. He is looking exhausted. The *Love Actually* film is sapping him. They have had some continuity issues with Samson Night and have had to put a hold on filming his scenes. He has started losing his hair and as his hair is his power, in a panic he flew to Dubai, without telling anyone, to see a surgeon to attend to his receding hairline. Now the scars across his forehead are still too deep and pronounced; they have to wait for them to fade. He has to wear a cap to hide his surgery as he wants no one to know that The Lion is losing his mane.

Kush and I work well together. With his experience from New York he works by Western standards, which, coupled with his inexperience as a feature-film director, means that he researches and organises everything thoroughly, leaving as little as possible to chance. I am completely involved and thrilled that I can use my experience. Kush's respect for my input makes the weeks of waiting and staying in India worthwhile.

Kush works on the script while I meet with the costume designer and make contact with an art director in South Africa. She sends us some ideas. Kush loves her work. She is hired.

The actress is incredibly difficult, rude and obnoxious. She takes an instant disliking to Kush and refuses to deal with him. The costume designer has a terrible time with her. She rejects all the outfits that initially she insisted on. Alisha comes on board as the production manager as The Producer and Spy are too busy on the other film. She brings harmony to the production, getting the actress to start cooperating.

The art director from South Africa is put up at the Grand Hyatt. She is easygoing and does not seem too disturbed by India and its chaos. She is given a local art department team and The Producer hires a driver to drive my car. This means I no longer drive myself, I get lifts with Kush and Alisha – my car now belongs to the art department.

The director of photography that Kush has chosen is a legend in India. His stage name is ACDC. He lives in Chennai and comes from the same school of directors as Kiran Cooper. He has worked with Kiran Cooper before. We put him up at the Hyatt as well.

For his role, Bly wants his look to resemble Karl Largerfeld. All the outfits have to be copied and made up by the little magician tailor from the game show shoot. House of Chanel in Paris sends a selection of Karl Largerfeld's designs. A gorgeous black-velvet jacket with suitable fabric, with a tight white T-shirt, boot-cut Armani jeans, pointed black leather shoes and the special grey ponytail flown in from London produces the look. I am nervous as the time draws near for me to go and meet Bly for the shoot at his home. The Producer has replaced my broken lens and has got me an extra 85mm lens with a 1.4 aperture, a dream lens for portraits. Kushi has complete faith in me. The director of photography from Chennai calls me as we are driving. He sounds more nervous than I do.

"You only be having one chance and one chance only, don't be blowing it! You sure you can be doing this? You must be getting lighting right."

"I thought I would be using natural light."

"Aaa ... you see you blowing it already! Why you not taking lights?"

I now feel even more nervous, but I know that natural light is right. "ACDC, let me take the photos my way, if they are not right we can talk."

"I'll kill you if they are not right! I am praying for you, dear."

Kush looks at me encouragingly.

"You are the photographer and you know what's right. Go with your gut, you will be fine."

He truly believes in me.

We are escorted through a modern Western-style house, guided up a wide marble staircase where the wall is covered in paintings, through to the Louis-Vuitton-everything dressing room in the west wing of the house. Bly Avibath has come a very long way since I saw him last. He career has turned around since the game show and people have found places to put him in their films again without making him the dancing queen. He is sitting in front of a mirror framed with lights, attended to by his makeup artist and his hairstylist, who is putting on the ponytail that we had flown in from London. He recognises me in the mirror and stands up.

"*Gini,* I am so glad you are doing a film with me."

He gets up and hugs me. He looks down at my camera and the one lens.

"That's all? No lights?"

"I want to shoot in natural light."

"Excellent choice, I love a confident photographer who knows what they want."

I have never been this nervous.

"Let me show you the dining room, one of my favourite rooms, where the light comes in beautifully."

Kush and I follow him to a large dining room. There is a heavy twenty-four-seater dining table with high-backed chairs. I am finally standing at Bly's dining room table. Kush winks at me, nodding towards the table.

Bly is only walking with one crutch at the moment. He seems far more stable than before – his health has improved considerably. He walks over to the window and opens the curtains. A beautiful shaft of golden light illuminates India's resurrected star.

I put my 85mm lens on. Bly stands in front of me. I am 60cm away from him and he is staring straight into the lens. If looks could kill, I would be dead. I take a deep breath to steady my shaking hands. I look straight into his crocodile-green eyes through the lens and direct him gently as I click away, making him turn into and away from the light, getting him from every angle possible. He suddenly stops.

"Okay, enough! I'm late for another meeting."

Before I lift my head from the viewfinder he is already out the door waving over his shoulder.

"Thank you, I hope you knew what you were doing. I'm not giving you another chance."

I had a minute and a half and that's all I'm getting. Magic.

Kush looks at me, unsure.

"You think you got it?"

"Of course I did!"

I am elevated and excited. I got it, I just know I did. Kush drops me at the lab and I agree to meet him at ACDC's hotel room in an hour. ACDC has instructed me to have them printed on A3 sheets so that he can stick them up in his hotel room and study them.

When I arrive at the hotel room everyone on the crew list is waiting to see them. As I enter the room ACDC grabs the envelope and pulls the pictures out.

"I need you close, if you wanting me to be killing you *yaar*!"

He looks down.

"*Arrey*, these are working, *yaar*! Look at the intensity in the man's face and what all. This is working, Kush ... Look, Kush ... Look!"

He gets off the bed and excitedly begins to hop around the room. He turns to me.

"Your photographs are fantastic. I could not have done better.

I was so nervous sending you without me being there." They are stunning portraits; even I'm impressed.

"I was wrong, you are bamboozling me with your goodness."

He sticks them up on his ceiling so that he can study them when he's lying in bed and wake up to them in the morning.

I have gained ACDC's confidence, India's greatest director of photography. What a wonderful film to be working on. Give a dog a bone!

Kush now insists that I deal with continuity, the costumes with the help of dressman Sashi, the photographs and of course Bly Avibath. Another assistant, Avi, will run the floor and another two will manage the script and the props. The responsibilities are clear and everyone is happy with what they are given.

From intelligent and productive conversations with Kush and my magical moment with Bly, I return to the apartment. I shut my bedroom door behind me and drown out the house troll's abdominal sounds with Michael Jackson's "Man in the Mirror". I grab my hairbrush and my teddy bear and I dance with Bly in front of the mirror. He spins me around and does a dip with me in his arms. My street children dance behind us in a choreographed sequence. My photographs and paintings of these children are pinned up everywhere in my mind. Today I lived my dream.

Wake up call

I wake up to a hard knock on my door. The house troll is incapable of knocking with such force.

"Open the door."

It's The Producer. He looks past me into the room. An ashtray with cigarette butts in it sits on the night stand.

"You smoking?" he hisses. He walks into the living room with my phone and starts to go through my messages. I have kept all the messages from my musician friend, the ones he sent to get me out of bed.

"Remember that I love you. Remember that you are beautiful. Remember that you are worth everything and more. Remember that there is someone who loves you waiting for you to return."

"Are you fucking him?"

"Who?"

"This friend of yours in South Africa."

"He's a friend, and anyway logistically it is impossible."

"There are many ways to skin a fucking cat."

"He's just a friend."

"Men and woman are never just friends, you think I'm stupid?"

"Maybe not in your books. He's just a friend who helped me through a hard time."

The Producer leaves without another word, slamming the door behind him.

"Destroy yourself, I don't care," I hear him shout while he waits for the elevator.

I whisper back at him.

"You destroy me. You stop me dreaming."

Sugar free

Everything comes together beautifully. Kush, ACDC and I do a final walkthrough on the beautiful set. The South African art director has created an outstanding London apartment. I have not seen or spoken to The Producer for over a week. He will be here to break the coconut. Hopefully he will not stay for long; his other film is keeping him very busy.

Kush gives the entire team a motivational speech. He ends it with a little banter aimed at me.

"Tomorrow is it possible to have you with us on set or will you be going out for Sunday lunch at your boyfriend's house?"

ACDC answers for me.

"You will not be having time for Sunday lunch and all, tomorrow, my dear, they will not see the work they will only see the economics."

The South African art director invites me back to her hotel for dinner. We have not had time to socialise since she got here, and she would like to buy me dinner and share a bottle of wine with me. We are driven in my smelly little maroon Ford to the Hyatt. At dinner the art director asks me about The Producer. I try to avoid the subject. She tells me that she has had a few arguments with him about the budget and her payments. I say nothing. I don't want her to know about our past.

She makes a joke about him.

"He reminds me of those buns with the deep-fried potato fritter in it that they sell on the side of the street. What do you call it?"

"A *vada pao*."

"Exactly, he looks like a fat deep-fried fritter, a *vada pao*!"

I cringe. May my secret never come out.

We shoot for five weeks in the studios that the South African designed at Film City. Things happen gently on our set and our working hours are reasonable. Bly insists that we get one day in a week off and we never shoot for longer than eight hours a day, which is usually unheard of in Bollywood. Because we are working with Bly, who is in every scene and will not work unreasonable hours for health reasons, we find ourselves in a very fortunate position. On our off day I spend time with the art director at the Hyatt. We sit at the pool, read and sleep. The chef of the hotel, an Italian called Roberto, always sends us something special to eat. I start receiving little notes written in Italian.

ACDC hates waiting and gets very impatient. Everyone relies on me to get Bly onto set as fast as possible. Sometimes it's not that easy, given his situation.

ACDC gets incredibly excited when Bly walks onto set.

"Kush, call it! Call it! It is all going wanky here. Movie making is simply called time pass, if we carry on like this! We are on top of the world only."

Sometimes I get phone calls from Bly in the evenings asking me about the following day. Sometimes he asks me to change the order in the schedule, explaining that logistically things would work better that way. Bly has been doing this all his life. He knows better than any of us how to schedule accordingly. His opinion always makes more sense. I never get used to his calls – at first when I hear his voice I always think that it is one of the crew members playing a trick; everyone is aware of my adoration for the man.

On our last day of the Bombay schedule The Producer talks to me for the first time in six weeks.

"How is it going at your apartment?"

"Fine, why?"

"I was there this morning, I see you have continued to defy me; I found cigarettes again."

I walk away and take my place next to ACDC. I get teary with anger. ACDC leans in, noticing how upset I am and whispers with a smile, "Down, down Producer! Down, down!"

We wrap the Bombay schedule and the South African art director goes home. We have a ten-day schedule in Delhi. While we are in Delhi, Roberto the chef calls me every day. I am starting to develop feelings for the guy. He makes me feel good. The idea of a relationship excites me. I am careful though and I delete all messages and phone records.

The Producer leaves Delhi early, leaving Alisha in charge as he needs to get back to the other film where things are going horribly wrong. When I land in Bombay I hang back at the luggage belt. I know Roberto will be waiting for me and I do not want Alisha and the other crew to see. It's my birthday and we have planned to do something special together. Roberto is waiting for me with a bunch of red roses. I have not been given flowers in almost six years. I'm sold. We go back to Roberto's hotel room where he has a crayfish dinner waiting for me. I don't intend for whatever this is to last for too long. I have two months to go and then the film will be done. I want to go home for good. Roberto is being transferred to Japan around about the same time that I finish my film. Neither of us wants to give up our plans in order to be together. It's an arrangement of convenience and it's fun. We both want to be with someone who comes from the same 'bread recipe'.

Doctor dirty

We have a full month's break. Bly has other commitments. We will go to London and complete the film there in four weeks' time. I have time to work on my photographs. Roberto asks me to move in with him at the Hyatt. I don't want to go back to my house troll so I'm willing to take the risk of being caught. I wake up to buffet breakfasts. I have a large swimming pool to lounge at, a gym to work out at and an Italian restaurant where I can order anything from crayfish to Kobe beef. I don't return to my basket even once. The Producer is in London with his other film; he will only be back in two weeks' time.

There is an Italian girl named Roberta who lives permanently in the Hyatt. She works for Roberto Cavalli, the famous clothing brand, travelling between Mumbai and Milan on a monthly basis. In her early forties, she is extremely vivacious and bold. I'm drawn to her positive energy; we become good friends. At night we eat the food that Roberto prepares for us, we have a very happy and full table. People often join us, international guests are also drawn to her presence.

The monsoons are back, but living in the luxury of the Hyatt makes it easy to cope with. I have been putting my regular injection on hold. I know I have to have it, but I cannot bear the idea of leaving the comfort of the Hyatt. I ask Roberto to come with me, but he has to stay at the restaurant. His busiest hours clash with Dr Bollywood's consulting times. I call and find out he can only fit me in after 9pm. I take a rickshaw. The roads are flooded and it takes forever. I call Dr Bollywood in a panic, I don't want to have to come back. He tells me he will wait for me. I reach his rooms after 10pm.

He is alone. I lie on the bed and pull the side of my jeans down across my bum cheek, he asks me to unbutton the jeans I tell him it's fine as it is. He gives me my injection and asks me smoothly and slowly how my new apartment is. He brushes a piece of hair away from my face and kisses the air between us. I get up quickly and push past him. He grabs my arm, spinning me around and forcefully pushing me up against the wall. He flicks the light switch off. His hot mouth presses up against mine, his moustache is moist and salty. I squirm. His thick tongue pushes into my mouth. I cannot move; he has me pinned. I grab beside me, there is a solid metal trolley with instruments on it. I pull it into the side of his leg and poke him with a long instrument. He falters and I lift my knee into his groin and scramble for the door. It's unlocked!

I run into the raging street. I am instantly drenched, the rain comes down hard like a solid sheet of water. I wipe my face as I run looking for a tuk-tuk. I cannot believe what just happened. I cry all the way back to the hotel. I pull myself together as I walk through the Hyatt doors as if everything is as it should be. So much for The Producer's choice in who he can trust with me. That Bastard!

Roberto is in the restaurant. I sneak up to the room and call Nisha. I dare not tell Roberto or The Producer, but I have to tell someone in order to move on. She tells me she does not go to Dr Bollywood because the exact same thing happened to a friend of hers. She tells me that she is getting married to the guy in London that works for Mittal. They will marry in Delhi after we are done with our film. She asks me to be at her side when it happens. I promise to stay for it, it is literally a week after we finish the film. I shower and join Roberto and Roberta for dinner.

Instead of telling her about the doctor, I tell Roberta about my problem with The Producer and that his servants are snooping. Roberta comes up with a fantastic plan. She tells me to knock the wind out of the rumours immediately and call him and say that my cousin, who is a chef in Italy, and his wife have been transferred to the Hyatt in India, and it is all so wonderful because I now have family here and I am staying with them all the time and they would love to meet him when he comes back. They have heard so much and ...

I stop her mid sentence.

"And the wife?"

She puts her arm around Roberto's.

"I'm the wife. We get him here and we pretend we are a couple. What's your mom's surname?"

"Cantamessa."

"Perfect! I am from the Cantamessa side! I am your cousin and this is my husband."

She pulls me closer.

"We look like family, no?"

I call The Producer. He buys my story.

Optical illusion

The Producer calls me as soon as he lands.

"So when and what time shall we meet?"

"Tomorrow?"

It's obviously been eating him.

Roberto, Roberta and I rehearse the dinner and tell all the hotel and kitchen staff to stick to the story. Roberto's staff adore him so they will do anything he asks them to without bribe money. Roberto says he doubts whether The Producer will ask. It would make him look stupid. We agree not to drink on the night in case something slips out.

The Producer arrives at the hotel wearing the yellow Banana Republic Hawaiian shirt that he wore when I first arrived in India. His skin always looks a shade darker in that shirt, the buttons bulge around the stomach area and a few 'curlies' escape through the gaping holes. We exchange pleasantries. Roberta executes a superb rendition about our childhood together and my mother, her aunt. It's so convincingly dramatic that even I start to believe we're related. She holds my face against hers.

"We look alike no?"

She does not give The Producer a chance to doubt the situation. Roberto does not sit with us much as the restaurant demands his attention. He watches us from his workstation.

"Thank you for taking such good care of our baby cousin. Please, you come to Italy we look after you too."

She smiles at him and speaks to me in Italian.

"You think daddy's concrete boots are heavy enough to sink him?"

I try not to blush.

"She says you have very nice eyes."

The Producer is flattered, he laughs and leaves. He waves to Roberto as he goes past the kitchen.

Once he's gone we celebrate with a bottle of Lambrusco. Give a dog a bone!

London Bridge is falling down ...

There are no tears when I leave for London. Roberto and I knew from the beginning how this was going to end. When I return to India he will be here, but not for long. I want to get to Delhi, attend Nisha's wedding and get out of here as soon as it's done. I must avoid my apartment at all costs. I cannot stomach the idea of being trapped up there again.

London tastes like home. I feel free and independent. Kush, ACDC and I fly in first; we spend a week prepping and doing recces with the facilitating producer, Daniel.

Daniel is a Pakistani Brit. Although he is not very tall, he dresses in smart suits, and his soft face always bears a smile. He speaks gently, he never raises his voice and always stays extremely calm no matter how hectic our shooting days become. When Alisha, the rest of the crew and Bly arrive, everything is ready and shooting goes smoothly without any hiccups for the entire six weeks.

The Producer comes back to London with his other film. Things are not going as well on that side; we hardly see him. The other film crew are staying in a different hotel to us across town. The Producer stays with them. I am so grateful for this arrangement. I don't have to see any of them. I have my own room and don't have to share with anyone. The closer we get to the end, the more confident I become. I have done good work on this film and I am going home soon with two feature films, ninety-seven commercials and five years of experience under my belt. I am bound to get a job. Alisha and I spend a lot of time together. We shoot a scene in London's top hair salon where Bly cuts his ponytail off. When we are done, I go back to the salon, cut my hair and dye it black. Goodbye Bollywood Blonde. We have two days left and I have already packed my suitcase, it sits on the nightstand ready to go. I receive a phone call; it's Daniel, the producer.

"Got any dinner plans tonight?"

"No, not yet."

"Mind if I take you for dinner? I've got something I would like to discuss with you."

He's got my attention.

"What's the problem?"

"No problem, let's meet say around seven-thirty? I will pick you up, meet me in your hotel lobby."

Daniel offers me a job. He wants me to come and work permanently for his production house in London. I'm surprised.

"Right now?"

"As soon as you can."

"I need to think about it."

"Of course."

"I really need to go home first. I have been desperate to go home for almost a year."

"It's already November. Why don't you go home, spend Christmas with your family and come back in January?"

"Let me think about it."

"Tomorrow's our last day. Since we are shooting in Bath I'm going to leave really early to make sure everything is ready for when Bly arrives. Why don't you drive with me instead of in the crew bus, we can discuss it a bit more?"

"I will need a proper contract."

"Of course you will. I will have it drafted before you leave. You can take it home with you and mull it over. We can discuss changes over the phone. You don't have to sign until you are completely happy."

Daniel and I walk through Notting Hill after dinner. We pass the famous 'blue door' from the *Notting Hill* film. I don't want a repeat of Romania, but walking straight into a production job in London is far more inviting than trying to sell myself in South Africa having come from Bollywood. Daniel has had six weeks to see how I work and I have obviously managed to impress him. Whether he has ulterior motives, I don't yet know, but this time if there are, I will know how to handle them. He does have a wife and two young children, but then again that doesn't mean anything, does it? With a signed contract in place and working on English soil I have a far better chance of survival than before.

I will sleep on it.

We spend our last day shooting in Bath. It's Bly's birthday. He buys us all an ice cream. Everyone is in very high spirits, we are wrapped and it's been a fabulous film to work on. Daniel quietly comes up to me with an envelope and an elegantly wrapped gift. I put it into my bag. Alisha and I drive back to the hotel together. When I open the bag to unwrap my gift Alisha looks surprised.

"Who's that from?"

"Daniel."

I read the card out loud.

"Thank you for your hard work and excellent performance. You made our job so much easier. Hope to work with you again ... soon. Daniel."

Maybe he does have ulterior motives?

Alisha raises her eyebrows.

"And now?"

"He wants me to come and work for him."

"Really, what did you say?"

"I told him I need to think about it."

I tear the wrapping paper, a bottle of Calvin Klein Obsession glows amber in the palm of my cupped hands.

When we get back to the hotel, The Producer is waiting for me in the lobby. He looks angry.

"Get your bags, you're moving into my room for the night."

"But you're in the other hotel."

His teeth are barred. He hisses. "Don't you dare fucking argue with me. Just do what I say!"

He throws a key card at me. "We wrapped the other film yesterday. I've moved to this hotel. I'm on the fifth floor."

I know better than to say another word.

He shouts after me as I climb into the elevator. "Get showered and meet me down here in half an hour. I'm taking you all out for dinner."

I don't understand what is going on. We fly back to Mumbai tomorrow – why has he moved me into his room for one night when I've been on my own for six weeks? Why is he acting so strange?

I move my bags to his room. I don't want to go for dinner with him and the crew. I have made arrangements to see some South African friends who live here. I dare not tell him, he needs to calm down first. I call them and tell them that I will have to meet them after dinner. They are disappointed. The Producer takes us to a Lebanese restaurant on Kensington High Street. Everyone is drinking and having a good time, but I can't relax. I notice The Producer watching me closely. He starts downing shots. His glares from across the table get more intense.

My phone rings. It's Daniel. I block the call and turn it onto silent. I look at my watch. I'm going to have to cancel with my friends. As I write the message, my phone rings again. It's on silent, but The Producer can see it vibrating in my hand. It's Daniel again.

"Who keeps calling you?"

The Producer's tone is intentionally aggressive. His fist hits the table. Everyone stops what he or she is doing. Silence.

Kush breaks the silence, passing The Producer a shot.

"Lighten up, what's got you in such a bad mood? Cheers everyone."

Everyone throws themselves back into celebration.

A message comes through on my phone; it's Daniel: "Did you like the gift?"

I have to stop him. I'm going to be spending the night in The Producer's room. He cannot keep trying to contact me. Something is wrong with The Producer and I think Daniel has something to do with it. I have not seen The Producer to tell him about the job offer. Anyway, what does it matter? What I do after this is my business not his. However, looking at The Producer's stewing face it obviously does matter. I need to get through one more night without a fight. I excuse myself and go to the bathroom. I call Daniel from the booth, whispering.

"Please you have to stop calling me, and no messages, I've been moved to The Producer's room for the night, I can't talk to you, you will get me into a lot of trouble."

"Why, I don't understand? Why are you whispering?"

"Please Daniel?"

I start pleading.

"Okay, okay. Call me when you can."

"I'll call you from South Africa, we can discuss things then."

When I go back to the table The Producer has paid the bill and everyone's leaving. We all walk back together. Then The Producer holds me back, pinching hard into my upper arm. I can feel it bruising immediately.

"Give me your phone now."

I dig into my bag, there's nothing else I can do.

He lets go of my arm, pushing me forward. "Go."

I stumble forward. Shit!

I link my elbow into Alisha's. I'm scared. I start pleading into her ear, panic-stricken. I whisper as fast as I can.

"Please don't leave me alone with him, please?"

"Who?"

Kush has started walking with The Producer, chatting loudly, oblivious to The Producer's raging mood. I continue whispering into Alisha's ear, getting more and more desperate. We are almost at the hotel.

"Did you say something to The Producer?"

"About what?"

"Please Alisha, I'm in so much trouble please, please, please help me. Don't leave me with him please?"

"With who?"

"The Producer."

We enter the hotel lobby. The Producer comes up to me as I pull myself away from Alisha's ear. He digs his thumb into my bruised arm again, it burns.

"Come."

He pulls me into an elevator. I look back pleadingly at Alisha. She turns away, answering to Kush's jocular banter. No one is aware of what's going on.

The Producer pushes me into the room.

"You're hurting me."

"Oh, you don't know what hurt is!"

He walks into me, his enraged wet face against mine, spitting mad. I move backward, he keeps coming. His alcohol breath and his condemning words lay into me.

"You fucking him?"

"Daniel?"

"No ... Sai!!!" His sarcastic smile guts me. I am so scared. That look, I've never seen that look. This fight is different. I start shaking.

"Of course not, he offered me a job."

"And the dinner? Strolling around Notting Hill in the middle of the night like two fucking courting pigeons?"

The only person that knew I was having dinner was Alisha. Was I followed? How does he know we walked through Notting Hill? Did Daniel tell him?

"And why the fuck were you driving alone with him in his car up to Bath?" His face becomes gruesomely contorted, his shouting fades in and out, I can't listen to him and the questions coming from my head at the same time, I only have one working ear.

How does he know all of this?

"Answer me. If you don't I will have to ..."

His fist curls into my chest, gripping my top. His nails scratch, I am up against him, I can't look at him, I look down. Two very different bodies up against each other, scrunched up shifting clothes my only shield against him.

"And the Obsession perfume? You think he really gave that to you because you did a good job? If he has not fucked you yet he sure intends to!"

Only Alisha and I were in the car when I opened the gift. I put it straight into my handbag, showing and telling no one.

I try to push him away.

"Leave me alone. I want to go home. Let go!"

My voice gets shrill with panic; it's so weak and pathetic compared to his. I twist around and he loses his grip of my shirt. I grab my laptop bag, it's all I need. It has my passport in it.

He grabs it off my shoulder.

"Not the laptop."

"It's mine, my father bought it for me."

"I said give it to me."

Of course he wants it. It holds all the photographs from the film.

"Take it, I just want my passport." I scratch in the bag, grabbing my passport. He snatches it from me.

I lose it. "The passport is mine!"

I lash out, grappling for it. Black-and-white arms waving wildly towards the ceiling. Twisting. Turning. Clawing. Hitting. He lashes out to stop me and his fist connects with my jaw. I register a spark of pain. My knee goes up into his crotch and then I run for the door. I'm out in the long passageway, a long royal-blue patterned carpet follows me as I run toward the stairs. The passage feels too long now. I shout Alisha's name over and over. She is on the third floor. My voice is faint. I am scared. I bolt down two flights of stairs. Is he following me?

I find Alisha's door. I pound on it; the urgency consumes me.

I look back, nothing.

Alisha's husband opens sleepily. I rush past him. Alisha is sitting on the bed painting her nails. She looks shocked.

"Hide me please? Hide me, hide me – don't open when he comes please? Hide me!"

"Calm down. What's going on?"

She stands up and touches my arm. She brushes the back of her hand against my jaw. I start to cry.

"Sit down."

Before my arse hits the duvet, The Producer's clenched fist is pounding on the door.

"Alisha, open this fucking door, I know she's in there."

I whisper desperately to her, pleading for her not to open. She walks toward the door. I go down onto my knees and cling to her leg but she wriggles free. She looks down at me.

"I'm sorry, I have to."

She opens the door and The Producer barges in. Alisha's husband moves forward.

"Please calm down, we can ..."

"You stay the fuck out of this."

He spins around, sticking his finger in Alisha's face.

"And you too."

His hand slaps down onto the top of my head, his fingers curl into my hair, scratching my scalp. He pulls me up by my hair and drags me out of the room. I cannot see where I am going. I am led by my head, my hair pulled taut ahead of me. My watering eyes try to focus on the moving patterned royal-blue carpet. I feel dizzy.

The Producer pulls me into the corner of the room. I crouch down next to the television.

"Now you stay there!"

He lies down on the bed staring at the TV. I don't know what he intends to do with me. For now, nothing. He switches channels, Manchester vs. Liverpool.

I sit for what feels like hours, my jaw throbbing. I stare at the floor, looking up randomly at The Producer.

"What you looking at?"

I look down again.

His eyes seem to be getting heavy. He falls asleep. I can reach the volume button on the television and I turn it up slightly. I wait ten minutes and turn it up again. If I can get the ambient noise up without him noticing, then he won't hear the door click when I make a run for it.

It's after 4am. I must take the chance and run before he wakes up. He is snoring. I have to go now. I dash for the door, I don't look back. I run, taking nothing with me. I don't wait for the elevator, instead I take the stairs and go straight to reception.

The reception clerk sits reading a book. Now that I am here, all my defences go. I break down and tell him what's happened. I ask him if I can phone my parents. He tells me that he will call the police. I wait in the luggage room for the police because I don't want to be seen. I go to the bathroom and look in the mirror. My jaw is swollen purple. I feel so little, so inferior, so beaten.

The police come and take my statement. They take pictures of my jaw and ask me if I want to press charges. They explain to me that if I do, he will be arrested. I don't want that, I just want him to get on the flight with the rest of the crew and go back to India. They go upstairs to talk to The Producer. I refuse to go with them. I tell them that there's a red laptop bag, a handbag and a blue suitcase that I need. They also need to get my passport. I call my parents from reception. I book myself into another room and ask them for a ticket home. My mother insists that I go back to India and get my possessions. She sends someone from the Italian Embassy to see me. They agree to escort me back into India and help me pack up. My mother has contacts in shipping, she will arrange for my trunks to get shipped back. My mother calls The Producer, informing him that I will be returning to India under the protection of the Italian Embassy and that he is not to come near me or enter my apartment until I have left India. I watch the crew leave with The Producer from my room window. The sight of The Producer makes me ill. I stay in London for two days before I leave for India. I do not contact anyone.

I am escorted into India and go straight to my apartment to pack. I call Nisha and tell her what has happened. She is sad that I will not be at the wedding, but she understands. She brings a bottle of rum and a pack of cigarettes and helps me pack. My apartment and everything in it has mould growing everywhere, the house troll is officially obese; he's eating himself to death. He has not lifted a finger since I've been gone. The house is piled high with body odour and rotting bins. We stay up all night packing. Things feel better when I'm drunk. By morning I have twenty-two trunks, mostly clothes – payment from The Producer. A guard, sent by the embassy, stands at my door 24/7. The shipping agent comes to fetch the trunks. I call Kush – I need to say goodbye and give him the photographs. He tells me to come and see him.

"What happened? I heard the shouting in the passage – you woke ACDC up."

"What, you and ACDC sleeping together now?"

He laughs.

"He complained about the shouting at breakfast the next morning."

"You could have helped."

"Can't get involved when it comes to love arguments."

"It's not love."

"Of course it is. You two are made for each other, you're good for The Producer. Can't you just kiss and make up, please?"

"It's different this time, Kush, I just want to go home."

"Okay, come have lunch at my house. I make you a great vegetarian meal in exchange for the pics."

I call Alisha and say goodbye, not a word is said about the night in London. I don't need to see her; maybe in another life.

I don't want to stay at the rotten apartment, so I check into the Hyatt. Roberto has left early for Japan, but perhaps it is better that way. Nisha stays with me. I fly out the next day so we plan to clean out the mini bar tonight.

I receive a phone call. It's Bly. He asks me most sincerely if I am okay and I start to cry.

"Is there anything I can do for you? You were so wonderful to work with and so wonderful to me, it's my turn to do something wonderful for you."

"A letter of referral so that I have some proof of the past five years?"

"Done, you can pick it up from my secretary tonight. Do you need help getting your possessions back to South Africa? I'm sure you have plenty."

"No, it's been organised."

"Okay, well, all the best, safe travels, and thank you once again."

"Thank you Bly, you are my magic man."

"Pardon?"

"You are my magic man," I whisper.

I put the phone down quickly. I start to cry again.

When I get to Kush's house, The Producer is sitting on the sunflower-yellow sofa. He looks so dark against the happy colour. I turn around and walk out the door. Kush runs after me.

"Please? For my sake? He wants to apologise and then you can leave. Don't leave like this. Almost six years together, it's not worth it. Don't leave with such a heavy heart. I know India means far more to you than holding onto a bag full of bad memories."

I let The Producer apologise. He seems genuine, but I will never trust him again. He asks me to stay for Nisha's wedding.

Without hesitation or thought I say yes. I just can't say no.

When I leave, my heart is lighter. I stop by Bly's offices. I read my reference letter in the tuk-tuk. "Gené is an extremely hard-working individual. Despite being a foreigner she easily adapted to local conditions. On many occasions I found her doing multiple jobs to assist in departments not necessarily hers. She has an extremely pleasant nature and is a thorough professional. I often found myself seeking her assistance ..." I cry.

Finally saying "no"...

Before I leave, I receive a phone call from Bollywood's best film poster designer. He is doing both of The Producer's films. He says he is blown away by my photographs and asks me if he can put me forward for other films, he says he has so much work lined up for me.

Not a chance! I am going home.

The last week before I fly home I attend Nisha's wedding. The ceremony goes on for five days. It starts with an engagement party where Nisha meets her husband for the first time and he puts a ring on her finger. After the party the groom and his London friends come back to our room. The rum gets the best of us. The last thing I remember is Nisha kissing me goodnight and telling me not to worry. When I wake up and she returns to the room after lunch I do not ask her where she spent the night.

Nisha's husband has been transferred to a Mittal plant in Algeria for seven years. They will leave as soon as they are wed. On the morning of the last day, The Producer's mother arrives at our room with a makeup artist, a costume supervisor and a trolley full of long-life milk cartons. We fill the bath with the milk and bath Nisha in it. She is teary and does not seem to be the radiant bride I expected her to be.

Her husband arrives on a horse. The Producer tells me that for his wedding he arrived on an elephant. How fitting. Nisha has to hold onto her groom's outfit, walking behind him around the fire seven times like a slave. It upsets me. She cries a lot, clinging to her mother and sister.

As I wave goodbye to my distraught friend being driven away in a Mercedes I think of Balkran taking me to the airport in The Producer's BMW to start my new life in a new land.

I find a recommendation letter waiting for me at The Producer's house from Kush and read it during take-off.

When I arrive home in October 2007, I find it hard to adjust permanently to the Western world, but I figure it out reasonably quickly. It is good to be home.

The Producer calls me just after Christmas. He wants to buy me a ticket to Hong Kong to spend New Year's Eve with him, for old time's sake. He is a very lonely man. I have not spoken to him since I left and I have to know if we are okay. I lie to my family, telling them that it is for work and that the money is too good to turn down. I don't think any rational mind would ever understand why I said yes; I just cannot say no.

When I get to Hong Kong I feel like I did when I first got to India. What the hell have I done? Am I addicted to The Producer? Or is he addicted to me?

We share a room, respect each other's privacy and have a really good time together as friends. There is no sex involved. We are okay.

I do not take Daniel's job offer. I have no inclination to find out if he has other intentions or not. Instead, I move back to Cape Town and get an agent. I am put on their books as a second assistant director. I pack my camera away though because I don't feel like taking another photograph for a very long time. The competition among photographers in South Africa feels too overwhelming for my jaded soul to handle right now. I stood out in India, the only white female photographer that everyone wanted. Here in South Africa I'm just another photographer, another face in the crowd. I don't want to have to prove myself. I don't have the energy for it. Fortunately, I find work quickly and start a new career as a second assistant director.

Nine months later, I receive a phone call from The Producer. He is doing a commercial with Kush in Portugal, Pierre is directing, they want me to do the hoarding photographs.

We meet in Portugal. The Producer flies Nisha in to be with me. She is unhappy in her marriage; she says her husband is a beater and a cheater. I worry for her, but she begs me not to tell. Kush tells me that he is planning a second film with Bly. His previous film was a huge hit – it went to Cannes. He is ready to do another one. He has been the catalyst in Bly's newfound success because he has started a new genre of Bollywood film without the dance, focusing on incredible acting. Bly is in his seventies and his newfound fame has only just begun. It's never too late. He is adored and wanted by everyone in Bollywood thanks to Kush and his dream to reinvent Bly. He promises to call me when his new film starts. So I am not quite done with India after all.

In 2009, two years after I have left India for good, Kush calls me. He is ready to do his second film with Bly Avibath. I am ready to go back. We are scheduled to shoot in Malaysia, Oxford, Cambridge and India.

We shoot in Malaysia first.

I am called into Bly's makeup trailer on our last day in Penang. He gifts me a brand new MacBook Pro. Almost four years later I write this book on it.

We return to Bombay for three weeks to shoot at Film City before going to England for the final schedule.

To thank Bly, I do a painting to add to the wall in his home where hundreds of paintings hang, painted for him by adoring fans. I paint a huge rooster standing in the chaos of Bombay traffic. I don't know what to write to India's biggest star in the thank you note. I steal an appropriate piece from *Eat, Pray, Love* by Elizabeth Gilbert.

"Dearest Bly ..."

I incorporate the stolen piece in my letter, justifying the subject matter in the painting. I am the chicken. The chicken story resembles how I fit into India.

> "The thing is, you must be very careful when introducing a new chicken to the general flock. You can't just toss it in there with the old chickens, or they will see it as an invader. What you must do instead is to slip the new bird into the chicken coop in the middle of the night while the others are asleep. Place her on a roost beside the flock and tiptoe away. In the morning, when the chickens wake up, they don't notice the newcomer, thinking only, 'She must have been here all the time since I didn't see her arrive.' The clincher of it is, awaking within this flock, the newcomer herself doesn't even remember that she's a newcomer, thinking only, 'I must have been here the whole time.'

Bly comes to thank me.

"I really liked the story about the chicken, did you write it?"

I am caught off guard and before I can stop myself, I say, "Yes."

"It's very good."

"Thank you."

I walk away, my cheeks burning tomato red. What the hell did I just do? I console myself. What are the chances he will read *Eat, Pray, Love*? Never!

Eat, pray, do not steal or lie ...

We wrap the film in Oxford. I will not go back to India or South Africa. Instead, I stay on for another Bollywood film being shot in

London. The poster designer insists I do it. The money is good so I agree.

I go to Bly's trailer to say goodbye, knowing I will never see him again. As I step into his trailer he looks up from a book in his hand. *Eat, Pray, Love* by Elizabeth Gilbert.

Never! I cannot believe what I am seeing.

"You reading that book?"

"Yes, I thought I should. Julia Roberts and the author are coming to have dinner with me next week. They will be in India shooting the Indian part of the film at an ashram on the outskirts of New Delhi. You've read it?"

"Umm ... Yes!"

We say our goodbyes. I hug him for a long time, thanking him over and over for the laptop. This will be the last hug we ever have. As I climb down the steep steps of his trailer, my mind still in the *Starry Night* whirl, he calls my name. I look back. He holds up the book and winks at me.

"I see this author also has a thing for chickens."

Several years have past, but in writing this book I have written the people who meant so much to me in India all back into my life. Nisha has divorced her husband. The beatings get worse and his appetite for prostitutes increases. She cannot bear the thought of going back to India, so she finds work in Dubai instead.

Alisha and The Producer part ways. Alisha is a freelance producer, still married to her new husband. Kiran Cooper still directs. The Producer does not produce anymore; he has started a new venture involving the rental of film equipment. Sai, Kutty and Balkran are still with The Producer. Roti sadly passed away, his epilepsy got the better of him. Kush still lives with his secret sexual preference, his life would become too complicated in India if he came out as being gay. His life partner waits for him in New York between filming, undiscovered.

While writing this book in December 2013 Alisha contacts me.

"I am calling to see if you would be interested in doing Kush's third film with us again, starring Bly of course?"

They will need me on the film for eleven months, in Bombay and Boston. A whole year away from my new life suddenly seems impossible. I am engaged to someone so divine that even Kush and Bly Avibath cannot persuade me to be apart from him for that long and I have two dogs that complete my new package. This is my life now. I take a month to think about it. I struggle to say 'no' but I say it. I say 'NO' so that I can get on with my life and write this book. I say 'NO' because I know from experience that chasing old dreams and trying to resurrect them is dangerous. I say 'NO' for me.

I send the original draft of this book with all the characters' real names still unchanged to Bly Avibath. I would like his approval and possibly have him on the cover of the book with me. Although my publishers are against me sending it, I do not see anything wrong with it. This was how I experienced India and Bollywood.

After reading the manuscript, Bly turns me down. He requests that I remove his name from the book completely. He kindly warns me that if I do not adhere to these conditions, it shall entail legal action that would become messy.

I understand. I remove all names from the book, but I am still entitled to tell my story as Bollywood happened to me. It was not Tinsel Town, where we burst into song and dance without the reality of life. Their films are an escape from the real India, where the dirty side of life is never portrayed. People are greedy and self obsessed and create an illusion of who they are that is completely the opposite of what they are like offscreen. I cannot expect to burst their inpenetrable bubble. I reply to him and tell him that I understand his request. I know that tomorrow all names will have to be changed, including his. What I don't know is that tomorrow does not come as easily as I thought and that publishing this story becomes far more complicated than I ever imagined.

Bly proceeds to send the first unchanged manuscript to two of the main characters involved, one of them being The Producer. The phone calls start coming in and I am threatened and told to never utter another word about India, Bollywood or any of the persons involved in my story. I have Bollywood up in arms and I have not even published yet, although Bly did take it upon himself to help distribute the first draft. I am warned by The Producer that if I pursue this book I will be sued by everyone mentioned and that Bly Avibath's legal team is ready to pounce. I consult with a lawyer and change what needs to be changed.

I understand the consequences of this book, but still I have no doubt that my story needs to be told.

I still have a recurring dream that keeps me dreaming. It involves the purest, most talented and honourable character in my book, Mr Kiran Cooper.

The dream is a combination of the two films *Casablanca* and *Pulp Fiction*. After all, Bollywood did teach me how to 'reference', didn't it?

The dream is in black and white except for a red patent-leather sofa set inside a pink Cadillac, and a red horse.

I sit on the red sofa in the interior of the *Pulp Fiction* diner. "Sweet Jane" by Lou Red crackles in the background. I swirl whisky in a tumbler with four ice cubes. I have my laptop that Bly Avibath gave to me on the table in front of me. Sam from *Casablanca* sits behind the piano on the stage next to the dance floor. He plays along with Lou Reed's "Sweet Jane" loudly distorting through the jukebox speaker. Kiran Cooper comes through the door on a red horse. He wears an eye patch with the Union Jack on it.

He gets off the horse, holding this book in his hand.

"Play it again, Sam," he says as he walks past the stage, taking a sip of Sam's whisky that sits on top of the piano. He does the waltz across the black-and-white checked floor. He holds up my book. Stretching his other hand out to take mine, Kiran Cooper speaks first.

<u>Kiran Cooper:</u>

"Shall we dance? I want to discuss turning this book into a film with you."

<u>Gené:</u>

"Here's looking at us kid."

Glossary

achcha! – exclamation of surprise
aṅkuśa – a sharp tool employed in the handling and training of elephants
arrey – a slang expression of exclamation
bachcha – child or baby
baingan bharta – grilled and mashed egg plant
barfi – *diamond-shaped* sweet confectionary with silver leaf topping
bhang – a preparation from the leaves and flowers of the female cannabis plant consumed as a beverage
bhangra – upbeat popular music associated with Punjabi culture
bhenchod – sister fucker
chapati – unleavened flat bread also known as roti
chikki – peanut brittle
dal – a dried pulse (lentil, pea or various type of bean)
dhobi – a washerman
firangi/firang – foreigner
ghee – clarified butter
Hinglish – a mixture of Hindi and English
jaldi – sooner rather than later
kapadā – clothes
khānā – food

khatam – finished

kurta – generic term used in Asia for several forms of upper garments for men and women

madarchod – mother fucker

mahout – a person who rides and looks after an elephant

makichod – uncle fucker

paan – betel nut or betel leaves that are chewed and then spat out

palak paneer – a popular north-Indian curry made with puréed spinach and cubed cottage cheese

paneer – a fresh cheese common in South Asian cuisine

pani puri – a popular Indian street snack consisting of a round hollow puri, deep fried and filled with a mixture of flavoured water, tamarind chutney, chilli, potato, onion and chickpeas, generally small enough to fit completely into one's mouth.

pani puri wallahs – a man who sells pani puri

petti – tin trunk

pujari – Hindu temple priest

peon – a foul and unpleasant state of being which in India refers to the underdogs working in the office or on set, similar to a spot boy.

putain – French word for whore

salwar kameez – a pair of light, loose, pleated trousers tapering to a tight fit around the ankles, worn with a long shirt by women

tandoor – a cylindrical clay oven used extensively in north-Indian cooking

tikka – red dot

yaar – Hindi word for 'dude', used to refer to acquaintances casually

vada pao – an Indian street snack consisting of a potato-filled patty in an unsweetened burger bun, served with coriander chutney and a spice mix.

Acknowledgements

To my darling Christo, thank for standing so close beside me during this very long and trying year while making my dream come true. Thank you to my beloved dogs, Pepsi and Tequila for not leaving my side while writing.

To my dearest friend Martine who put me in touch with my publisher Melinda, you were the catalyst and my sounding board for this project every step of the way. Thank you Melinda for believing in my story and letting my ideas run wild and free. You inspire me so much.

Thank you to my parents Nadine and Elio for unconditionally investing so much into this project and believing in my dream while I made endless mistakes doing it. Thank you to my family Gianmarco, Candice, Cindy, Mark, Greg and my godmother Aunty Lynn.

Also thanks to: Neill for all your musical inspiration, Tarryn, Debbie for taking the time to read my first draft in the bath, Miki, Peta for making me get back on the horse, Darryl inspiring me while walking our dogs, Toni taking my first steps with me to write this book, Megan for being such a sound editor, Peter and Richard at the George Hotel, you guys gave me the most inspirational space to work in and Cian for shooting my promotional video for the book.

Thank you Eric Mabius for your amazing shout out and encouragement to get this book turned into a film.

I have undoubtedly caused an uproar in Bollywood with my story, and for this I am sorry, but India is part of who I am now and I apologise for any anger or hurt caused.

Roll sound ... And Action!